LEGENDS

OF THE POND

Stories of
Big Island Pond,
Atkinson, Derry, and Hampstead

by
ALFRED E. KAYWORTH

Al Kayworth 8/10/00

Branden Publishing Company
Boston

Library of Congress Cataloging-in-Publication Data

Kayworth, Alfred E., 1920-
  Legends of the pond : stories of Big Island Pond, Atkinson,
Derry, and Hampstead / by Alfred E. Kayworth.
    p. cm.
  ISBN 0-8283-2053-5 (alk. paper)
  1. Rockingham County (N.H.)--History, Local.
  2. Big Island Pond Region (N.H.)--History.
  3. Big Island Pond Region (n.H.)--Folklore.
  I. Title.

F42.R7 K39 2000
974.2'6--dc21   00-037868

BRANDEN BOOKS
PO Box 812094
Wellesley MA 02482

To:
WALWORTH AND MARY LOU WILLIAMS

Two roads diverged in a wood and I--
I took the one less traveled by
And that made all the difference.

Robert Frost

ACKNOWLEDGEMENTS

T he stories that make up *Legends of the Pond* are from sources as diverse as one could possibly imagine. These sources range from 17th Century chronicles of the Jesuit historian for King Louis 14th to the youthful exploits of Herbie Herold--a 1920s rumrunner. Books based exclusively on library research can sometimes be dull reading. It is the happenings of "real people" that vitalize a story. Those who I mention here are the people who helped me to bring the history of Big Island Pond to life.

The publication of *Legends of the Pond* in a professional format would not have been possible without the support of my publisher, Adolfo Caso and his wife, Margaret. Adolfo is the author of 15 published books and the owner of Branden Publishing Company of Brookline, MA. Their waterfront cottage overlooks Escumbuit Island from the Atkinson-Derry shoreline. I am so pleased that "Maggie" found the "Legends" interesting and I am delighted that Adolfo decided to publish my story.

Mary Lou Williams' old valise full of letters, papers, magazines, and news articles is the backbone of this book. 100-year-old poems and fascinating details about the pond and its surrounding communities were mined from that valise. Thank you Mary Lou and Wally for your help and encouragement during the four years it took to complete *Legends of the Pond*. Richard Jones of Hemlock Heights became my researcher, consultant, editor and sounding board for George Whitney and the legend of Lover's Leap. His out-of-print copy of *America's Steam Car Pioneers* and his yellowed clipping of a 1949 Haverhill Gazette article about an Amesbury couple's flight from witchcraft charges were a bonanza! I met Christine (Kukukuo) Dube through *Abenaki Warrior*. My chapter entitled *The Hidden Nation* is about her. Through her I met Becky (Soft Talker) Jackson and Onkwe Tase who appear in their regalia in these pages. To them

I say, the old oak trembles, but still stands: K'chai wliwni nedobak! (Great thanks my friends!)

Many thanks to Bill & Claire Chase for allowing me to examine and write about a family whose roots in the New World go back to Colonial days. In our search for the truth we became friends. It took a couple of years, but in the end Dennis and Pate Stone made it possible for me to write a unique parable about the original builders of Mystery Hill and their encounter with The *Walking People*. Thank you Bob, Dennis, Pat, and Dawn for your patience and your help.

Through his dogged restoration of Whitney's hot air engine Russell Dickey continues to perpetuate the legend of *The Steam Pioneer*. It's a curious thought, but if I had not researched Whitney I would have never met Russ, and that would have been a loss. My research on Hampstead history led me to Maurice Randall, the town historian. His book on the 250th Anniversary of the Town of Hampstead was published in time for the celebration. He graciously shared several stories that I used in *The Legends*. My family has long left the nest, but I can still bank on their support. My sons, Steve and Pete, did some crucial editing for me and I used Tim, Tami and Andy as a sounding board for some of my ideas. Thanks guys—I love you all!

In one way and another, the following people contributed to the publication of *Legends of the Pond*. My apologies to anyone whose name I have inadvertently omitted:

Herb & Dee Lippold, Warren Kruscwitz, Ken Heinrich, Herb & Effie Dixon, Arthur McEvoy, Roland Korb, Bill and Jessie Banton, Mary Minzner, Virginia (Meier) Krauklin, Tim Chase, Patsy Goodrich, Al Craig, Bertha Smith, David Williams, Lillie Cleveland, Jack and Lois Sieg, Dennis O'Riordan, Joanne Lambert, Arthur & Rita Rother, Anne and Alfred Teischmeier, Warren Stickney, Dave Schneider, Dot Conley, Karen Wilkins, David Sherman, Steve Smith, Dick & Gladys Emery, Dr. Keith Emery, Dr. Brad Smith, Lorna Drew, Joe Davies, Lorne and Kathy Woods, Edith Sweeney, Franz Schneider.

ABOUT THE COVER

The cover is a digital collage of historic figures superimposed on a photograph taken by Doctor Keith A. Emery of Derry in 1972. As the sun rose behind the island the fog parted just long enough for him to capture this mystic image of the pond and Escumbuit Island. Pearl Associates of Boca Raton designed the cover.

The ghosted image of the Indian Warrior is a photo of my friend Onkwe Tase in his regalia. He is a Mohawk and a member of the Turtle Clan who lives in Lowell, MA.

Benning Wentworth's image is taken from a painting of the First Royal Provincial Governor that hangs in the statehouse in Concord, New Hampshire.

George E Whitney appears sitting at the tiller of a steam carriage with his daughter Ida. His handwritten caption describes the scene: "My first horseless carriage, 1896."

The astronaut is a representation of the most famous legend of them all. Alan Shepard spent 12 childhood summers at the family summer cottage on Escumbuit Island.

This photographic composite is a symbol of man's progress from Indigenous Man to Man in Space--in less than 300 years!

CONTENTS

INTRODUCTION

In the spring of 1996 I drove up to New Hampshire from my home in Florida intending to research and write a story about Big Island Pond. I had previously written *Iceman to the Internet* as a personal chronicle of my experiences, and my family encouraged me to continue writing. Since my son Peter and I bought our place on Escumbuit Island in 1987 our entire family had developed a passion for island living that surprised and pleased me. My goal was to write interesting stories about the pond that my grandchildren and even their children might enjoy. I suppose I was really looking for a way to keep my name alive in their memory.

In the course of my research, I discovered many new fascinating details of Chief Escumbuit's remarkable life. It occurred to me that I had accumulated enough information on Escumbuit to write a story that would stand on its own merit. I set aside my original project in order to work on *Abenaki Warrior....The Life and Times of Chief Escumbuit*. Through an incredible series of events my story was published and was well received by the general public and by the Native American community. Christine Dube, an Abenaki Indian descendant and former resident of the pond, suggested that I might have been subtly influenced to tell Escumbuit's story by lingering spirits on Escumbuit Island.

There was nothing spiritual about my motivation to write *Legends of the Pond*. It began when I told Wally and Mary Lou Williams that I was thinking about reviving my original story about the pond. Mrs. Williams presented me with an old suitcase crammed with news clippings, magazine articles and correspondence about the area:

This is all material about the pond and the local area. Wally and I think you are the one to organize it into a story about our pond.

I spent many nights going through this material and found much of it fascinating reading. This treasure trove of information gave me an excellent start, but I subsequently had to do a great deal of research at the libraries of Portsmouth, Derry, Hampstead and Atkinson.

Research for a book is a little like trying to negotiate a labyrinth. Sometimes a small clue will turn up a major story. Other times, a hot lead will fizzle. I met Dick Jones at a book signing and intended to call him but lost the information. Fortunately he followed up and provided me with two major stories. He sent me a copy of a Haverhill Gazette article in which a 1692 suicide pact was the focal point of the story. He also uncovered extensive information about George Whitney that enabled me to write a full chapter on *The Steam Pioneer*. His celebrity clearly placed him with the other *Legends of the Pond*. Warren Kruschwitz gave me access to his records on the history of the BIPC (Big Island Pond Corporation) water rights. Everything I needed to reconstruct events from 1878 to 1978 was there in his files. Several times I turned up stories by putting together bits of information from different sources. The Hampstead town historian, Maurice Randall, mentioned a place on North Island Pond Road where a woman sold whiskey and female companionship in the early 1900s. I combined that with information on the Rockingham Hotel that I got from Arthur Rother and Ann Teischmeier to write the piece about *The Brothel*. Information about a black man named Francois in Elizabeth Schneider's 1962 chronicle tied in with Virginia (Meier) Krauklin's fascinating story about an old house on North Island Pond Road that was a *Way Station* for run-a-way slaves.

The Last Rumrunner was an unexpected bonus. When I first talked to 90-year-old Herb Herold he didn't want to talk about his days as a bootlegger. I went down to see him anyhow, and I ended up with a story that is one of my personal favorites. The vignette entitled *The Assignation* tells how the loss of a Cadillac through winter ice spoiled an island tryst of illicit lovers. The fascinating legend about a 1692 suicide pact at Wellman's Ledge was little more than a local myth until Dick Jones sent me a Haverhill Gazette news clipping that confirmed the story. The chapter on Governor's Island is based on fact, as is the chapter on *The Steam Pioneer*. That holds true for the historic details of Escumbuit's meteoric career and the chapter on

Alan Shepard. *Mystery Hill* opens with a parable about *Stone Building People* from Europe. An episode from Paula Underwood's extraordinary 10,000-year-oral history of *The Walking People* reveals what happened when her ancestors encountered *The Stone Hill People*. Among Mrs. William's papers I discovered a journal written by Elizabeth Schneider that described her experiences camping on the big island in the late 1800s. Edith Sweeney of Freeport, Maine and Franz Schneider of Marblehead, Massachusetts provided the background material that I needed to complete *The First Campers*. Researching material for a book can be hard work, but it often turns out to be a stimulating experience.

Legends of the Lake had the sound of a good title until Russell Dickey reminded me that it was a story about a pond. *History of the Pond* did not fit because the book is not pure history. Certain historical characters may become known as legends or myths, but not all legends and myths are historical. This collection of stories and anecdotes is a composite of history, legend and myth with some pure fiction thrown in. The parable that opens the chapter about *Mystery Hill* is imaginary as well as the fictional conversation that I attribute to the proprietress of *The Brothel*. Some will dispute my version of local history, and others will wonder how I failed to include their favorite anecdote. This is the risk that comes with choosing a subject that resides so close to the hearts and minds of so many people.

Having been associated with the pond for 72 years, I couldn't resist recalling some of my own experiences. Some were memories that helped to sustain me during World War II when it seemed like I might never return to the pond. These personal anecdotes vary from my carefree days camping at Chase's Grove to my recovery of a dead body between Escumbuit Island and the mainland. The pond has always been my refuge from the pressures of contemporary life. I know that there are many others who share my love for this special place. It is my hope in the new millennia that succeeding generations will want to review the history of Big Island Pond through these pages.

Chapter 1
THE ORIGINAL PEOPLE
8000 BC--1600 AD

There is something about the natural confluence of wilderness, water and sky that soothes the human psyche. Man, in spite of his genius, has yet to create anything to surpass the beauty of a sheet of water guarded by wilderness and framed by the blue bowl of the sky. The pressures of modern society fade to insignificance in nature's milieu. Simple events can provide rare moments of beauty that remind us that bigger, faster, and louder is not necessarily better. In the age of miracle drugs, psychiatrists and spiritual gurus it is ironic that, by renouncing the material icons of modern society and returning to nature, man can find inner peace. The trail to this ideal state of mind becomes clear when he or she learns to recognize the inherent beauty in very simple events.

Perhaps one's attention is captured by the sight of a family of newly hatched ducklings, shepherded by anxious parents, cruising at the shore, tranquil in their passage, their tiny webs paddling furiously beneath the surface. Or, cruising the back side of the big island, a blue heron rises from his fishing perch and soars majestically down the shore with a backdrop of pines and hemlocks framing his effortless flight. Then, as if to remind us that man does not order the elements, the New England weather surprises with an abrupt wind-shift that causes the temperature to plummet 40 degrees overnight. By daybreak tendrils of fog, stirred by a cold east wind, rise from the water and the distant tree line is now a vague outline against a leaden sky. By afternoon the wind shifts once again and reveals a wedge of blue sky on the northwest horizon. An hour later, the scene is transformed. Now a brisk northwest breeze visits the surface of the pond and the sun's reflection from its ruffled surface is blinding. The leaves on the nearby birch trees dance in the breeze, and high above the pine boughs sway and sigh in concert. Now, like a well-composed portrait, all is distinct and clear; the air is dry and a distant ridge traces a dark silhouette against the sky. Perhaps it is at this moment that one pauses to reflect and think; this is really a special place.

The pond offers unstinting and impartial glimpses of these snapshots of beauty and, if we fail to see them, it is our loss. We may be prompted to conjecture what ancient eyes have shared these same views and to ponder how they might have reacted to such splendor. It is useful, therefore, to examine the past and to try to reconstruct how this special place came to be what it is today.

The first people to walk the shores of Big Island Pond were spear-carrying indigenous people in search of the mastodon, the woolly mammoth and the giant sloth. These small nomadic bands roamed vast, grass-covered tundra that was exposed when a global warming trend caused immense glaciers to retreat to the north. The pond basin into which water from the melting ice flowed was created by the glacier's relentless advance during the *Wisconsin Ice Age*. The pressures created by this advance gouged the earth pushing up moraines of crushed rock and earth during its slow southward advance in about 13,000 BC. Before this great thaw, New Hampshire was covered by a mile-thick ice cap. The uneven terrain left by the retreating glacier was treeless permafrost that provided a natural habitat for these large Ice Age animals.

In a time beyond memory a great human migration began in Asia. Colossal climatic changes produced frigid winds that converted vast quantities of sea water into a massive build-up of ice that was more than two miles thick in some areas. Ocean levels dropped dramatically, and the 57-mile seabed between Siberia and Alaska dried up and exposed a crude land bridge between the two continents. Archaeologists called this land bridge *Beringia*. Bands of Asiatic hunters eventually traversed this land bridge in their never-ending search for food. For many years archaeologists and anthropologists have believed that these nomadic bands were the first human occupants of this continent. Recent archaeological discoveries suggest that Polynesians may have navigated to this continent in crude sailing rafts thousands of years earlier. Nevertheless the weight of established knowledge suggests that human occupation of this continent occurred in the manner described in this chapter.

By 12,000 BC, a warming trend came to pass, and water from the melting glaciers once again covered the land bridge. Cut off from Asia, these hunters probably didn't know that they were the first humans to occupy a vast new continent. Over the next several thousand years these *Paleo-American Indians*, in their perpetual search for food, managed to occupy every corner of the New World. Archaeologists have concluded that there were three main migration routes. Some made their way down the California coastline into Mexico and South America. Others wandered into the central plains after their passage down the eastern slopes of the Rocky Mountains. A third culture continued to hunt in the far north as far as Labrador from where they migrated through the Canadian Maritime Provinces into Northern Maine. And, wherever these *Original People* went, they demonstrated a remarkable ability to adapt to the climate and the available food supply.

As the warming trend chased the glaciers northward, the cold-loving animals began to decline. The bogs and swamps that replaced the grass covered tundra proved to be difficult terrain for these large animals. This new environment made them easy victims for spear-wielding hunters and, over a period of time, they became extinct. The conifers (evergreens) that gradually filled the areas left by the retreating glacier were joined by nut-bearing hardwood trees. The gradual northward proliferation of these trees attracted a variety of smaller animals that came to forage on the varied fare. By 8,000 BC, the *Early Archaic Age* began and scattered bands of *Paleo-Americans* began to settle in these areas where they were able to supplement their meat diet with plants, roots, berries and nuts.

Two thousand years later, in the *Middle Archaic Age*, individual bands began to settle into their own traditional lands where they began to show some signs of tribal unity. Artifacts from the period demonstrate that they had begun to use their leisure time to fashion ornaments to wear or to bury with their dead, providing evidence that they were preoccupied with the possibility of life after death.

During the *Late Archaic Age* extending from 4,000 to 2,000 BC, the tribal concept seems to have become solidified. During this period the Northeastern Woodland Indians developed their Algonquian language. Three distinct northeastern cultures developed during this period. *The Lake Forest Indians* were located in the Great Lakes region where they navigated the lakes in dug-out canoes using gill nets, seines, harpoons, gaffs and three-pronged spears. They also discovered copper nuggets along the shore of Lake Superior that they learned to work into weapons, ornaments and implements.

The *Narrow Point Culture*, also known as the *Mast Forest Archaic*, comprised the largest group who occupied New England. Archaeologists identify them by their unique, narrow atlatl dart points with squared bases. The atlatl was a short throwing stick that had a notch at its tip to accept the butt end of the spear. They learned that a spear launched by an atlatl flew further and penetrated its target better. The spear was the delivery device for the flint point that was designed to pierce the hide of a mastodon. Archeological digs have uncovered remains identified as those of an intact mastodon skeleton with dart points buried between its ribs, all held together by a matrix of soil which preserved the evidence for more than 12,000 years. Through discoveries like this, dedicated scientists can re-construct a fairly accurate picture of how these ancient people lived. Through thousands of years of trial and error these prehistoric people perfected the spear, the atlatl and the detachable dart point. The bow and arrow, which we associate with Native Americans, did not come into use until 400 to 700 AD

The third culture to inhabit New England did not have Algonquian origins. They were probably descendants of those Ice Age hunters who ranged across northern Canada in search of game. They migrated south from Labrador into the Canadian Maritime Provinces and settled in Central Maine. They were known as the *Red Paint People* for their custom of sprinkling their grave sites with red ocher powder. The fine stone sculptures, slate arrowheads, rare colored stone woodworking tools and fire making sets buried with their dead, reveal an unshakable belief in life after death. The Maritime Indians learned to harvest the bounty of the sea from their dugout canoes. They fished with nets, drop line and sinker. They learned how to take seals, porpoises, walruses and even whales with barbed and toggled harpoons. Oddly, studies of that period show no evidence that they harvested the plentiful supplies of shellfish in the coastal areas.

During the *Terminal Period*, which lasted from 2,000 to 1,000 BC, the Woodland Indians lived well and their diet and life style became much more varied. The Ice Age prey of their ancestors gave way to smaller game like caribou, deer, bears, and moose, and they became gatherers of nuts and roots; they even learned how to extract the sap from maple trees. The lakes and streams attracted small fur bearing animals such as beaver and muskrat that also became a source of food. They developed techniques for netting fish and taking them with drop lines and spears. They learned how to carve soft soapstone bowls that were used for cooking and as cups and plates from which to eat.

The Iroquois, who spoke their own language, began to involve other cultures in their intertribal warfare. Their nation was located between the Lake Forest tribes in the Great Lakes region and the Maritime Indians in the east. When their internal squabbles began to spread to the Lake Forest tribes, these Algonquian speaking Indians fled eastward to seek refuge with the Maritime Indians. These refugees eventually became the Micmac, Maliseet and Abenaki tribes that occupied Maine and New Hampshire. It was they who originated the birch-bark canoe and, judging by the shell middens left by them, they took full advantage of the shellfish that had been ignored by the Maritime Indians. The Abenaki Indians of Maine and New Hampshire split into many smaller bands that generally were identified by names that described the area in which they lived. For example the Amoskeag Indians of Manchester were "The people at the good fishing place." The Pawtucket Indians of Lowell were "The people at the tidal rise in the river." There was a flint quarry in Swanton, Vermont where New England Indians went to secure flint for their scrapers, knives and arrowheads. The Missisquoi who lived there were known as "The People at the Flint." The Passamaquaddy of northern Maine were "The Pollack Spearing People."

By 1,000 BC the *Early Woodland Period* began and the culture of the Northeast Woodland Indians remained virtually unchanged until the arrival of the Europeans in the early 1600's. By 700 AD many Mayan customs were being adopted by the Native Americans of the Mississippi Valley. As these southeast religious cults assumed power, their priests began to practice Mayan customs including the sacrifice of humans to appease their gods. A caste system developed, and this religious elite dominated the ordinary Indians until the arrival of the Europeans in the sixteenth century. Their efforts to influence the Northeast Woodland Indians met with little success since these tribes preferred to follow their own traditions.

The Iroquois, who occupied the territory between the Central Algonquian tribes and the Coastal Algonquian tribes, were eliminating each other in inter-tribal conflicts until wiser heads prevailed and the Great League of the Iroquois fashioned a lasting peace through council representation. They have been portrayed as a warlike and bloodthirsty people, but this portrayal may not be entirely accurate. Having learned the benefits of living under the umbrella of The Great Law of Peace they tried to extend this law to their neighbors in order to deny them the right to wage war. By the time of the Revolutionary War, they were the largest representative democracy in the world, and their confederacy extended from the Great Lakes to the Hudson Valley and from the Canadian border down into Mississippi. However, they were unable to entice the Abenaki Indians of Maine, New Hampshire and Vermont into their powerful league and the two remained enemies. During the French and Indian wars, the Iroquois were allied with the English and the Abenaki Indians fought with the French against the English and the Iroquois.

The close of the sixteenth century witnessed the end of the isolation of the *Late Woodland Indians*. But the arrival of the Europeans signaled their doom. Viking fishermen, curious as to what lay beyond Greenland, made contact with the Woodland Indians of the Maritime Provinces. Other fishermen, explorers, traders and colonists followed and the natives were overwhelmed by their presence. Initially awed by the newcomer's technology and trade goods, they were decimated by foreign diseases for which they had no immunity, and many became addicted to the white man's alcohol which caused them to give up their land for trinkets of little value.

The Whampanog and Narragansett Indians of Massachusetts, disillusioned and embittered by their dealing with the newcomers, went to war with the English settlers in 1675, but learned too late that they were no match for English muskets and cannon. The genie had been let out of the bottle and, in 1676, Chief Metacom also known as King Phillip was killed in a Narragansett swamp. This event marked the end of *King Phillip's War* and the end of Indian resistance south of the Merrimac River. Those Massachusetts Indians who were not killed or sold as slaves in Jamaica and other far off lands, took refuge with sympathetic Abenaki tribes in Northern New England.

The relentless Colonial expansion followed a course destined to bring them into conflict with the Abenaki Indians. The English built new settlements at river outlets to the ocean from where they could explore inland and claim fertile farmland. But these same rivers were the Indian's highway and a vital source of their food supply. By the first week of May, the annual migration of salmon, smelt and shad began at the falls in Lowell where the Pawtucket Indian tribe lived. By the second week of May, the Amoskeag Indians of Manchester occupied their traditional stations at the falls wielding their nets and spears. The supply of smoked and dried fish taken at this time was vital to the survival of the Indians.

Through many millennia these semi-nomadic tribes had used the Merrimac, the Saco, the Kennebunk, the Kennebec and the St. Croix to reach the seashore in their canoes. These coastal sites coveted by the English settlers and the Indians alike, became the tinder that exploded into the firestorm that enveloped the English and the Woodland Indians in sporadic warfare for 88 years.

At the center of the dispute was the fur trade that was important to the two European powers. Beaver pelts were in great demand in Europe where beaver coats and hats were popular. The Indian's thirst for European goods was equally strong. Metal pots and pans, steel axes, metal hoes, trade blankets, and colored glass beads were finding a ready market with "The Original People." A more negative influence were the muskets, gun powder and musket balls that dealt death to animal and man alike. Alcohol, the final, insidious commodity, was the ingredient that spoiled the stew. Its effect on the Indians was almost as disastrous as the European diseases for which they had no immunity. In the end, the white man's unbridled appetite for Indian land overwhelmed a people who did not understand the concept of property rights. To the Indians, man belonged to Mother Earth. In their thinking man did not own the earth; he was merely a strand in the web of life that makes up the earth.

This mere glimpse at 13,000 years of pre-history brings us to the juncture where we can turn our focus on Big Island Pond as it was in the 1690's. At this time, the Merrimac River defined the frontier between the settlers and the Indians, and Dunstable, Massachusetts was the western frontier. Adventurous frontiersmen had also settled along the coast in settlements as far north as Newfoundland. The Indians ruled the interior and constantly harassed the border settlements, spurred on by the French who contrived to keep the Indians at war with the English. To that purpose they had sent Jesuit priests to take up residence in all of the important Indian villages with the mission of converting the natives to Christianity. In this the Jesuits were extremely effective, and it was only later that some of these missionaries were pressured by Canadian authorities to incite their Indian converts to take up arms against the English. Some of the Jesuits were accused of favoring the English because of their refusal to urge the Indians to take up the tomahawk against the Colonists. Others openly incited their converts to go on the warpath against the settlers.

The pond was very much as we know it today if one can imagine it without a single cottage on its shores. A boat tour along the south shore of the big island offers a good example of how the mainland must have appeared. The natural level of the pond was much lower than it is today. There was no reason to restrict the flow of water from the pond and there were actually two bodies of water. The smaller pond was on the Hampstead shore, and the passage that extends from the cliff at Lover's Leap to the main pond consisted of shallows and swamp.

The Indians living on the pond have been variously described as living at Sanborn Shores, the Big Island, Conley's Grove and Escumbuit Island.[1] They had gardens where they cultivated their

---

[1] *Abenaki Warrior*, by Alfred E Kayworth, (page 94); In this "historical novel" Chief Escumbuit persuades his small band of 40 Indians to move to Escumbuit Island in order to be better prepared against a possible attack from the south. It also placed the band closer to their garden that was located in the small cove that is formed by the dam at the outlet of the pond. Before the dam was constructed, this low-lying area was an ideal site for a garden. Two man-made changes drastically altered the character of the area. Mathew Taylor built a dam there in 1878 to control the flow of water to mills on the Spickett River and, in 1958, Walter Stickney dredged the swampy area in order to create water front lots that he quickly

traditional "Three Sisters." The corn was planted in hills instead of rows and the corn stalks held the climbing pole beans and the wide leaves of the squash acted like moisture saving mulch. They also grew tobacco and sunflowers. They used their birch-bark canoes to fish with drop lines and at night they speared fish lured to the surface by the glare of resin torches held over the water. In the winter they went north bundled in wolf and bear skins, traveling on snow shoes in quest of moose, deer and bear. They returned pulling toboggans loaded with deer and moose carcasses from which meat was cut in strips then smoked, dried and stored for use during the winter. In the summer they lived in bark-covered domed wigwams, but in the winter they moved into long houses which were insulated by mats woven from cat tails and swamp grass. During the warm summer months they set up camp at the seashore in the Seabrook area where they harvested the bounty of the sea. There were seals and porpoise to hunt as well as clams and oysters to harvest. They speared fish and lobsters from their canoes and they netted thousands of passenger pigeons and other waterfowl. Like other Indians of the interior, they traveled to the seacoast via the rivers on which their villages were located. Big Island Pond Indians probably loaded their belongings into canoes and traveled down the Spicket River to the Merrimac from where they could reach the ocean. Summer was a time for eating well, enjoying the weather and trading furs with seafaring English traders for pots, pans, blankets, fish hooks, axes, hoes and of course--rum. When the days began to shorten in September, they returned to the pond to get ready for the oncoming winter. The semi-nomadic culture of the Indians made it appear to the English settlers that they had no permanent home and that the land was theirs for the taking. Actually, the various tribes had established the boundaries of their hunting territory, still boundary violations resulted in skirmishes between competing tribes. Rivers, brooks, animal trails and other topographical features were used to mark their territories. Most animals of prey mark the boundaries of

---

sold to the public.

their territory and will attack intruders with ferocity; the Indians protected their traditional hunting grounds in much the same way.

The code of the Abenaki Indian was simple but rigorous. The Spartan virtues--to speak the truth--to scorn fear and exalt valor--to endure pain and hardship and--to repay in kind good for good and evil for evil; these were the marks of a man and warrior. Like many so called civilized people, these Indians could be ruthless with their enemies, and history tells us that their torture of their captives could be ingenious. They shared a deeply held belief of good and bad spirits and they also believed that inanimate objects, such as rocks and trees, were living things. Their great mythical spirit was "Glooscap" whom the Indians believed to be capable of prodigious feats and who was their great teacher and hero. They believed he was capable of flying from the North Pole to the South Pole in a single day. He taught people how to inhabit the earth and how they should live, about spiritual power and how to fight the forces of evil and overcome the obstacles that are against the nature of mankind. If an Indian drowned, they believed that evil spirits had taken him to the bottom of the lake. They believed that the evil spirit "Pomona" lived at the summit of Mt. Katahdin in Maine. The summit of Mt. Washington was believed to be the home of the Creator of all Things whom they called "Agiochook"; they appeased their evil spirits and gave mythical powers to the good. They shared a deep reverence for the physical world about them. They believed that The Creator had given the physical world to the Indians and they also believed that he had prepared a Spirit World for those Indians who departed this physical world. Many present-day Native Americans embrace the beliefs of their ancestors. One of these concepts is that we dwell on the back of a great turtle island that is floating in the universe.

The Indians formed strong family units and most could recite their patrilineal origins through many generations. The important events in their lives were celebrated with elaborate ceremonies in which the participants chanted and danced to the beat of drums. They placed great store in the medicinal brews and incantations of their tribal shaman who acted as both spiritual and medical advisor. Through thousands of years they developed ingenious methods of sustaining themselves, and they had learned how to live very well off the land without the white man's accoutrements.

Given these beliefs, we can only speculate on the wonder experienced by the Indians who first saw the strange collection of stone structures that we know today as American Stonehenge. In what circumstances did the builders of the site and nomadic bands of Indians make contact? How did the Indians react to the light-hued strangers who used their magic to create great structures of stone? What thoughts passed through their minds as they pondered the 4½-ton sacrificial stone? However, no one has ventured an opinion as to what happened when East met West. Although Winkler and others speculate that *Northeast Woodland Indians* may have used the site for their own purposes, they do not address these questions.

For 100 years, many scholars, and the media, have argued the origins of the enigma that is Mystery Hill Caves. The following chapter describes a virtual eye witness account of a meeting between *The Stone Building People* from the East and *The Walking People* from the West. This momentous meeting of two ancient cultures changed the destiny of *The Stone Building People* forever.

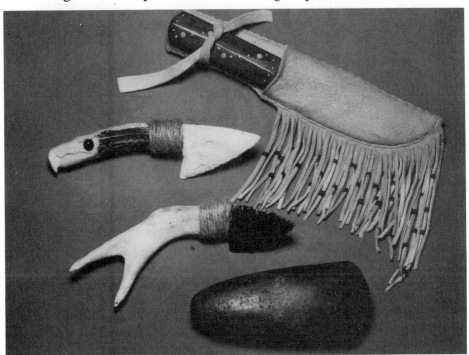

Chapter 2
MYSTERY HILL
2000 BC--2000 AD

Far back in the dim mists of time a group of pre-historic humans gathered near the summit of a barren rocky hill and pondered, what was for them, a momentous decision. Their animal skin and fur apparel together with their bearded faces and long hair made them appear like a species of animal, but their upright posture identified them as human. Their gestures and communication with one another marked them as progenitors of modern man. Their bronze-tipped spears and their apparel indicated that they hunted animals for their subsistence. At their center, holding their rapt attention, stood a man whose manner and attire set him apart from the others. Unlike them, he carried a long intricately-carved wooden staff. The white fur cloak that covered his shoulders together with his white hair and beard were a marked contrast to the drab attire of his followers. There were wise men and soothsayers among them, but they all deferred to this man whom they called "The Oracle".

They had arrived in this land after a long, arduous sea voyage from their homeland that lay to the east. The stories of a vast new land to the west told by their elders had been proven to be true. They had been exploring the coastline of this unknown continent for weeks at the whim of The Oracle. As they traveled southward there had been numerous sheltered bays where they were able to go ashore and replenish their water supply.

When they first saw the large bay, they continued south to explore the land beyond. They made their first contact with native hunters south of the great bay. Although the natives were friendly, their sign language revealed little about them. Their skin was dark in hue and their speech was foreign and they had women, children and elders among them. They were clothed with the skins and furs of animals, among them. They were clothed with the skins and furs of animals, and the spears they carried marked them as hunters. There was nothing of metal about them. Their spearheads were fashioned from stone and the pendants they wore were of bone or stone. Their painted faces and the use of colored beads and feathers to decorate their clothing lent them an exotic appearance. The natives were in awe of the people from the sea; they appeared to be fascinated by their metallic possessions. The long ship and its great sails provoked astonishment, but they were loathe to board the ship when they were invited. They kept their women and children well apart during the brief contacts, and the seafarers noted that the women did not wear clothing above the waist during the warm days. The women and their men seemed unconcerned by this strange custom. The seafarers traded salted codfish for fresh meat and berries but, except for the exchange of food, the natives kept to themselves. Their round dwellings made of boughs and animals skins and their diet of dried meat, roots, berries and nuts marked them as Gatherers and Hunters. There were no signs of a permanent village. After a third encounter with these timid strangers, The Oracle declared them to be peaceful and his followers believed it must be so.

"We have met the people of this land and you see that they are a peaceful people. Unlike ourselves, they are a primitive people who do not possess tools of metal and who do not threaten us. Yet, we did not cross a great sea to live with primitive people. Neither is this flat land suited to our purposes. Our signs made our quest for stone clear to them and they pointed to the north--always to the north. That is why I have turned our search towards where we have been. We have no desire to share our new home with these people."

As they retraced their course, The Oracle gave the command to explore the large salt-water bay. The strange ship they sailed was about 100 feet long with sharply upturned bow and stern. The profile and enclosed deck resembled seagoing ships that dominated trade in the Mediterranean during *The Bronze Age*. The Vikings and other Northern European cultures copied their efficient design. After tacking all day, the lookout spied a small stream feeding into the bay that gave promise of fresh water to fill their large clay water jugs and skin bags. It was an inviting place to rest after months at sea. The water was clear and good and game was plentiful and there were edible roots and berries to harvest. On the second night, as they sat around a campfire, The Oracle pointed to the silhouette of a low hill to the east and declared, "Yonder hill shows promise. Tomorrow we will climb to the summit."

They discovered that the fresh water stream originated at a large fresh water pond about two miles from their camp.[2] But it was the hill that held the attention of The Oracle. They climbed to the summit from where they could see their ship and the bay beyond. When a soothsayer approached to describe what he had seen on the eastern slope of the hill, The Oracle quickly strode in that direction at the head of his followers. As he walked about the barren hillside among the profusion of rocks and boulders he stopped occasionally and surveyed the horizon and the position of the sun. Despite his calm demeanor there was something about his manner that conveyed excitement. The wise men and followers wondered, "Could this be the place The Oracle has sought for so long?"

The treeless landscape gave wide range to a view of rolling, tundra like land. Having already explored the surrounding terrain, they were familiar with the nearby body of water whose overflow formed the stream they had followed to this hill. Who were these people? Where did they come from? What were they looking for? The rocky terrain may have been exactly the environment they were looking for. Like any group of people seeking a place to live and worship their deities, they were looking for a site with special characteristics. If it were merely a place to live, the shore of the nearby pond might have served them better, but they were looking for a site with certain geological characteristics. Like many primitive people, their spiritual beliefs influenced the way they conducted the mundane activities of their daily life. Their preoccupation with

---

[2] Author's note: Skeptics question why the Mystery Hill builders would choose to locate their site so far from the ocean. Some researches theorize that ocean levels were much higher 4000 years ago than they are today. It is possible that the Merrimac River watershed may have been a very large salt water bay. I have found fossilized shark teeth and whale bones in abandoned phosphate pits in Central Florida 50 miles inland from the Gulf of Mexico. I am suggesting that ocean levels may have been high enough for a sailing vessel to land quite close to Mystery Hill.

earthly activities such as agriculture, hunting, food gathering and shelter were inextricably tied to their spiritual beliefs. Deep superstition and subordination to the commands of their soothsayers and The Oracle ruled their lives.

Their deference to the head soothsayer they called The Oracle revealed how he held them with his power. They saw him as their only protection against the non-believers whom they feared. He was their icon of stability in a hostile and uncertain world. They had been selected for the deep fervor of their belief in their leader and they could be counted upon to support any decision he made. The astrological sages among them saw that this location had the necessary elevation and unobstructed view of the surrounding horizon they needed to create the astronomical calendar they planned. The horizon would provide the sharp delineation between sky and tundra they needed to design a giant calendar that used vertical stone monoliths to mark the occurrence of important celestial events. These singular-standing stones would be placed to serve much like the sight on a rifle. When the sun rose or set on an alignment marked by a monolith, it would signal a significant celestial event that controlled the lives of these ancient people. And the basic building material needed to create these alignments lay in profusion on this rocky hillside.

They were standing on a hill of granite that had been carved down to bedrock by the advancing glacier of the *Wisconsin Ice Age*. The mile thick cap of ice that had once enveloped the area had long since retreated to the north leaving in its wake a rough, uneven landscape of tundra similar to the terrain in parts of Alaska. The lowland had a profusion of grass and shrubs that provided cover for small animals, but the side of the hill on which they stood was devoid of trees and bushes. It was littered with thousands of rocks and boulders called erratica that had been left by the retreating glacier. They stood in silent respect as The Oracle pointed to a fault in the granite that had been sheared by mighty forces.

"Witness, my people, the power of Our Gods who have created the substance for our temple. We are a favored people because we are A Stone Building People, and it is our never-ending labor that proves our fealty to Our Gods. Here we will offer our sacrifices to those who will favor us with plentiful game and bountiful harvests. Through these rituals and by our labor and sacrifice, our children and their children's children will earn the right to reside with our immortal ancestors midst the stars."

As they listened intently to their leader, the soothsayers, the wise men and the lesser followers murmured their agreement with their leader's wisdom for, after all, was he not The Oracle? Who among them would question his declaration that it was those who ruled the stars who had sundered the rocks and slabs of stone that lay in profusion about them?

Indeed, an earthquake **had** created a rift in the granite that left loose slabs of stone that crude quarry methods would put to good use. What might appear to be a hostile landscape to a different culture in a different time now caused the pulse of the followers to quicken in anticipation of the ceremonial site they planned to build here. The Oracle and his soothsayers were already imagining solemn processions and rituals performed amidst a massive stone complex built around a central sacrificial stone. At nightfall the crew of the ship gathered around the campfire to hear The Oracle speak. They sat silently as he outlined his broad and far-reaching plan.

Tomorrow we will begin to build shelters for those who will stay. We will build our home on this rich soil by this stream where our planting will provide us with food. The foul matter of our daily activities must not desecrate our sacred place. Those who return to our homeland will tell our people that we have found a new home. Tell them that the natives of this land roam their land as nomads. They make no claim to permanent homes. Those of the tormented world must built ships to carry our people to a new home in a New World. Here they will be safe from those who persecute us for our beliefs. At our sacred place our wise men will interpret the heavenly signs that control the sacred rites of our people and they will pay homage to The Gods who rule our destiny.

So it was that A Stone Building People, driven by the relentless will of a man they called The Oracle, began a massive endeavor that lasted for centuries. A thousand years passed and more, until one-day descendants of The Oracle and his followers encountered a people who came from the west. Their journey had been long and arduous; it was a journey of 10,000 years. They called themselves The Walking People and they possessed knowledge that would change the destiny of *The Stone Building People* forever!

The foregoing parable is based on the many theories that have been advanced about Mystery Hill since 1907. The design of the ship, the large inland bay that provides passage to the site, the barren rocky hillside, the divine earthquake and The Oracle's decision to live apart from the ceremonial center are based on previous speculation about this fascinating complex. In the sense that historical fiction is not history it can be said that this illusory parable is not science, but that evades the issue. It is to open our minds to the possibility that this wooded rocky hillside in Southern New Hampshire may have been the theater for one of the great human dramas of history. This much seems certain; at some point in a time beyond memory, human beings came to this site and made a colossal expenditure of time and energy to build a celestial observatory and a site for ritualistic sacrifice. If Mystery Hill is an enigma inside of a riddle, as some people say, then this fiction may be more accurate than some of the individual theories previously offered. I leave it to the reader to judge which theory makes the most sense and to judge whether Mystery Hill is a sham or one of the most important archeological sites on this continent. To attempt to tell the whole story of Mystery Hill in a single chapter would be a fool's errand. Besides, the tour guide and other written material available at the gift shop do an admirable job of presenting the known facts in an interpretive way. Nevertheless, after extensive research and careful thought, it is my personal opinion that Mystery Hill is truly an important archaeological site.

The earliest known reference to Mystery Hill was made in Edgar Gilbert's book entitled *History of Salem NH-1907*. Jonathan Pattee and his family occupied a house built on the site from 1826 to 1855. It appeared that part of the ancient ruins provided a ready made foundation for the house, and that one of the stone structures served as the back wall of a "cold cellar" that was located in one corner of

Descendants of Pattee revealed that he was an Abolitionist. This supports evidence that he was involved in the illicit traffic of run-a-way slaves. Prior to the Civil War, a clandestine movement took place in America that historians refer to as, The Underground Railroad. The name came from the voluntary efforts of sympathizers along the Eastern Seaboard to aid in the escape of run-a-way slaves. The North Star became a symbol of hope for these run-a-ways during their long journey to Canada. Those who supported this movement by supplying shelter, food, and transportation were known as Abolitionists. The slaves traveled mostly by night and were hidden during the day to shield them from bounty hunters seeking to recover and return them to their southern slave masters. The places where they were sheltered were called "Way Stations" and the individuals who operated these stations were known as "Station Masters." *The Fugitive Slave Law of 1850* was passed to mete out swift punishment to anyone caught concealing or assisting slaves in any way. Those who helped, both publicly and undercover, did so at great personal risk.

Slaves were concealed inside false bottoms built into wagons, and they were concealed in secret rooms in houses and barns. Natural caves and ditches were also used to conceal fugitives. Many slaves were transported from the South to New England in ships that discharged their human cargoes in Boston, Salem, Marblehead, Newburyport and other ports. Researchers on this subject have had great difficulty identifying the routes used and learning the names of the individuals involved; records of this illegal traffic are non-existent. Like a well-organized spy ring, each link in the chain knew only the details of his or her own involvement. The only records are the information that has been passed down by individual families to succeeding generations.

William Siebert wrote a book entitled, *The Underground Railroad in Massachusetts*. He described a branch route of The Railroad that followed the Old Boston Post Road with stations in Woburn, Reading and Andover. From Andover it went through South Lawrence and on to North Salem. The Old Boston Post Road in North Salem later became known as Pope Road. Traces of this road are still discernable near the lower parking lot parallel to the path that leads to the Watch

House. Siebert described the transfer of slaves from Andover to the North Salem site in the following passage:

> Being pronounced abolitionists, Joseph W. Poor, Elijah Hussey, and William C. Donald, had separated from South Church and organized the Free Christian Church in 1846, and could perhaps be counted on to speed the black wayfarers on their journey. When Mr. Poor heard a gentle rap on his door or other subdued sound in the night, he dressed quickly, went out, harnessed his mare Nellie into a covered wagon and started with his dusky passengers, probably for North Salem, New Hampshire. On the top of a hill at that place were several large excavations, lined and covered with slabs of stone, which had furnished retreats for neighboring inhabitants when the Indians were on the warpath, but which now afforded refuge to fugitive slaves. Mr. Poor was always back in time for breakfast.

An iron shackle recovered at the site by archaeologists is displayed in the Mystery Hill museum. One can imagine Pattee with his hammer and chisel cutting the shackle from the leg of a black slave before sending him on to freedom after a night's rest in one of the stone caves that surrounded his home. Although North Salem did not see as much traffic as more traveled routes, it nevertheless played an important role in this clandestine railroad to freedom. William Siebert wrote that, "there were also stations in and near Haverhill eight miles to the southeast."

For years after the Pattee house burned, the site was used as a picnic area and one of our older residents remembers hearing the story that farmers in the area used to store their surplus potatoes, turnips, and carrots in some of the stone caves.[3]

---

[3] Author's note: This information comes from Roland Korb, who has been on the lake for 80 years. In his early teens he used to visit the site with other youngsters from Germantown. The highlight of their picnic came when they used the Oracle Chamber to play "Post Office."

There was never any attempt to do research on the site until William Goodwin purchased the property in 1937. He had a genuine desire to establish the identity of the original builders of the site, but his enthusiasm led him to conclusions he was unable to prove to the scientific community. He spent years trying to prove that the site had been built about 1,000 AD by Irish Culdee Monks. He learned from ancient Irish sagas that Irish Monks fled Ireland and moved to Iceland to escape Norse invaders of their homeland. His research turned up an 800-year old History of Iceland that described how Christians had fled Iceland in 750 AD because they did not want to live among heathens. Ancient documents convinced Goodwin that these Irish Monks had gone to Vinland. Although scholars of the period could only place Vinland somewhere between Labrador and Florida, Goodwin was sure he had pinpointed its true location. He was convinced that Leif Ericson had established a settlement at the mouth of the Piscataqua River in Portsmouth, NH, and it took only a small leap of his imagination to believe that the Irish Monks must have following Ericson's route to the mythical Piscataqua settlement. He theorized that their search for an ideal location eventually brought them to North Salem.

He hired a mining engineer named Roscoe J Whitney and a crew of local laborers to help him excavate the site. Lacking the supervision of a trained archeologist, the workers dug with great zeal discarding anything that did not support Goodwin's Culdee Monk theory. Fragments of pottery, stone scrapers, and a stone mace they uncovered were not even cataloged and have since been lost. When Goodwin took over the site the large sacrificial stone lay flush with the ground. Modern scientific methods would require painstaking screening of each layer of soil in order to study the age profile of the accumulated leaf mold and atmospheric dust deposited through centuries. When the workers discovered that stone legs supported the large stone slab, they committed a giant blunder. They carelessly dug out the accumulated soil and discarded it thereby destroying any chance to study the vital soil profile for clues of age. Goodwin then instructed them to clean out the rubbish that had collected in the Y-cavern that lays adjacent to the sacrificial stone. When this had been accomplished with the same disregard for scientific method, Whitney made a personal investigation of the interior of the chamber.

Intrigued by the hollow sound he heard when he tapped a rectangular shaped stone at head height, he pried it loose and found a stone lined voice tube that extended 8 feet to an opening under the sacrificial stone. Further investigation revealed a similar stone near the floor that covered the opening to a 40-foot water drain that led to the outside. The accumulated silt at the end this drain might have held clues to the age of the site in its soil profile, but Goodwin's men unwittingly destroyed this evidence by using shovels when hand trowels and small paint brushes would have been appropriate.

Whitney traced his New England ancestry to 1635 and he reflected his Yankee roots. A skeptic by nature, he would not buy the colonial cellar theory. His comments about the site are revealing. In response to the suggestion that the site was nothing more than the remnants of Colonial cellars he said, "Not even a New Hampshire farmer is that stupid or that stubborn" adding, "But there was one curious thing. I measured every wall and every ramp and every building in that site and I found no place where the measurements were in feet or yards or inches. Whoever built that place either didn't give a damn about standard linear measure, or he didn't know it existed."

Goodwin's investigations continued for 10 summers and, in 1946, he published a book entitled, *The Ruins of Great Ireland in New England*. Dogmatic to the end, his book identified the builders of the site at North Salem as Irish Culdee Monks who he theorized had come there from Iceland to practice religious freedom. His book and his findings were universally rejected by contemporary scholars of the day. By denying Goodwin his triumph while accepting the easier colonial cellar explanation, these experts discredited themselves when they should have been seeking the true answer to the mystery. Goodwin deserves credit for turning Pattee's Caves into a scientific controversy. Although experts rejected his theory, he managed to expand what had been a local curiosity into an archeological mystery.

For more than 100 years local people referred to the site as Pattee's Caves. Local residents and summer visitors to Big Island Pond played there as children and used it as a picnic site. People said Pattee was a local eccentric who built the caves to harbor runaway slaves for the Underground Railroad. Some claimed he was a bootlegger who stored hundreds of gallons of cider in the caves ignoring the fact that the open-ended caves would allow the cider to freeze. Others said that he and his five sons built the place as a whimsical gesture just to mystify people. These rumors were untrue. He and his wife had five daughters and only one son. There is evidence to suggest that he did shelter runaway slaves in stone caves that were there long before his family bought the property. To suggest that Pattee built the site as a whimsical gesture to confuse his neighbors recalls Whitney's response— "not even a New England farmer is that stubborn or that stupid."

In 1945, Junius Bird and a young Yale archeology student named Gary Vescelius were invited by Goodwin to investigate the site. After spending five days digging for artifacts, they gave up their search for lack of material results, but they left still intrigued by what they had seen. In 1955, after Goodwin's death, they returned at the invitation of an Early Sites Foundation that had been created to investigate the stone village. After spending six weeks digging 10 test pits and, after sifting tons of dirt for artifacts, the 67-page report failed to confirm anything earlier than Colonial origin. Furthermore, the report flatly rejected Goodwin's Irish Monk theory. Vescelius and the foundation, discouraged by the negative results, decided that further investigation was unwarranted and they gave up the project. However, one member of the excavation team did not share their opinion.

Frank Glynn, president of *The Connecticut Archeological Society*, felt privately that the search for answers on Mystery Hill had not gone deep enough, but he had personal reservations about pursuing his interest. In the face of Goodwin's obsession with proving his Culdee Monk theory, he knew that it would not be possible to continue his research with a open mind so he returned to Connecticut and resumed his study of Indian mounds in that area. He discovered a sunken Indian village that was estimated to be 4000 years old and, in 1954, he made a startling find in Westford, Massachusetts. Punched into the side of a buried ledge was the outline of a 14th century Scottish knight outfitted with a helmet and mail and carrying a sword and a dagger. As a result of this discovery he began a correspondence with British archeologists who were authorities on the *Mediterranean Stone Age*. On an impulse he included some photographs of Mystery Hill in his correspondence. The British noted a startling resemblance to ancient stone structures they had studied in ancient Crete, Malta and Mycenae. This revelation fostered numerous theories that concluded that the builders of the site came from Europe.

Glenn returned to North Salem where he resumed his search for facts to support the exciting speculation of the British authorities. He noted a growing number of similarities between the local stone structures and *Bronze Age* structures in Malta. The sacrificial stone and the stone voice tube resembled structures in Malta, as did the stone seats and niches. He found that the cells along the 106-foot ramp were equivalent to the chapels of the Malta site. Like Whitney he found that nothing was built to modern measurements but he carried that curious fact one step further. He discovered that all measurements at Mystery Hill conformed to an ancient Egyptian unit known as the cubit. He also found a shard of pottery with a pattern that was different from any of the Indian pottery he had previously found. The composition of the clay was unlike Native American pottery, but it did resemble the clay used in pottery made in the Mediterranean area. Frank Glynn eventually found 48 similarities between Mystery Hill and sites in Malta.

In 1250 B. C, the Mediterranean was dominated by Cretians, who were wiped out by an earthquake. Out of this disaster the Phoenicians emerged from their ports of Tyre and Sidon to dominate the Mediterranean with their ships and their trade. Known as *The Silent People* for their passion for keeping their trade activities secret, they were known for spreading tales of sea monsters and other horrors designed to scare off competitors. They were master navigators and seamen, and they are credited with designing the first keel for ships. Their seagoing vessels were 100 feet long with sharply turned-up-bow and stern and they had covered decks. Their design was widely copied by others. In 1957 a severe drought revealed a ship carving on a large stone at the bottom of Assawompsett Pond in Massachusetts that was a faithful replica of a Phoenician seagoing ship. The date of the carving was undetermined, but the discovery provided another clue to support the theory of exploration of this continent by Phoenicians.

One of the ardent supporters of that theory was Professor Charles H. Hapgood, of Keene College. He pointed to the obvious fanatical intent of the North Salem site as an indication that the Phoenicians could very well have been involved.[4] Fanatically religious beliefs shaped their lives and even drove them to human sacrifice as a manner of appeasing their gods. The sacrificial stone is completely consistent with this extreme practice and possibly explains why so much effort was expended to create the one-inch deep groove and spout in the perimeter of this 4½ ton slab. The process of shaping this groove without metal tools defies the ingenuity of modern man. Constant pounding at the same point with a hand-held stone weighing as much as ten pounds was required to create that groove. Scientists assure us that water dripping on a stone for thousands of years will wear a hole in a stone. It took one or more humans pounding with hand-held stones to laboriously carve this groove. Water drains in the bedrock of the site were also fashioned in this manner. There are no metal tool marks to indicate that these grooves were carved during the Colonial period.[5]

Hapgood also identified the carvings of a bull's head and a double axe discovered at the site to be favorite Phoenician designs. He referred to an ancient Piri Reis map discovered in 1513 that was found in a Turkish Harem. He claimed that the grid lines on the map

---

[4] "Mystery Hill: *Development of Theories Concerning its Origin.*" David Williams wrote this unpublished report in 1971 as a college project. His fellow researchers for the report were Stanley Parsons, and Mr. Marks. They invited Dr. Hapgood to examine some of the stonework at the north end of the big island and he became quite excited about the similarities between the two sites. However, his investigation was finally abandoned for lack of funds. David William's thoroughly researched and well-written college paper is the source for much of the information on the Phoenicians and the Island of Malta.

[5] Author's note: This method used to create this groove and to carve the drains in the bedrock of the site are confirmed by David Stewart Smith, the official stone mason for America's Stonehenge. I also saw a fascinating *National Geographic* demonstration conducted by an archeological team on a dig at Matchupichu, the stone city high in the Andes Mountains of Peru. The stones of the walls of the city are fitted to one another with a tolerance that will not allow the passage of the blade of a knife. They showed local workers hand shaping building stones by persistent pounding with a hammer stone to tailor the fit to the adjacent stone. The labor required to fit a single stone was incredible, but it worked!

proved it was drawn by the Phoenicians. Scholars theorize that this map may have been drawn as early as 1000 B.C. The implied conclusion was that Phoenician navigators might have traveled to North America as much as 2,500 years before Columbus made his discovery of America.

James Whittall, chief archeologist of *The New England Antiquities Research Association*, made some favorable comparisons with the sites he had visited in Malta and Portugal. Besides listing similarities in the physical structure of North Salem and these Mediterranean sites he noted that the pottery fragment found at Mystery Hill was very similar in texture and color to that found in Malta. The Mediterranean sites he visited were, like Mystery Hill, all built into the sides of the hills and never at the absolute top. One of the thought-provoking discoveries in North Salem was the unmistakable outline of a deer or an ibex carved on one of the walls in the Y-cavern. There is an almost identical carving on the wall of a cave on the island of Malta.

About 1965 a group of men associated with *NEARA (New England Antiquities Research Association)* began to investigate the possibility that Mystery Hill was an ancient stone calendar. Their interest was prompted by a CBS special about the British Stonehenge as well as a new book entitled *Stonehenge Decoded*. NEARA members spent the next three years cutting lanes through the trees to open viewing paths to the summer and winter solstice sunsets. On December 21, 1970, for the first time in at least a 1,000 years the group, led by Robert Stone, observed and photographed the sun setting directly over a large singular standing stone marking the winter solstice sunset. Continuing work confirmed that the site was a giant calendar designed to view important seasonal events marked by the position of the sun and the moon. This revelation represented a quantum leap in the importance of the site. Meanwhile many of the old time residents of the area dismissed the site as an area of old colonial cellars, and one "expert" claimed that the sacrificial stone was actually on old cider press.

Bob Stone decided to get a second opinion from a respected firm of consulting engineers and surveyors. B.V Pearson Associates spent over 350 hours checking the alignments of the singular standing stones that rise five to seven feet above the perimeter walls in which they are set. Two passages in the lengthy report compiled by B.V. Pearson Associates stand out and deserve to be quoted directly:

"As we stated in our earlier report of survey to your firm, we have been surveying stone wall and other features of the local and historical landscape for many years (over 15 at the present time) and with the broad experience of the various staff that worked on your job, have all come to the same conclusion namely that your site has many stone walls that do not appear to align with any Colonial or Post-Colonial boundary lines, that the detail of many of the stone wallsgeo at your site is different in appearance and construction from the known Colonial stone walls in the locality, that the large and significant standing stones in the outer walls of the central site do have obvious and proven alignments to many astronomical events and can easily be used as a calendar, and that many of the stone structures at the site are completely different in construction and appearance from the traditional cellar holes and root cellars examined in various other sites we have surveyed over the past 15 years."

The report concluded with a strong opinion: "During the field location of the various features at the site, we set drill holes in many of the stones at an assumed high point or centroid of the various significant stones. In some cases these stones were 3 or 4 feet in width, so there is some degree of latitude (possibly up to 1.5 to 2 feet) It is obvious that the major standing stones we have located were placed to indicate the significant astronomical events of the sun and moon, and it is difficult for us to imagine anyone reviewing the physical evidence at the site and on our survey plan and reaching any other conclusion. This is not any astronomical theory, but a straightforward geometrical analysis of measurements at the site."

Despite carbon dating studies suggesting that the site existed in 1500 BC, and despite solid evidence that a solar and lunar calendar was in place at Mystery Hill, the scientific community seemed unimpressed. For Bob Stone it was like trying to row a boat up a tidal river against an outgoing tide. Much of the skepticism was the result of the legacy left by the noted Samuel Eliot Morison of Harvard University. While he lived, Morison ridiculed any evidence that seemed to support any sign of exploration of the American continent before the arrival of Columbus in 1492. In his 1971 book, *The European Discovery of America,* he stated unequivocally that, up to that time, no one had discovered any evidence to support pre-Columbus exploration of America. His habit of dismissing any data that contradicted what he had previously published in books is reminiscent of Professor Evan's rigid opinion about the Mayan culture at the turn of the century. Evans assured the archeological world that the Mayan civilization was a peaceful agrarian culture and that the glyphs carved into the surface of Mayan temples were decorative designs without meaning. He too managed to squelch contrary theories for years until young maverick epigraph scholars cracked the mystery of the glyphs and completely discredited Evans after his death. The translations of the glyphs revealed that the Mayans were a warlike people who sacrificed humans in their rituals. Today their translations of the glyphs are universally accepted fact. But after Morrison died in 1976, his Harvard colleagues and students blindly affirmed his dogma and continued to discredit mavericks like Barry Fell, a Harvard professor emeritus and a leading epigrapher.

As we prepare to enter the 2nd Millennia, research continues at what is now called America's Stonehenge. Professor Louis Winkler, Ph. D of Penn State University, is the latest scientist who is involved in an ongoing investigation of the site. Of particular interest among his many articles is *Astronomically Determined Dates and Alignments* which appeared in the *1972 Journal of Physics*. His conclusions about the local site are based on the physical similarities between Mystery Hill and other Bronze Age sites and the results of his analysis of other research performed at Mystery Hill by B V Pearson Associates and computer studies at Harvard University.

Winkler claims that Mystery Hill was constructed by Celt[6] (pronounced Kelt) immigrants in three phases beginning in 2000 BC. Construction continued until 1500 BC when, for unknown reasons, construction was discontinued. From 1500 BC until 500 BC there may have been some restricted use of the site by *Northeast Woodland Indians*. The Celts resumed construction in 500 BC and are thought to have occupied the site until 1600 AD. During this third and final

---

[6] Author's note: The Celts were a powerful race of Europeans who were known to the Romans as the Gauls.

stage Woodland Indians may have used the site for their own ceremonies. There are several radio carbon dating results that support Winkler's findings.

Various artifacts found on the site point to occupation by Indians. These include a typical Algonquin stone axe, a stone hoe, hammer stones, rubbing stones and pendants. An 1800 to 2500 year old clay pot was found in the cliff shelter at the north end of the site that is typical of the pottery used by Woodland Indians of that period. Pat Hume, a former president of *The New Hampshire Archaeological Society*, has identified a habitat site of Woodland Indians that she believes is 2000 years old.

There are over 200 stone structures scattered throughout New England in which artifacts have been found that are typical of the Woodland Indian culture. In the western part of the United States there are still remnants of stone calendar wheels that were used by Indians to time their planting cycles as well as to mark ceremonial dates. The use of the local site by Woodland Indians is consistent with what we know about their culture.

A Professor Winkler specialty is calculating dates and alignments of monoliths at prehistoric sites. These singular standing stones or monoliths were used like the fore sight of a rifle to mark calendar events. Over the course of 4,000 years precession of the earth's axis and changing earth tilt have altered the alignments of these monoliths. The earth does not spin precisely on its axis. Like a spinning top, its axis weaves in a circle that takes approximately 26,000 years to complete. This action is called "precession." The term "obligite" refers to the changes in earth tilt as it orbits the sun. This is a 41,000-year cycle. The amount of misalignment of a monolith calculated in degrees and minutes can be used to determine the age of megalithic calendars. Computer programs that take into account the effects of precession and obligate can calculate the period in time when a specific monolith would have been an accurate marker for a particular calendar event. The use of astronomy and carbon dating are the two best ways to tell the age of sites like Mystery Hill, but like DNA testing, they are difficult concepts to understand.

In the summer of 1998, Peter Kayworth and I were conducted on a tour of Mystery Hill by Bob Stone and his son Dennis. An amateur archeologist tagged along with us. Bob Stone suggested we visit the area where many of the monoliths were taken from what he called "the quarry." When Peter joined us after having taken a separate path, his first comment was "What is that long stone back there in the woods?" About a hundred yards away he showed us a long slab of granite with a squared base that measured about 3 feet across and came to a rough point at its other end. It had apparently fallen and broken into four pieces and the profile of the broken pieces matched. A reflexive comment by someone in the group mirrored my own thoughts, "This stone was once upright and when it fell it broke into four pieces." All of us had reached the same conclusion based on compelling visual evidence.

This 14-foot stone is the largest monolith on the site. Professor Winkler has calculated that, 3800 years ago, the grazing circumpolar star Izar would have appeared to graze the tip of this standing monolith just before it disappeared due to "atmospheric extinction." At its zenith point, it would have been possible to view Izar through a viewing hole in the roof of the Oracle Chamber as it passed overhead. The zenith sighting of Izar from the Oracle Chamber and its relationship to the monolith are intriguing, but what are the implications? This and other questions may be answered as the pieces of the puzzle are assembled but, for the present, it is part of the work in progress. It is encouraging to know that most of Professor Winkler's conclusions are based on the laws of astronomy and mathematics. The same cannot be said for the parable that I used to open this chapter. Entertaining maybe, but hardly scientific. Still, the weight of evidence tips the scale heavily in favor of the site being built by immigrants from Europe.

Assuming that people not unlike The Oracle and his disciples built Mystery Hill, one can only imagine the difficulties they faced in bringing their people to the New World. Decades and centuries of time must have passed in the building of such a massive religious site. One wonders how the Woodland Indians received these light skinned strangers from the East. Unfortunately, there were no written records of Woodland Indian history until Jesuit priests began to develop a written language for them in the early 1700s. Up to that time, Native Americans maintained the history of their people through stories handed down through succeeding generations. During long, cold winters, story telling was the principal means of entertainment for families confined to wigwams and long houses. And for people with a history that reaches back 10,000 years, story telling took the place of history books. It was their principal means of preserving the essence of their ancient culture. Wampum, also called "telling beads" was also used to record important events as well as pictograms. It is through such a Native American Oral History, written in the ancient way, that we gain insight into the fate of the Stone Building People. The credentials of the Lineal Keeper of this 10,000-year oral history are quoted directly from the jacket of an 859-page book called *The Walking People*:

> Paula Underwood is an author, lecturer, trainer and consultant in education cross-cultural understanding, and organizational methodologies based on lifelong training and experiences in a Native American philosophy. She has inherited the responsibility for this Oral History--which comes to her from her grandfather's grandmother who committed it to memory in the early 1800s and meticulously handed it down through the generations of Ms. Underwood's family.

Ms. Underwood has spent many years visiting and attempting to identify the probable locations of the many areas where her people may have established permanent homes. Unlike other groups of people who subsisted off the leavings of the great herds during the Ice Age, The Walking People were place keepers and farmers who lived in one place hundreds and even thousand of years. Then, for one reason or another, they moved on to seek their original destination--the edge of ocean. Through the years she identified many of the sites that are part of the history, but her search for a stone complex in New England eluded her. She enlisted the help of friends who eventually discovered America's Stonehenge. In 1985 she finally visited the site with Sherry Espar, who is part Mohawk, and they were deeply impressed with what they saw. The both had Spirit experiences with beings there, and to quote Ms. Underwood:
"I was profoundly convinced that this was Stone Hill."
Within the scope of this chapter it is impractical to provide a complete text of the dialog between The Walking People and The Stone Hill People. What follows is my interpretation, in an abbrevi-

ated form, of significant passages relevant to my story. I have italicized certain phrases to show where I have borrowed from Ms. Underwood's text. Also, complete passages from *The Walking People* are used to illustrate Ms. Underwood's unique way of story telling in the ancient way, and also, to provide dramatic impact to the narrative:[7]

10,000 years ago, The Walking People were driven from their home in Asia by cataclysmic forces of nature. In the face of earthquakes, avalanches and tidal waves, they left their edge of sea home with its mountain background to search for a new *Center Place*. They had survived *The Walk by Waters* (Bering Land Bridge) and *The Never Ending Mountains* (The Rockies) and they had lived for a time by the *Western Sea* (The Pacific Ocean). They had crossed *The Great Dryness* (The Desert) and *The Ocean of Grass* (The Plains) and they had finally encountered forests once again by *The Winding River* (The Ohio).

They survived all this as a strong, unified people with great wisdom. They had learned how to build round structures out of wood to give shelter. They had learned the secret of "The Three Sisters" (The planting of corn, beans and squash). They had learned how to solve problems as a group and they had learned that there is wisdom in the words of children as well as elders. They learned to use the best of what they saw in other cultures they encountered through thousand of years. They learned these things and much more that forged their identity as *A People* who continued to search for *A Center Place*.

During their long stay at The Winding River they were dominated by The Sun Disk People who wore metal discs around their necks that reflected the rays of the sun. They worked as Dig and Carry People for many years building a giant earthern mound for The Sun Disk People (The Ohio Mound Indians). The Sun Disk People were

---

8 Author's note: Ms. Underwood has given her permission for the use of selected portions of her book in *Legends of the Pond*. For those who, like myself, are fascinated by her unique telling of stories in the ancient way, her book is available at the following address: *The Walking People*, A Tribe of Two Press, P.O Box 913, San Anselmo, CA 94979.

very secretive, but one member of The Walking People learned much of their history and that their ancestors had been Builders in Stone across the ocean to the south and to the west (Mexico). After many years laboring in slave-like conditions, The Walking People left to seek The Eastern Sea (Atlantic Ocean) leaving most of their belongings behind in their haste to escape their oppressors.

Their eastern migration took 80 years and, when they arrived at The Eastern Sea, they found two disparate cultures. The Southern People reluctantly allowed them to live to the north as their neighbors in order to provide a buffer between themselves and another people to their north whom they called The Stone Hill People.

FOR THIS WAS A PEOPLE
WHO BUILT THEIR CENTER PLACE
WITH GREAT DIFFICULTY
THIS WAS A STONE BUILDING PEOPLE
A People
who raised with great difficulty
some solid pieces of Earth herself
cut it to suit some preference
or purpose of their own
and laid it in place
-one after another-
until some extraordinary assemblage
was attained

After The Walking People observed The Stone Hill People for a period of time, they arrived at an accurate assessment of these strange people. Though they were not hostile, The Stone Hill People remained aloof and they gave the impression that they thought their ways were superior to those of The Walking People. They noticed that individuals roamed about their stone hill in a random way but, when The Stone Hill People walked in a procession, they always approached their stone hill in a northerly direction (this ceremonial path exists today). They noted that these people were of a lighter hue than The Sun Disc People, and that they had implements made of the same material as the shining disks worn by The Sun Disk People. They learned that these people were not as numerous as they had once been, and they reasoned that they might be lonely for their own kind. After a lengthy council meeting, they selected five of their most learned tribal members who went to seek council with The Stone Hill People.

Although the five were lavish in their praise of the great works of The Stone Hill People, they found them reluctant to share their wisdom. In their eagerness to share their own history, the five told how their ancestors had spent many years working for The Sun Disk People. They described the shining disks and the giant earth mounds, and they told how the ancestors of The Sun Disk People had been great builders in stone in another land. Despite their feigned indifference, The Stone Hill People could not contain their excitement when they learned that the ancestors of The Sun Disk People placed great significance on the movement of celestial bodies.

AND ALTHOUGH
It seemed they thought much
of what we had said
It seemed also
that they had no will to show it
UNTIL AT LAST
they said we should go
seeking no further learning from them
for they had much to discuss among them
NOW IT SEEMED TO US
They showed-all unwilling-
great consternation
SO THAT IT SEEMED TO US
That what we had said
may well have had great effect
Perhaps even the effect that we sought
AND SO
We left this Stone Hill
walking in a ceremonial way to the South
and gave them time to consider

Through the period of three moons they heard nothing from The Stone Hill People, but one day seven delegates came to the camp of

The Walking People. They stayed well into the night, and The Walking People patiently answered all of their questions for they were anxious for their success. As they described The Sun Disk People ways, it was obvious that The Stone Hill People were enthralled by their account. Carefully guarding their intentions, they departed with a warning:

> If one day you arise
> and see no one at all
> on our Stone Hill
> Be aware
> that it is yet ours
> and to it we may yet return
> Be aware also
> that there are those you cannot see
> and yet who guard our Sacred Places
> Be aware
> and choose some other place
> for your living.

Sometime after this meeting, a delegation of The Southern People came to the camp of The Walking People to show their grateful hearts and to censure the strange and worrisome Stone Hill People. The Walking People counseled patience saying, "The seven who have gone may one day be followed by the remainder. On hearing this counsel, The Southern People protested with great humor:

> "You do not understand"
> -they answered us
> "We have been there and returned
> to their Stone Hill as you call it
> "We saw no one leave
> no one at all"
> And they laughed-
> and laughed again at our amazement
> "We show you many, many grateful hearts
> -they went on
> "We have been there and back

to learn what might be so
"And although we saw no one at all leave
surely many did just so
"FOR THEY HAVE ALL LEFT
THERE IS NO ONE THERE AT ALL"

And so, the stone structures and the stone walled ceremonial paths stood silent and empty for the first time in a multitude of centuries. And since The Walking People had no desire to leave their village of round dwellings made of woven branches and skins, they heeded the warning of The Stone Hill People. But, when they visited the sacred place, they found that all vestige of human living was gone. The intricately carved wooden totems and ceremonial staffs had vanished just as the people who held them sacred had vanished. Only the ageless, enduring stone remained, the caves with their ponderous cap stones, the stone-lined ceremonial paths, the oracle chamber with its stone speaking tube and the grooved sacrificial stone whose purpose remained an enigma. Their 10,000-year journey from the west had prepared The Walking People for any eventuality and, as it was their custom, they held a council to contemplate their future. In their wisdom they concluded that they had no wish to be a disparate people as had been The Stone Building People. They correctly divined that those who now welcomed them with grateful hearts might one day view them as a disparate people. And though they chose to respect the sacred place of The Stone Hill People, they did not covet their stone hill. And so, for one reason and another, they left The Central Place of a vanished people inviolate and began to dream of a day when A People might find a permanent home for the children's children's children. They were unaware at that time that a journey undertaken in a time beyond memory was nearing its end. But that is a story for another time, and it is a story better told by Paula Underwood, The Lineal Keeper of her peoples 10,000-year oral history.

Onkwe Tase, Mohawk and member of the Turtle Clan,
Lowell, Massachusetts.

Ceremonial center, Mystery Hill.

Sacrificial stone, Mystery Hill.

Chapter 3
CHIEF ESCUMBUIT
1665--1727

T he name Escumbuit has fired the imagination of Big Island Pond residents for many years. Youngsters have listened wide-eyed to campfire tales about the legendary Indian Chief who fought with the French against the English Colonists during the French and Indian Wars. During the 1950s his story was partially documented in research done by a local woman named Pat Howard. As Pricilla Lane she gave up her role as a movie celebrity to be the wartime bride of a local boy named Joe Howard. Joe grew up in Howard's Grove and, when the war began, he went through flight training and was commissioned as a pilot. He and Pricilla met in Hollywood where they were married during World War II. When the war ended, Joe returned to the pond with his movie star wife. The presence of Pricilla on the pond created a considerable stir. Despite her celebrity, Pat maintained a low profile and, in time, she was allowed to live the lifestyle that she preferred. After her husband Joe died, she still maintained her year-round residence at Howard's Grove and continued her role as a mother and resident of the pond.

Intrigued with local history, she did some research on the legendary Chief Escumbuit for whom the small island opposite Chase's Grove is named. Although her story was not fully researched, her findings created a mild sensation around the pond. She wrote that he was the most important Sachem of all of the Indians in the Merrimac Valley and that he had been an ally of the French in their wars with the English. Pat interpreted the meaning of Nescambiouit to be, "He who comes out of the woods." She reported that the French gave him a silver sword and a purse of gold in a ceremony in which he was knighted by the French King.

Others wrote that he was the leader of the band of Indians who spent the night on Escumbuit Island the night before they went down to Haverhill and carried Hannah Duston into captivity. Another version stated that the Indians stopped on Escumbuit Island with their captives after their raid on Haverhill. I was unable to confirm either of these stories by my own research.

Escumbuit is credited with the death of 150 English and he was famous for his war club on which he had cut 98 notches. Sebastian Clayton Francis who runs Penobscot Indian Art in Old Town, Maine provided the pictures of the traditional Penobscot root clubs that appear at the end of this chapter. "S C" told me that these ceremonial clubs are made from young birch trees that are dug complete with root ball and are carved and painted by native American craftsmen. The Original People threw these clubs with startling accuracy to bring down small game such as rabbits, squirrels and even game birds on the wing. On the warpath the clubs were used for close quarter mayhem.

The inspiration for Abenaki Warrior came after four months of research about Escumbuit's life in the summer of 1996. The information in Pat Howard's brief report convinced me that the life of an Indian of Escumbuit's renown must have been recorded somewhere in the history of that period. As it turned out this reasoning was well founded, and my persistence was finally rewarded by new discoveries. A rare book that was written in 1727 by New Hampshire militiaman, Samuel Penhallow, refers to the chief by his Indian name--Assacumbuit. I then located an English translation of the works of the Jesuit Historian P.F.X. Charlevoix that contained extensive references to Chief Nescambiouit.

Without the facts uncovered by Pat Howard, it is unlikely that I would have ever undertaken the research that enabled me to write Abenaki Warrior. The knowledge that he had been so honored by the French fueled my enthusiasm to learn more. I credit her for showing the way to the incredible details of Chief Escumbuit's life story. Writing Abenaki Warrior as a historical novel enabled me to describe what his life as a youngster might have been like as well as to describe the motivation that drove him to incredible heights. This chapter is a factual account of Escumbuit's career based on my 1996 research. In those cases where I make deductive assumptions about his motives and actions I have tried to make it clear that they are my personal conclusions. His connection to Big Island Pond begins after his visit to France in 1706 and 1707 and after his well-documented raid on Haverhill in 1708.

Chief Escumbuit was born in the beautiful valley of the upper Saco River in an area that had been the home of the Pigwacket Indians for thousands of years. The name Pigwacket resembles certain root words of the Abenaki language and appears to describe the sweeping turns of the river as it passes close by the beautiful sheet of water now known as Lovewell Pond. This valley, flanked to the west by the White Mountains, abounded in wildlife. Moose, deer, elk, bears, wolves, beaver and fish were plentiful, and the valley provided fertile soil for the Indian's primitive agriculture. Here they planted their corn, pumpkins, beans, squash and tobacco. At the pinnacle of Escumbuit's fame he was known by several names. His fellow Pigwacket warriors gave him the name "Assacumbuit." According to N.F. Maurault, the Jesuit missionary who wrote *Histoire du Abenaquis*, Assacumbuit meant, He who is so important and raised so high by his merit that thought cannot reach his greatness. Escumbuit undoubtedly earned this exalted name as a result of the daring and ferocity that marked his military campaigns. The Algonquian spoken by the Woodland Indians of the Northeast is a language of images. A single word can convey a rather complicated meaning. Certain English words like mob or crowd can also convey a broad meaning. The French called him "Nescambiouit" (pronounced Nescamboo-ee) and English historians referred to him variously as Assacumbuit, Escumbuit and Old Escumbuit. The "Old Escumbuit" version suggests that he may have been born as early as 1650 and that he could have been 77 years old when he died in 1727. Although the average life span for Indians of his era was only 45 years, there were notable exceptions. (Passaconaway, famous chief of the Pennacook Indians was 100 years old when he died.)

The ancestors of the Pigwacket Indians were nomadic hunters who migrated down from Labrador in the wake of the retreating glaciers of the last ice age. Little wonder that the Pigwackets believed that their tribe had occupied their valley since the beginning of time. Their culture and lifestyle was very similar to that of the Big Island Pond Indians. Saco Pond in Fryeburg, Maine was the locale for their large village and the Saco River provided a highway for their canoes to carry them to the coast in the summer. In the winter they hunted for moose, bear and deer in the White Mountains and their life was good.

Historians first singled out Escumbuit for special attention in about 1688. By that time the elders of his tribe had named him Assacumbuit and had made him a Sachem and a War Chief of the Pigwacket tribe. These honors were bestowed on him for his courage and daring in battle. His role as a leader of Indian raids vaulted him to prominence and attracted the interest of contemporary historians.

The English had an important fort at Pemaquid Point that was located at the tip of the peninsula south of Damariscotta, Maine. It was attacked and destroyed by the French and the Abenaki Indians in 1689 with the loss of 80 men, women and children. The surprise attack caught many civilians outside the protection of the fort. The Indians used the cover of a large rock outcropping to pick off half of the fort defenders with musket fire. Despite the heavy loss of life among the civilians surrounding the fort, Chief Madockawando persuaded the other Indian leaders to spare Captain Weems and five of his men. They were taken as captives to Canada from where they were eventually repatriated. Chief Escumbuit was among the 200 Indians who took part in that raid.

In 1696 Fort William Henry was rebuilt under the direction of Captain John March of Andover, Massachusetts. He had formerly been a boat builder on the Merrimac River. The walls of the rebuilt fort were unable to withstand cannon fire because there had not been enough lime available for the concrete used in the construction of the fort. Another Andover man named Pasco Chubb[8] commanded it.

---

[8] *Andover: Symbol of New England*, by Claude M Fuess (p 75): "The Strange Case Of Pasco Chubb." This man, with a name which Dickenson would have been delighted to immortalize, made his entrance on the colonial scene in unobtrusive fashion but ended as the central figure in a grim and sinister episode. Thomas Chubb arrived from England in 1663, bound to Samuel Maverick for his passage money. We have the record of the marriage, May 29,1689, of Pasco Chubb, son of Thomas and Avis Chubb, to Hannah Faulkner, daughter of Edmund Faulkner, one of the original proprietors of Andover. When and how he came to Andover is unknown; but he was listed in a "Rate made for the minister in the year 1692 for the North End of the Town Of Andover." The Chubb family had evidently come up

Having decided not to occupy the fort after demolishing it in 1689, the rebuilt fort stood once again like a bone in the throat of the chagrined French.

Twelve Indians including Escumbuit, Chief Egeremet of the Machias tribe and Chiefs Taxous and Abenquid of the Norridgwock tribe went to the fort under the protection of a white flag. The English and the French had agreed to a parley in order to discuss the exchange of prisoners who were being held in Boston as well as in Canada. Pasco Chubb, an unprincipled man, feigning the good host, plied the twelve Indians with rum and, when their guard was down, he and his eleven companions tried to capture the entire group. In the melee that followed, Chief Egeremet and two other Indians were killed. Two Indians were captured, but Escumbuit and Chief Taxous managed to escape.

Even the English Colonists were outraged by this betrayal of trust. The French soon took advantage of the Indian outrage resulting from Chubb's treachery. They had little trouble raising a force of 300 Indians to attack the newly rebuilt Fort William Henry. D'Iberville, the famous Canadian sea captain, came down from Quebec with the warships Envieus and Profond. At St. John, Newfoundland they engaged two British frigates and an auxiliary tender. They dismasted and took one frigate, but the other frigate and the tender escaped in the fog. At Saint Castin's trading post in Maine the Jesuit priests Thury and Simon joined them with Indians from the villages they served. The French sponsored a powwow and feast to get the Indians in the proper fighting mood. Then 500 Indians in canoes headed for Pemaquid by sea. D'Iberville caught up with them a day later with his two war ships. The entire force arrived at Pemaquid August 14, 1696. Escumbuit and his Abenaki warriors landed at New Harbor located about ½ mile from the fort. The Indian war party was under the command of the French trader Saint Castin, and Captains Villieu and Montigny. The Jesuit historian Charlevoix wrote that Montigny

---

in the world! Chubb must have accumulated some military experience, for in February, 1696, he was placed in command of the newly constructed Fort William Henry at Pemaquid, on the coast of Maine.

performed wonders with his faithful Nescambiouit always at his side. In his passage lauding the bravery of the French officers he singled out Nescambiouit for special praise.

Pasco Chubb and 95 soldiers, who were well supplied with powder, ball and provisions, defended the fifteen-gun fort. Although the fort had been rebuilt at great expense with stone and mortar, the quality of the workmanship was poor. Many of the soldiers had been permitted to bring their wives and children who now cowered inside the fort. The sole source of drinking water for the people in the fort was a spring that was located outside the walls of the fort.

Although Escumbuit and his warriors surrounded the fort in great numbers, their musket fire was ineffective against the stone walls of the fort. Nevertheless, they sent a message to Chubb demanding his surrender. In response Chubb is reported to have uttered these defiant but hollow words: "We will continue to fight though the ocean may be covered with French ships and the land by Indians."

That night, with great difficulty, the French unloaded two cannons plus two mortars from one of their sloops and moved them into position to fire on the fort. The two Jesuit priests labored alongside the Indians to move the heavy guns into position. The following day, at three o'clock in the afternoon, they fired exploding mortar shells into the fort with devastating effect. Shortly before the shelling began, Castin sent a message to Chubb to warn him that if he did not surrender he would be given no quarter and that the defenders of the fort would be turned over to the Indians. After five or six mortar shells exploded inside the fort, Chubb ran up a white flag and asked for a parley. He offered to give up the fort if he and his people were protected from the Indians and exchanged for French and Indian prisoners in Boston. D'Iberville agreed to Chubb's terms, and the occupants of the fort were transferred to a small island in the bay over the protests of Escumbuit and his Indians. A French sloop was deployed to protect them from the Indians

Upon entering the fort they found a chained Indian in a dungeon. His deplorable physical condition enraged the Indians who immediately wanted to take revenge on the English prisoners. The French discovered a letter from the Governor's Council in Boston that instructed Chubb to hang the chained prisoner. They withheld this intelligence from the Indians fearing they would be unable to control them. D'Iberville kept his word and the English defenders were eventually returned to Boston in a prisoner exchange.

When Pasco Chubb returned to Boston, he was tried for cowardice for surrendering the fort without a fight, and the Massachusetts authorities imprisoned him. They failed to recognize that, had he resisted the French to the end, the fort would have been demolished by cannon fire and its inhabitants left to the mercy of the Indians. Escumbuit was outraged by d'Iberville's treatment of Chubb, and we will learn later how he and his men meted out Indian justice to Chubb and his wife in Andover.

After demolishing the fort at Pemaquid and loading the captured cannons from the fort aboard his ships, d'Iberville sailed for Newfoundland taking Escumbuit and his Indians with him. They landed at Placentia, the main French settlement on the southwestern coast of Newfoundland. Mr. De Brouillan, governor of Placentia, was waiting there with a force of local men. Both France and England had bases on this large strategic island. The English settlement of St John's held a strategic advantage being located on the East Coast of the island. Whoever controlled the island controlled the massive cod fishing grounds in the North Atlantic. St. John's defenses had been designed to repel an attack from the sea. Perhaps the perceived hardships attackers faced crossing Newfoundland on foot made an attack from that quarter unlikely, but their oversight would cost them dearly.

On the first of November, d'Iberville left Placentia at the head of his troops and headed overland for St. John's. After a nine-day march, under the most severe winter conditions, they reached Florillon. They captured an Englishman who later escaped and warned St. John's that the French and Indians were on their way. De Brouillan, a vain and power-hungry man, tried to assume overall command, but upon learning that d'Iberville's troops would fight only under their own commander, finally agreed to share the glory. The entire army began to march on Bay de Toulle about six leagues away.

On November 26th, after advancing three leagues, they encountered a force of thirty Englishmen who immediately retreated to a defensive position from where they offered stiff resistance. In a brief action, the enemy lost six men and the rest abandoned the position and retreated to St. John's. When De Brouillan's force arrived that evening a fierce snow storm began that held them up for an entire day while they waited for more favorable weather. During the snowstorm the impatient Montigny and his favorite Indian Commander, Escumbuit, reconnoitered the area with a small force of warriors and captured several prisoners.

On the morning of the 28th they began to advance again with Montigny and thirty Canadians leading the way. De Brouillon and d'Iberville followed with the rest of the troops. After marching about 2½ hours, Montigny spied, within pistol shot, approximately 90 Englishmen positioned behind rocks. A fight broke out immediately in which Montigny and his twenty men held their own until the army came up to support him. De Brouillon and his men made a frontal assault while d'Iberville and the Indians circled and flanked the enemy. After about a half-hour fight, the English disengaged and made a fighting retreat towards St. John's with d'Iberville, the Canadians and Escumbuit in full pursuit.

St. John's was only three leagues away and, when the inhabitants saw their beaten force retreating to the fort, panic reigned. They had been counting on these soldiers to stem the enemy advance. Many boarded a ship in the harbor carrying their most valuable possessions with them. As the French and Indians approached the fort, they could see a ship putting on sail preparing to leave the port while consigning the defenders to their fate. The French commander sent a women prisoner into the fort bearing a surrender demand, but the commander held her without answering the ultimatum. The French, concluding that the English were going to defend the fort, sent men to bring up the cannon and mortars which had been left at Bay de Toulle.

On the nights of the 29th and 30th Montigny was ordered to burn the houses outside the fort. D'Iberville and Escumbuit advanced with thirty handpicked men to support them. De Brouillan provided additional cover in the event their assistance was needed and, on the night of the 30th, in the glare of the burning houses, a soldier came out of the fort carrying a white flag. The commander desired to meet outside because he did not want the French to see the deplorable conditions inside the fort. There were virtually no supplies and fishermen and civilians were the principal defenders. During the

meeting, De Brouillan submitted his terms, and the English commander asked if he could deliver his answer the following day. From
the height of the fort they had seen two large English warships
tacking to enter the harbor, but the French had also spotted the
ships. De Brouillan threatened to attack immediately if the commander refused to surrender. Presently, the English captains assessed the
situation on shore and they decided to put about and set a course for
England.

Again the French erred by not occupying St. John's. They decided
to burn the remaining houses and the fort and abandon the settlement. Montigny and Escumbuit had captured most of the outlying
settlements and had taken over 700 prisoners. Of the two posts
remaining, Bonnevista was heavily fortified and difficult to reach
over impossible terrain dragging the massive siege guns they had left
at Bay de Toulle. Three hundred Englishmen had reached safety on
Carbonniere Island over difficult terrain that made a winter attack
impossible.

In his analysis of this campaign[9], Charlevoix, the French Jesuit
historian for King Louis XIV, points out the folly of the French
commanders in giving up the settlement after having subdued it. The
French could not foresee that Chief Escumbuit would return in 1706
and that, on this occasion, the English defenders would suffer his full
fury.

In her book, *Historical Sketches of Andover*, published by Sarah
Loring Bailey in 1880, she examines the cowardice of Pasco Chubb

---

[9] *History of New France* by The Rev. P.F.X. de Charlevoix,S.J. (p.47), in the final
paragraph of his account of this action writes; "In this campaign D'Iberville gave
striking proofs of his ability, and was at every point where danger was to be met
or hardship undergone; next to him came Montigny, generally in the van and often
leaving little to be done by those who followed him. After them, the most
distinguished were Boucher and de la Perriere, d'Amor de Plaine, Dugue de
Boisbriand, all three Canadian gentlemen, and *Nescambiouit*. There is no doubt,
had there been force enough to complete this well-advanced conquest and guard the
posts from which the English had been expelled, they would have lost the island of
Newfoundland forever; but few men in France then saw how important is was to
secure the total possession."

at Pemaquid. She describes the imprisonment that followed his dishonorable discharge and the manner of his release from prison. The Massachusetts archives still contain a letter petitioning the court for his release.[10]

It has also been suggested that friends intervened on his behalf. The opinion has already been expressed here that, given a fort filled with men, women and children, it would have been folly to face cannon fire when it was possible to save all the occupants of the fort through a prisoner exchange. Aside from that single point, there is no doubt that his decision to live in Andover after his release put the entire town at risk of an attack by Escumbuit and his warriors. On February 22, 1698, less than two years after Pasco Chubb escaped torture and certain death at the hands of the Abenaki Indians, Chief Escumbuit led a war party of 30 Abenaki braves across the Merrimac River in order to settle accounts with him. What emotions must have festered in the mind of this driven man while he waited for this moment?

The winter of 1697-8 had been the most severe in the memory of the townspeople. Over the years they had experienced Indian raids and their militia still patrolled the south shore of the Merrimac on the lookout for Indian raiders, but patrols were now discontinued in the belief that no one would venture outside in such harsh weather.

---

[10] *Historical Sketches Of Andover* by Sarah Loring Bailey, (p. 181); "The Petition of Pasco Chubb late Commander of his Majestys Fort William Henry at Pemaquid, Humbly sheweth. "That yr Petitioner stands committed a Prisoner in Boston Goale for his Late surrendering & delivering up the aforesd Fort and Stores thereto belonging unto his Majestys enemies.

And whereas yr Petitioner is a very poore man, having a wife and children to Looke after wch by reason of his confinement & poverty are reduced to a meane and necessitous condition having not wherewithall either to defray his present necessary charges or to relieve his Indigent family.

Your Petitioner therefore humbly prays that this high and hon Court will please to consider the premises so as that he may now either be Brought to his Tryall or else upon giving sufficient Bayle be delivered from his present confinement, whereby he may be enabled to take some care of his poore family for their subsistence in the hard & deare winter season.

But once again English settlers underestimated the willingness of the Indians to endure extreme hardship. On the night of February 21, 1698 Escumbuit and his 30 warriors crossed the frozen river on snowshoes, dressed in wolf skins and bearskins to shield them from the bitter cold. Their mittened hands carried muskets, tomahawks and war clubs. Their Indian guide was familiar with the town having known Colonel Dudley Bradstreet who was a magistrate and colonel in the local militia. He had agreed to guide Escumbuit and his men with the understanding that Colonel Bradstreet and his wife would be spared. He had been treated well by the colonel in the past and, though he was willing to share in the loot taken in the raid, he felt indebted to the colonel.

At daybreak they attacked the unsuspecting village and they soon overwhelmed Chubb's house where Escumbuit took his revenge. Chubb's wife, bound by her vows, but not by his deeds, suffered his fate and, after taking their scalps, the Indians fired the house and barn. They burst into Bradstreet's home where they murdered Major Wade, a visiting relative from Mystic. They took the colonel and his wife some distance from the house as if to take them into captivity, but later released them to the safety of their own home. In the general melee that followed they burned two more houses and killed two more people. They burned a barn containing a large store of corn and a number of cattle. They ransacked the church and took the pulpit cushions outside and set them on fire. During the raid many of the Andover town records were destroyed.

When they heard sounds of the militia mustering, they retreated over the Haverhill Road towards that city loaded down with loot from the raid. On the outskirts of Haverhill they encountered Jonathan Haines and Samuel Ladd and their two sons. They killed and scalped the elders and took the boys captive, but the Haines boy managed to escape. It was the second time he had escaped his Indian captors in two years. They also invaded and burned the house of Mr. Timothy Johnson of Haverhill and killed his nineteen-year-old daughter Penelope. They skirted Haverhill and headed north over the Pentucket Trail that went north through Atkinson. Although this was the last and worse Indian attack on the City of Andover, the town reacted by building two blockhouses on the shore of the Merrimac

River. They were well supplied with munitions and the militia was provided with snowshoes that facilitated their winter patrols.

Spurred on by the French, the Abenaki Indians continued to harass the frontier but there is no historical reference to any specific actions by Escumbuit until 1703. During this period small groups of Indians killed unwary farmers working their fields, or carried off stray children to captivity in Canada. The earlier "no quarter" slaughter of the settlers was tempered somewhat by new policies in Quebec and Montreal. They began to offer bounties for women and children captives delivered to Canada. There were five males to every female in Canada; some of the female captives married Frenchmen and others married Indians and lived in Indian villages. The children were placed in convents and Catholic orphanages where many converted to Catholicism.

Governor Dudley was appointed Royal Provincial Governor of the Massachusetts Colony in 1702. Inasmuch as the Indians were described as being in a "tolerably good mood," he decided to declare a Congress in Casco, Maine where he and his Massachusetts delegate met with all the important chiefs of the Abenaki tribes.[11] On June 20, 1703 hundreds of Indians, many in full war paint, came to Casco in their canoes. A New Hampshire militiaman named Samuel Penhallow wrote a fascinating account of the intrigues that took place at that famous meeting.[12] Escumbuit, famous Pigwacket Sagamore, is not listed among the participants having been given an undercover role in a plan to assassinate all the English at the meeting. After a great deal of speechmaking and, after declarations of everlasting friendship by both sides, the participants placed new stones on a monument that had been named "TWO BROTHERS." After this

---

[11] *Abenaki Warrior* by Alfred E Kayworth (p. 63), Gives a detailed account of the intrigues that took place at that Congress.

[12] Author's note: Samuel Penhallow was a well-known figure in New Hampshire history. He wrote a book entitled *History of the Indian Wars* that chronicles the 1703-1713 period. This 1727 book was used as a reference for this chapter on Chief Escumbuit. He later became a New Hampshire judge and was a close associate of Benning Wentworth, the first Royal Provincial Governor of New Hampshire.

ceremony, the Congress was adjourned having accomplished nothing of lasting importance.

On August 10, 1703, scarcely six weeks after the declarations of brotherhood and everlasting peace, five hundred Indians, together with their French sponsors, struck simultaneously from Casco to Wells. Thirty-nine people were killed or taken captive at Wells. Cape Porpoise was overwhelmed and burned. Winter Harbor defended itself well for a time, but was forced to surrender under terms. Saco Fort was taken with a toll of eleven killed and twenty-four taken captive. Perpooduck, Maine, home of nine families, suffered the worse. All their men were gone when the Indians butchered twenty-five and took eight captives.

One of the important Maine forts was located at Casco Bay where Major John March, former Andover boat builder and re-builder of the fort in Pemaquid, was in command. He was unaware that all the settlements south of him were under Indian attack. Therefore, when he saw a party of three Indians approaching the fort carrying a white flag, he decided to go out and meet them. The three Indians were the Sachems Escumbuit of the Pigwacket tribe, Mauxus from Norridgewalk, and Wanungonet from the Penobscot tribe. Prior to hailing the fort, warriors had moved into concealed positions close by. As part of a rather foolhardy arrangement, two elderly inhabitants of the surrounding settlement went with the Major to see what the three Indians wanted to talk about. As March left the fort in the company of the two elders he said to the defenders, "Keep a sharp eye!"

The parley had scarcely begun when Escumbuit and the other two chiefs drew tomahawks concealed beneath their mantels and attacked the three Englishmen. March, being noted for his agility and strength, wrested a hatchet from one of his assailants and held the others off until Sergeant Hook and a few soldiers came to his aid and managed to get him back to the fort. However, both Kent and Phipenny were dispatched with Indian tomahawks in the melee. Despite being wounded in the attack, March rallied his men and prepared to defend the fort. When properly equipped with food and water and aggressively defended, palisade forts and garrison houses were impregnable against Indian attacks. The Indians used all sorts of subterfuge in their attempts to force an entrance to these strongholds.

The Indians soon appeared in force and began to burn all the cabins and property around the fort. After a few days, their numbers increased to about five hundred Indians and a few Frenchmen under an officer named Beaubassin. They had completed their ravages down the coast and now they proposed to take this fort. The fort was on the shore of Casco Bay and Escumbuit and his warriors took shelter behind a steep bank that shielded them from English musket fire. They dug trenches towards the palisade intending to tunnel under the logs and launch a surprise night attack. Three days of hard work brought them very close to their objective when they suddenly came under cannon fire from the Province Galley commanded by Captain Southack. He had sailed into the harbor and captured three small vessels that had been previously captured by the Indians and he also destroyed many of their canoes. Escumbuit and his warriors were forced to abandon their efforts to breach the fort defenses and, by daybreak the following morning, they had disappeared into the forest.

The failure of the Indian plan to ambush the Governor and his council during the peace conference in Casco was balanced somewhat by their successful attacks against the coastal settlements. The decisive action by Captain Southhack of the Province Galley saved Major March and his men at the fort in Casco, Maine. These actions marked the beginning of Queen Ann's war that raged until 1713. After this massive, coordinated attack, the Indians launched smaller hit-and-run raids with small war parties on individual garrison houses. Although Escumbuit was undoubtedly in action during 1704-1705, his activities were not reported until he was re-united with Montigny in Newfoundland in January 1706. The English historian Samuel Penhallow wrote an excellent account of the Indian Wars that chronicled the 1703-1713 period. This rare book, published first in 1727, is firmly pro-British as one might expect from a former member of the New Hampshire militia.[13]

---

[13] *"History Of The Indian Wars"* by Samuel Penhallow, (p.40) "But of the Indians that was ever known since King Phillip, never any appear'd so cruel and inhumane as *Assacambuit,* that insulting monster, who by the encouragement of the French went over to Paris, and being introduced to the King, lifted up his hand and in the most arrogant manner imaginable, saying "This hand of mine has slain one hundred

By 1705 the English had rebuilt their settlement and fort at St. John's, and once again posed a threat to the French in the area. The Frenchman De Subercase got permission from King Louis XIV to sail to Canada in command of the warship Wesp and mount a new attack on the English at St John's. He took aboard one hundred Canadians in Quebec and landed them at Placentia, the main French settlement on Newfoundland. Among his officers was the famous Montigny and it appeared that wherever he went into action he had Escumbuit at his side. These Canadians joined Subercase in his attack on St. John's on the 15th of January 1706 at the head of 450 well-armed men. Among them were soldiers, Canadian civilians, privateers and Indians led by Escumbuit. Each man was given a blanket and twenty day's provisions. One has to wonder what motivated this motley assortment of men to undertake a two-week march through the bone-chilling cold and snow to risk death at the hands of an enemy protected by the walls of the fort at St. John's. Surely they were not motivated by ideology. The presence of privateers in their ranks tells us that they were probably in it for the money.

Unlike the 1688 raid, the inhabitants were not forewarned of the attack. Escumbuit and his braves were obliged to lay all night in six feet of snow waiting for the daylight to illuminate their attack on the houses surrounding the fort. The ordeal seems to have created a rage in Escumbuit that he continued to vent on the captives even after they surrendered. Only the intervention of the French commander, Monsieur de Beaucourt, prevented the wholesale slaughter of the defenseless civilians. The description of the action by the Englishman

---

and fifty of your Majesty's enemies, within the Territories of New England & C. Which bold and impudent speech was so pleasing to that Bloody Monarch, that he forthwith Knighted him, and order'd eight Livres a day to be paid him during life; which so exalted the wretch (having his hands so long imbrued in innocent blood) as at his return, to exert a sovereignty over the rest of his brethren, by murdering one and stabing another, which so exasperated those of their relations, that they sought revenge, and would instantly have executed it, but that he fled his country, and never return'd after."

Penhallow[14] contrasts sharply with the account written by the French historian Charlevoix.[15] The contradictory stories demonstrate how Escumbuit, the French hero, was at the same time termed a monster by the English. The differences remind the thoughtful reader to examine the background and motives of any writer in order to detect a strong personal bias or hidden agenda.

They had taken one hundred and forty prisoners in the area surrounding the fort. There was no humanity in their decision to send these prisoners into the fort. First, they no longer needed to guard and feed them, and secondly, by sending them into the fort,

---

[14] *History of the Indian Wars,* Samuel Penhallow, 1727 (p 30). "The Descent that the enemy made on Newfoundland was more terrible and surprising than the former; for on January 21,st 1707, at break of day, Monsieur Supercase, Governor of Placentia, came with five hundred and fifty French from Canada, Port Royal, and other places adjacent, and a company of savages, of whom Assacumbuit was Chief and laid waste all the Southern settlements in a few days and then fell on St. John, where in the space of two hours all were become prisoners of war, excepting those in the castle and the fort. The night before the enterprise they were obliged to lye on a bed of snow, six foot deep, for fear of being discovered, which caused such cold and numbness in the joynts of several, that **Assacumbuit** vow'd revenge, and accordingly executed his resentment, for that he destroyed all before him, and gave no quarter for some time; till Monsieur de Beaucourt, who was a gentleman of more humanity, did interpose and abate his fury.

[15] *History Of New France,* The Rev P. F. X. De Charlevoix, S.J. (p.174) "On the 5th of March the army decamped and marched along the shore to Ferryland, where the inhabitants at first made a show of defense, but they soon changed their minds and surrendered as prisoners of war. That town was burned, after which **Montigny**, who had brought his faithful **Nescambiouit** on this expedition, was detached with the Indians and a part of the Canadians to go in the direction of Carbonniere and Bonavista, with orders to burn and destroy all the coast, which he executed without losing a single man, so great was the terror among the English. His very name made the arms fall from the hands of the most resolute, and gave him a number of prisoners whom he had only the trouble of binding. But he had to reserve Carbonniere Island for another time. It held three hundred men, and was, as I have stated, inaccessible in winter. Every other place was carried or submitted; Messrs. De Linctot, de Villedonne and de Beletre, thoroughly supported **Montigny**, and **Nescambiouit**, as usual, distinguished himself. In fine, this campaign completely ruined the English trade in Newfoundland."

they counted on drawing down the food supply of the garrison by forcing them to feed additional mouths. They then laid siege to the fort for thirty days, but the fort under the command of Captain Moody, and the Castle commanded by Captain Lotbarn, rejected all demands to surrender. Much of their gunpowder had been rendered useless during river crossings and they were unable to bring their heavy guns and mortars into action against the fortifications. Montigny and his Canadians, accompanied by Escumbuit and his Indians ravaged the outlying communities and took many captives, but in the end, they were obliged to withdraw to Placentia, leaving the fort and the castle to the enemy.

The most amazing event in Escumbuit's career was his trip to France in 1706[16]. He may have traveled to France with d'Subercase on his return voyage aboard the Wesp. What thoughts must have gone through the mind of this Aboriginal Indian when he was told he was going to be presented to the King? What was his reaction to the wonders of Paris: the Palace of Versailles, Notre Dame Cathedral, The Champs Elysees, the cabaret life and the wine and the women of Paris? How did the Parisians react to Le Sauvage, dressed in his native regalia and carrying his war club with its 98 notches? During his stay in France he met The Reverend P.F.X. Charlevoix who wrote The History of New France. The high regard that Charlevoix had for Montigny and Newcambiouit is reflected in the praise he lavished on their fighting ability in his reports.

When Escumbuit was presented to the French monarch he raised his right hand and declared, "With this hand I have slain one hundred and fifty of Your Majesties enemies in the territory of New France." The King then knighted him and presented him with a beautifuly-crafted sabre and a pension of eight livres a day for life.

---

[16] *Abenaki Warrior* by Alfred E Kayworth (p.74-83) In this historical novel, an entire chapter is devoted Escumbuit's trip to France in the company of his idol, Montigny. He and Montigny became favorites of the Paris café society where they mingled with the elite. After being knighted and given a pension by King Louis XIV at the Palace of Versaille, he was entertained by the French historian Charlevoix at Notre Dame Cathedral. During an exhibition dueling match with an expert French swordsman he stunned the spectators by suddenly reverting to his killer instinct.

The effect of all the presents and attention heaped on him by the French must have had a profound effect on Escumbuit, because we learn that upon his return to his village in Maine he became quite haughty and arrogant in his relations with his fellow tribesmen. In the course of a dispute he stabbed one brave to death and wounded another. The Abenaki code demanded that the relatives of these men avenge these deeds, and Escumbuit fled his village in order to escape retribution from the aggrieved relatives.

He dropped out of sight at this juncture, and history does not record his whereabouts until he vaulted to distinction the following August during a French and Indian attack on Haverhill. He may have gone up to the French missionary village on the Saint Francis River. This village, now called Odanak, was established to harbor Indian refugees and descendants of the Abenaki Indians still reside there. This, of course, is where those seeking revenge would have expected him to go and would have been the first place they would have looked for him. The association of his name with Big Island Pond suggests that he chose to join the isolated band of Indians who lived there. At Big Island Pond he was beyond the reach of his Pigwacket enemies and safe in a stronghold from where he could harass the English.

Big Island Pond was called Lake Escumbuit as late as 1926. Proof of this comes in the form of two postal cards owned by Patsy Goodridge of Hemlock Heights. One card displays a photograph of the lake with the caption: "West Shore near Conley's Grove, Lake Escumbuit, Island Pond, New Hampshire. The other is a picture taken of a rocky point on the west shore of the big island that is captioned: "Menagerie Rocks, Lake Escambuit, N.H. Today, the imaginative observer can still make out what appears to be the outline of an elephant with a lion reclining in the foreground. Magnification of the postmark on this card clearly shows a 1926 postmark.

Escumbuit Island and the post cards are the only solid evidence tying Chief Escumbuit to the history of the pond. However, a considerable amount of legend, rumor and speculation connect him to the pond. There are solid reasons to conclude that Escumbuit transferred his headquarters to Big Island Pond after his banishment. He had ranged along the Merrimac River from 1680-1689 preying on border towns. During these forays he was a long way from home for extended periods. The familiar environs of Big Island Pond provided an ideal base of operation. From this isolated area he was within easy striking distance of many border settlements while avoiding his Pigwacket enemies. When he was driven from his native village in Maine, it was natural for him to seek the shelter of this home away from home. In Haverhill, the following year, he was described performing great feats of valor with the sword given him by King Louis XIV at the Palace of Versailles.

Early in 1708 the Canadian Governor Vaudreuil called a great council in Montreal which included all the chiefs of the Christian Indians settled in the colony. These Indians decided to join with 100 Canadian soldiers and other volunteers to make up a force of 400 men. Messieurs St. Ours des Chaillons and Hertel de Rouville commanded the French, and Sieur Boucher de la Perriere planned to lead the Indians. They planned to split into several small parties, each of which was to make its way to the south end of Lake Winnipesaukee by separate routes to avoid discovery by the English. At a rendezvous, near what is now Wolfeboro, they were supposed to be joined by a large force of Abenaki Indians from the Pigwacket tribe. From there they planned to descend on the Pistcataqua settlements of Berwick, Salmon Falls, Dover, Portsmouth, Oyster River, Durham and others.

When the French reached the rendezvous they were chagrined to learn that the Pigwackets and other Abenaki tribes had failed to show up so they were forced to scale back their plans. Instead of a general attack on the previously mentioned settlements, they turned their attention to the town of Haverhill. Despite all the secrecy, word had gotten to Governor Dudley in Boston that something was afoot, and all of the settlements had been reinforced with militiamen and outlying roads were being patrolled. By Saturday night, August 28, 1708, the French and Indian raiders lay in the woods on the heights above the village of Haverhill. As he waited with the others,

Escumbuit must have been keenly aware of the attention his silver saber attracted from French and Indian alike.[17]

As the sun rose above the eastern horizon August 29, 1708, the people of the small village were enjoying a day off by sleeping in. Most planned to attend church at midmorning and spend the rest of the day at leisure. The village still consisted of no more than thirty houses grouped down by the river with a few more scattered up on the hill. On the crest of the hill, a garrison house owned by Jonathan Emerson guarded the approach from Little River, and another one flanked it in the opposite direction. Although the garrison houses had recently been reinforced with militia from towns up the river, the raid caught them completely by surprise. The French, who were painted like their savage allies, infiltrated via the banks of the Little River without alarming the outlying garrison houses. A lone settler, who happened to be up at the early hour, spotted the assailants filing silently out of the woods. Shouting an alarm, he fired his musket as he ran for the protection of a nearby garrison. It was too late. Whooping and yelling, the invaders descended upon the houses of the town in a maelstrom of destruction and terror. The inhabitants, still in their beds, were awakened by the hellish sounds and made desperate attempts to save themselves. Unrestrained burning and mayhem went unchecked until the attackers heard a drum roll and a trumpet signaling the approach of the militia from the outlying garrisons. The raiders fired the meetinghouse and began to retreat, driving their captives before them, forcing them to carry plunder from their own homes.

After they put out the fire in the meetinghouse, the militia mustered a force of men to pursue the retreating raiders. When this force of about 70 men caught up with the retreating force they

---

[17] *History Of New France* by Charlevoix (p.206): "Our braves were not dismayed on learning that the enemy were so well prepared to receive them, and no longer trusting to a surprise, resolved to make it up in valor. They rested quietly all that night and the next day, one-hour after sunrise, drew up in battle array. Rouville made a short address to the French to exhort all who had any quarrels with each other to be reconciled sincerely, and embrace, as they all did. They then prayed and marched against the fort. Here they met with a vigorous resistance; but at last entered sword and ax in hand, and set it on fire."

pressed the attack. In the fierce engagement that followed, the French and Indians lost nine men killed, but managed to drive the militia back with their superior force and they resumed their retreat carrying their wounded and prisoners with them. They had to abandon most of their plunder and two French officers, Chambley and Vercherer, were killed in the skirmish. In all, the French admitted to having eighteen of their number wounded during the day. In his *Border Wars of New England*, Samuel Adams Drake wrote,

> French accounts add that the monster Assacumbuit performed prodigies of valor with a sabre given him by Louis XIV."[18]

Between thirty and forty persons were killed or taken captives in this raid. Sixteen of the slain were inhabitants of Haverhill. The soldiers were mostly from towns up the river. Had the pursuit been bolder and better sustained, it is likely the raiders could have been scattered and the prisoners recovered.

During this raid Escumbuit was wounded in the foot. Like Archilles, seemingly indestructible to his enemies, he finally proved to be merely human. After this raid on Haverhill, historians appeared to have closed the book on Chief Escumbuit. The typical comment was, "After being wounded in this raid he seems to have dropped out of sight." The French appeared to have bit off more that they could chew when they undertook this raid. Their original plan to raid the coastal settlements of Maine and New Hampshire was abandoned when some of the Indian allies failed to show up at the rendezvous at Lake Winnipesaukee. Although they made it back to Canada with a few captives and some plunder, the sad news of their fallen comrades and the loss of their most famous War Chief cast a pall over their return.

---

[18] *History Of New France*, by Charlevoix (p 207): "Nescambiouit, who had returned from France the year before, always fought near the commandants performing wonders with the sabre presented to him by the King. He received a musket-ball in the foot. In the two actions we had eighteen men wounded, three Indians and five Frenchmen killed, among the last two young officers of great promise, Hertel de Chambly, Rouville's brother, and Vercheres."

Driven from Haverhill by the local militia, and crippled by a wound to his foot, Escumbuit's last raid on the English was an anticlimactic event in a meteoric career. Over a brief span of years, like a rocket, he had risen to the heavens where his fame had blossomed in the court of Louis XIV at Versailles. Then, with the brief glow of a spent rocket, his flame was extinguished at Haverhill.

Escumbuit was restless when there was no war, and it was rumored that, during a lull in the New England border wars, he had gone to fight the English on the lower Mississippi with d'Iberville. Others suggest that he went up to the Jesuit mission on the Saint Francis River in Canada. It is unlikely that he returned to Canada with a crippled foot where he would encounter vindictive Pigwackets. With his foot smashed by a musket ball, it is more likely that he chose to return to his adopted band at Big Island Pond. He was known to be friendly with Chief Ezekial who lived in the Atkinson area. His fame as a warrior and his frequent forays along the border made him well known to these local Indians. It followed that the pond, known in 1926 as Lake Escumbuit, got its name from its most famous (perhaps infamous) resident. The navigation chart of Island Pond, published by the New Hampshire Public Service Commission, clearly identifies the small island opposite Chase's Grove as Escumbuit Island.

The Border Wars of New England, by Samuel Adams Drake, provides the final chapter to Escumbuit's career. At the end of his description of the French and Indian raid on Haverhill he reveals the date of Escumbuit's death and relates the strange circumstances under which he died. His cryptic reference to Escumbuit's silver mine in that account makes it important to learn about one of the big mysteries of The Border Wars. During these protracted wars, the English discovered that some of the musket balls used by the Indians contained a high silver content.[19] Apparently the Indians had their

---

[19] *Colby's Indian History* (Chapter21) Silver bullets: During the long and bloody struggle between the English and the Indians that drifted back and forth between Maine and New Hampshire and the French rendezvous in Canada, the Indians sometimes used bullets which contained more than half silver. These remarkable missiles became the wonder of the whites and the source from whence they were obtained was a mystery. To this day the secret has not been learned, but how near

own source of lead which they melted down to make musket balls without realizing the real value of the material. This story is confirmed *in Colby's Indian History* and his reference to silver bullets gives credence to the strange circumstances of Escumbuit's death in 1727.

It is ironic and a little sad that the death of the Pigwacket warrior whose name meant, "He who is so important and raised so high by his merit that thought cannot reach his greatness" should attract so little attention when it occurred. An obscure footnote in *The Border Wars of New England*, by Samuel Adams Drake makes the following reference to the death of one of the most famous Indian leaders of his era.

THE NEW ENGLAND WEEKLY JOURNAL of June 19, 1727, had the following notice of Escumbuit's death:

---

it once came to being known is told by an old resident of Berlin, New Hampshire.

Some years before Berlin was settled, Mr. Benjamin Russell came through the woods from Newry, Maine on a hunting excursion as far as what is now called Old Goose Eye Mountain, but not meeting the success anticipated, he started from that mountain to go back through to Newry, but got lost. It was four or five days before he at last found where he was, but when he did he came out on Bear River, nearly famished with hunger. When wandering around, about to descend a very steep place on the side of the mountain, and finding his hatchet a hindrance, he threw it ahead of him down the declivity. To his surprise the tool embedded its edge in what looked to him a solid rock. Upon reaching the place he found it was stuck in a vein of lead, so soft that it could easily be chipped. He stopped to cut out three or four pounds of the ore, and, putting it in his pack resumed his journey, thinking it would be an easy matter to find the isolated spot again. He did succeed in finding his way out of the wilderness, and soon after, he sent some of the ore to Boston to be assayed. It was found to contain more than sixty percent of silver. It was now evident where the Indians had found the ore for the "silver bullets." Elated over his accidental discovery, Mr. Russell started to find the place again, but after days of anxious search, he failed to find any sign, which revealed the rich vein of ore. This search he repeated from time to time, but he was never able to find the place, and to this day it remains undiscovered. Without a shadow of doubt somewhere between Old Goose Eye Mountain and Newry lies a vein of ore which would be a fortune to him who should find it.

We hear from the eastward that some days ago died there Old Escumbuit, who was formerly the principal Sagamore of the (now dispersed) tribe of Saco or Pigwacket Indians....He, Hercules-like, had a famous club, which he always carried with him, and on which he made ninety-eight notches, being the number of Englishmen that he had killed with his own hands.....He had formerly made discovery of a very fine silver mine up Saco River, but could never be persuaded to tell whereabouts it was till very lately he was prevailed with to promise to carry an Englishman (who had several times been in quest of it) to the spot, and endeavored to do it. But upon their way, when they got within a few miles of it, he fell sick, and in a short time died; having first gave the Englishman all the directions he was able for the finding out of said mine, who is resolved to prosecute the matter, hoping still to make discovery of it.[20]

The first contact between the Europeans and Aboriginal Indians reminds one of a Star Trek episode in which Time Travelers encounter a older culture with primitive weapons. After the Indians befriended the Colonists and helped them survive the hardships of their first winter, their relationship began to deteriorate. Awed by the newcomer's technology, and unable to comprehend the English concept of legal transfer of land for consideration, some Indians sold their land for mere trinkets. Their belief that they were merely granting the right to the use of their land resulted in them trying to recover their land through warfare. They belatedly learned that their traditional ferocity and valor were no match for the muskets and cannon of the paleface.

---

[20] Author's note: The #I question directed at me after I wrote Abenaki Warrior was: "Did they every find Escumbuit's silver mine?" I met an Abenaki Indian at a pow wow in Brunswick, Maine who told me about an old lead and silver mine near Route 2 between Gilead, Maine and Gorham, N. H. He told me that the Indians mined silver there in the 1700s and that the English had mined it for lead. Since Old Goose Mountain and Newry are in that area I am satisfied that this is the site of Escumbuit's mine.

Having been born into this unending conflict, Escumbuit fought the invaders of his homeland with fierce courage using the guerilla tactics he knew best. By English standards he was a monster, but to his people he was a hero and a patriot. He was simply trying to preserve a culture that had served him and his ancestors well for 12,000 years. In the final analysis, he should be judged in this context.[21]

---

[21] *Abenaki Warrior* by Alfred E Kayworth (p.104), Escumbuit's dying statement to his family expresses the frustration of his people:

"Hear me speak, my family. I am like an old oak that has withstood the storms of a hundred winters. Though the winds and frost have stripped me of my leaves and though my branches are weak, I still stand--but soon I must fall! But when I was Ottucke, young and strong...no young brave of the Pigwacket could bend my bow and my arrow could fell a deer at a hundred strides. Then the English trembled at the sound of my warwhoop...the scalping cry of Escumbuit rang from the Merrimac to Newfoundland. The scalps on my cloak and on the pole of my wigwam told the story of why I was named Assacumbuit.... "He who is raised so high by his merit that thought cannot reach his greatness."

We burned their villages...we took a thousand scalps...we carried off their women and their children and still they came to steal our land. Our Shaman tried their most potent magic against them, but their sorcery was stronger.

I won many honors with the French. Their generals wanted only Escumbuit at their side in battle. The French King touched me with his sword and made me his knight. Yet the French have forsaken our people and their treaty gives the land of my ancestors to the English. Now the Indian fights alone against the English who multiply like the leaves of the forest. I, who as a boy killed the bear with my war-club... I, who no warrior could defeat... I, who speak to the Great Spirit and take his counsel...I...I found that I could not turn back the paleface.

The oak bows before the storm; Even now it trembles! ...soon its trunk must fall to the ground!...the birds and squirrels will forsake it and the ant and the worm will consume it! So think my family of what I say; The Great Spirit counsels me now;"

"You must tell your people---peace with the paleface is their only hope. I have given mighty ships and cannons to the paleface for their weapons. As your numbers dwindle, so shall they multiply like the mushroom of the forest. Soon they will till your gardens with their horses and their plow. Your forests will fall for their dwellings. The deer, the moose and the bear will be driven from your hunting grounds and the stone building of the paleface shall occupy your fishing places."

"These things, The Great Spirit tells me and I must listen to his counsel. Our warriors are few and our will to fight falters. Now the fierce north wind blows! It feels cold! The old oak is weak! Its branches fall to the ground! Its sap rises no more! It leans! It falls! The Great Spirit whispers to me now.... The last hope for your people is peace; it is the command of The Great Spirit, and it is my wish---the

Even today those attuned to nature and history can sense the spirit of Chief Escumbuit on Escumbuit Island. The best time to commune with this ghost of the past is the window of time in which the sun lowers itself to meet the silhouette of the ridge behind Dixon's Grove. From the pine-needle-covered-knoll on the north end of the island the sun still performs the same pageantry of colors that once captured the imagination of the great Sachem. In 1727 Escumbuit sat entranced by the shimmering path of silver that began at the distant shore and ended virtually at his feet on Escumbuit Island. He believed his spirit would surely follow this trail to the afterworld when he died. As he watched, the silver slowly transformed to a rippling, jagged band of bright gold that held him with its brilliance and then revealed at its center a river of magenta that seemed to flow towards the setting sun. Then, as if controlled by the magic of an alchemist, the magenta faded and the gold turned to bronze and then to pewter as the sun sank below the horizon. In the gathering dusk Escumbuit felt the presence of The Great Spirit and he reflected on his mortality.[22]

Today, the sun performs its brilliant ballet of color and movement against the same backdrop of water, forest and sky as it did for Escumbuit 275 years ago. In the magic instant that the sun hangs motionless before plunging below the horizon, one may reflect on his or her own mortality and be transfixed by the beauty of the moment.

---

last wish of Escumbuit."

[22] *Abenaki Warrior*: (p. 227) In this scene Escumbuit, forced to face his mortality, finally makes the decision about his silver mine that he hopes will insure the future of his family.

Traditional Abenaki root clubs
(Courtesy of Penobscot Indian art, Old Town, Maine)

Fort William Henry, Pemaquid Point, Maine.

Chapter 4
GOVERNOR'S ISLAND
1700--2000

T here is little about the serene, natural beauty of Governor's Island to suggest that it was once the focal point of important events. 250 years ago the north end of the big island was the summer residence of the first Royal Provincial Governor of New Hampshire. Today, in the cathedral-like quiet of old forest, ghosts of the past linger still among the long abandoned foundations and relics of an elegant bygone era. After the King of England appointed Benning Wentworth governor in 1741, he and his friends founded a dynasty that survived for 25 years. On this island Wentworth entertained important political figures from Portsmouth and Boston and even from England. His children played at the shore of the pond as workers cleared forest, and built stone corrals to confine horses, cows and sheep. Here at this pond, Wentworth and his family established New Hampshire's first summer resort.[23]

The fascinating details about Wentworth's 25 years as governor, and the scandal he created by marrying a maid from his own household after his first wife died, is the subject of this chapter.

Two ill-considered decisions by diverse men ignited a series of events that propelled Benning Wentworth to fame and fortune. The Massachusetts Provincial Governor made a tactical error when he appointed John Wentworth Lieutenant Governor to handle his affairs in New Hampshire. He became tired of the long carriage rides from

---

[23] Author's note: For years Wentworth Hall in Wolfeboro has claimed to be New Hampshire's first summer resort. However John Wentworth built that estate in 1766 **after** he succeeded Benning Wentworth as governor. The title of "New Hampshire's First Summer Resort" should actually be applied to the summer estate built at Big Island Pond by Benning Wentworth in 1741.

Boston to Portsmouth, NH to visit his rural constituency. John Wentworth immediately exercised his authority by sending his son Benning to England to cultivate advantageous friendships. By the time the boundary dispute between Massachusetts and New Hampshire came up for resolution, the Wentworth family had a close relationship with influential people close to the British Crown. Had the Massachusetts Governor not let the fox into the chicken house, the settlement of the boundary dispute may have favored the State of Massachusetts. Through the efforts of a wily English agent named John Tomlinson, New Hampshire was awarded additional land measuring 14 miles by 50 miles for which they had not even bargained. By deferring to his personal comfort, the Massachusetts governor allowed the Wentworth family to develop political allies in England. It was these friends who arranged to have Benning Wentworth appointed the first Royal Provincial Governor of New Hampshire and Surveyor of the King's Forests.

A second fiasco developed when young Wentworth schemed to make a financial killing by borrowing money from English backers to pay for a shipload of New Hampshire oak for delivery to Spain. A modern exporter would have insisted on advance payment by means of a letter of credit. Instead, when the original Spanish agent was fired, the newly appointed agent rejected the shipment and young Wentworth had to set a course for Portsmouth with his unsold cargo. Misfortune turned into calamity when his ship foundered during the return voyage. Although he and his crew survived the shipwreck, he was forced to declare himself bankrupt upon his return to Portsmouth. The events that followed suggest that forces close to the monarchy had a financial stake in the venture. Out of the protracted negotiations to recover the lost value of the ship and its cargo came a promise to name Benning Wentworth Provincial Governor of New Hampshire with the proviso that he drop his claim for the $56,000 lost in the deal. His creditors in England then used their influence with the Crown to have him appointed as Governor and Surveyor of the King's Forests in order to provide him with a source of income from which he would be able to repay their loan. In a strange way, he had become Governor through his own miscalculation of risk. He was a keen student, however, as his subsequent accumulation of wealth and power affirms.

Benning Wentworth's rise to fame and fortune, and his decision to build an elaborate country home at Big Island Pond, are an important part of the history of the pond. His political machinations, and the peculiar circumstances of his marriage to a housekeeper forty years his junior after the death of his first wife, suggest that his story rivals that of the famous Indian Chief Escumbuit.

He was born in Portsmouth, New Hampshire on July 24, 1696. He was the first of three sons born to Lt. Governor John Wentworth and his wife Sarah Hunking Wentworth. John Wentworth had been appointed Lt. Governor to serve as a proxy for the Royal Governor of Massachusetts in New Hampshire who, as previously mentioned, chaffed at having to make frequent long carriage rides to visit his remote New Hampshire constituency.

Benning graduated from Harvard in 1715 ranked fifth in his class. This high ranking was considered a social coup at the time, and was an early sign of his natural talent for business and politics that he would demonstrate throughout his life. He went to work for his father in his "counting room" where he began to learn the financial details of his father's activities in the timber trade.

At the age of twenty-three he married Abigail Ruck, the daughter of a wealthy Bostonian. Their two sons served in the military and both died relatively young. Their marriage, to all appearances a happy one, lasted thirty four years ending with the death of his wife Abigail after a ten day illness of what was called "The Dead Palsy." According to eyewitness accounts, the 60-year-old Governor was inconsolable over the loss of his lady.

As a young man, he borrowed money to finance an export venture. His family's background in the timber business prompted' him to accumulate a shipload of fine New Hampshire oak with which he sailed to Cadiz, Spain, where he discovered to his chagrin that an agent who refused the shipment had replaced the original surrogate. Given modern communications, this unhappy outcome could have been avoided if Wentworth had been forewarned of the change in agents, but in the 1700s information traveled at the speed of a sailing vessel. Obliged to reverse course for America, he and his crew encountered a storm in which the ship and its cargo were lost. Wentworth and his crew were rescued, but his family must have greeted his return with mixed emotions; his financial losses and the resulting bankruptcy tempered the joy of his safe return.

The actions of the British Crown following this debacle hint that sources close to the Crown had a financial stake in this deal. At the root of the matter is the fact that the shipment of oak timber, cut from the New Hampshire forests for shipment to Spain, was the property of the British Crown and the loss of the shipment cost them money! Benning returned to England to try to recover the cost of the vessel and its cargo. After being sued by England for the losses, Spanish authorities promised to reimburse Wentworth, and subsequently reneged on their commitment. He again petitioned the British Crown for favor and Spain once again refused to follow through on her promise to pay. Other British merchants had experienced the same litany of failed promises by the Spaniards, and their complaints were one of the reasons that England finally declared war on Spain.

Wentworth changed his tactics and petitioned the British Crown for favor in recognition of the loss, in that a grievance against Spain became a matter of state. His agent, John Thomlinson helped him to obtain a promise from the Duke of Newcastle that, should New Hampshire be put under a district governor, he would be appointed to the post. As a tradeoff Wentworth promised to give up his $56,000 claim against Spain. It was a very clever work of diplomacy by the young Benning, and one is constrained to admire him for his persistence. However, renouncing his claim against Spain still left him owing money to the financial backers of his ill-fated venture.

Back home, he enhanced his reputation as a politician by supporting his father in a nasty dispute with Johnathan Belcher, the Massachusetts Governor. Uncertain as to whether the ailing Governor Shute or Jonathon Belcher was going to assume the post of Governor of Massachusetts, John Wentworth sent letters of congratulations to both. Belcher was infuriated by the affront. He, in turn, snubbed Wentworth's invitation to visit his mansion in Portsmouth, but the insult cost him politically. After John Wentworth died, Benning and his brother-in-law Theodore Atkinson formed a party to oppose Governor Belcher. Standing up to the Massachusetts Governor earned him the approval of the New Hampshire public as well as attracting the favorable attention of powerful English interests. These developments, combined with the promise he had extracted from the Crown for his lost timber, vaulted him to the governor's office in 1741.

The Assembly voted him a salary of 250 pounds a year, and he was promised a loan of $25,000 that never materialized. His London agent bribed a man named Dunbar to resign his position as "Surveyor of the King's Forests" in order to appoint Wentworth to the position. As King's Surveyor he received a salary of 800 pounds ($1,294 at current exchange rates) out of which he had to pay four deputies. A final allowance of 250 pounds ($404) was provided to pay his personal expenses and house rent. By all appearances, the position he had aspired to was not a financial bonanza. Nevertheless, we shall learn how it became a base from which he achieved great wealth and power.

In 1741 the long-standing boundary dispute between Massachusetts and New Hampshire was settled. The settlement placed the southern boundary of New Hampshire roughly where it is today giving New Hampshire a great deal of new territory north of the Merrimac River. The British agent Thomlinson had done his job well. It was he who arranged for Massachusetts and New Hampshire to have Provincial Governors with equal stature. Benning Wentworth was named the First Royal Provincial Governor of New Hampshire and the state became the third Royal Colony joining Massachusetts and Virginia. At a later date, the territory of Georgia became the fourth.

The supporters of the two New Hampshire political parties were distinguished by their religious preferences. Benning Wentworth founded Portsmouth's Anglican Church and it was charged that his motive in doing so was purely political. The Anglican Church was Episcopalian as opposed to the Congregational Church that had been founded by the English dissidents who were the original Puritans. Wentworth's Court Party was associated with the Anglicans and the Country Party was made up of Congregationalists. After assuming office, it appeared his actions were directed more towards achieving commercial success than with insuring his own spiritual salvation and that of his associates. The Wentworth oligarchy brought all the trappings of a monarchy to Portsmouth in the form of liveried carriages drawn by thoroughbred horses that carried important personages to political meetings resplendent in their periwigs and silver buckles. Puritanism seemed to be in a state of decline.

Wentworth steadily consolidated his power and, through a variety of favors to friends, relatives and political associates, he managed to virtually eliminate opposition. His regime ruled for 25 years and, at the apex of his reign, his powers were formidable. The Governor was not only responsible for the moral and religious conditions of life in New Hampshire but, as an Anglican Church member, he represented the King as head of the Church of England. Besides his duties as Surveyor of the King's Forests he was responsible for keeping "fair books of accounts" which he sent to the Treasury and the Board of Trade. He recommended appointments to his own council. This council served as the highest court of review as well as the probate court. It had the power to veto any law and review any case brought before it. It could suspend its own members with concurrence of its own majority. The Royal Governor also established and maintained the local court systems and his title of Vice-Admiral of the Colony gave him naval jurisdiction. He appointed all other judges and justices of peace and other provincial ministers. He appointed all military officers above the rank of captain. In short, his power exceeded that of any other Royal Provincial Governor. Only the King of England had the power to remove him from office.

Having established that Benning Wentworth wielded immense power, it is natural to be curious as to how he used that power and how he managed to keep his constituency happy for the better part of 25 years. Wentworth appointed several members of his own family to his council. At the suggestion of the English agent Thomlinson, they raised the 300 pounds required to secure the Governor's appointment. With sympathetic ears in England, and his base secured at home, Benning Wentworth was now positioned to capitalize on his spectacular rise to prominence. His appointment as Surveyor of the King's Forests was designed to help him pay off his creditors in England. This was probably the impetus behind the Crown's diligent legal maneuvers attempting to recover his losses from the Spanish government. The money he had borrowed to finance the shipload of oak destined for Spain had come from people close to the Crown, and these speculators had been petitioning the King to recover their money from Spain.

His appointment as Surveyor of the King's Forests stabilized Wentworth's finances since the position permitted him to arrange contracts and collect commissions and other fees. His brother Mark Hunking Wentworth became the official mast agent who arranged to cut the trees and float them down the Piscataqua River and the Merrimac River to be loaded on ships for transport to England. He was paid about 100 pounds ($162) per mast and Benning collected a fee for each mast shipped during the 24 years he was in office. Wentworth's agents combed the state of New Hampshire for straight trees with a 24-inch butt diameter to reserve them for King George's navy. The farmer who owned one of these trees had to leave it standing as he cleared his land. Mark Wentworth became quite wealthy during his brother's time in office and, by the time his brother's popularity began to fade towards the end of his long term as governor, Mark had become a silent supporter of the opposition Country Party. It is unclear whether he cynically sought to ride the ground swell of negative sentiment against his brother or whether he had actually adopted the ideology of the anti-Royalist Country Party.

Most of Wentworth's wealth was accumulated after his associates bought the Mason Land Grants. At one point in the history of the colonies, the King of England had given a large area of New Hampshire to a man named John Mason. He, in turn, gifted smaller grants to individuals with the stipulation that they had to build a mill, a meetinghouse and appoint a minister within a certain time limit. In 1746, in spite of the recommendation of Governor Wentworth, the New Hampshire Assembly refused to buy these Mason Land Grants. Thirteen of Wentworth's friends seized the opportunity that had been rejected by The Assembly and bought the grants for 100 pounds per share. After acquiring the grants, they immediately gave quick claim deeds to the yeomen who had previously been given Mason grants. Having silenced potential protest from that quarter, they were left with hundreds of thousands of acres of valuable New Hampshire land that they had bought for a mere trifle. In the years that followed Benning Wentworth approved requests for more than 200 townships in New Hampshire and it became a routine practice for each of these new townships to deed back 500 acres of prime land to Wentworth as a gesture of their appreciation. Having granted these townships, Wentworth then loaded the New Hampshire Assembly with personal supporters from these new towns. As an added favor to him, many of these new towns were named after his associates. The town of

Atkinson was named after his brother-in-law Theodore Atkinson. Eventually, his awards of townships west of the Connecticut River brought him into conflict with New York. The Crown, casting a favorable eye to their burgeoning colony in New York, settled that dispute in favor of that colony, but many of the townships he had previously awarded in Vermont were not affected. These included Bennington, Vermont, which was named to honor the governor.

The fierce resistance of the Abenaki Indians tribes was steadily waning, and they were gradually abandoning their villages and moving up to the French Jesuit missionary settlement on the Saint Francis River in Canada. The population of the New Hampshire Colony mushroomed from 11,000 in 1730 to 62,000 in 1770. The bulk of these newcomers were Scotch and Irish farmers who were followed by other Europeans who yearned for land they could call their own. The Abenaki Indians, whose ancestors had roamed the mountains, valleys, rivers and the coastal estuaries of Northern New England for 12,000 years, made a valiant attempt to stem this human tide of invaders of their land. Now, with their population decimated by paleface diseases, and outgunned by European technology, their doom was certain.

While all this was going on, Benning Wentworth managed, not only to keep his New Hampshire constituency happy, but was also able to convince The Crown that everything he did in the province was done in The Crown's best interest. He enlisted the support of the locals by turning a blind eye to their smuggling activities; he was known to engage in a bit of smuggling himself. He managed to convince the British Crown that he wielded a big stick in enforcing The Crown's policies while he continued to tread softly on the local scene. It was only in the late stages of his regime that he came under heavy criticism for enriching himself through the medium of his township grants.

His political party was known as the Court Party. On the surface they appeared to support whatever position the British Crown favored. Although the leaders of the opposition were city folk who lived in Portsmouth, they named their party the Country Party in order to draw the support of the people in the countryside.

During his administration he led the province successfully through two wars. In 1745 Wentworth joined with Governor Shirley of

Massachusetts in his military actions against the French. Their victory at Louisburg, on Cape Breton, united the Colonists, but in 1749 the English signed a treaty in which they returned the Louisburg fort to France. New Hampshire people were enraged by the terms of this treaty, but the loss of Wentworth's son in the war earned him their sympathy. During the French and Indian War from 1755 to 1763, he diligently promoted military action against the Abenaki Indians and their French allies.

The scope of Wentworth's political and moneymaking activities might suggest a lack of interest in the finer things in life. On the contrary, he is also remembered for his ambitious building projects such as the mansion at Little Harbor in south Portsmouth. (This 55-room mansion is still open to public view.) His country estate, or hunting lodge at Big Island Pond in the southern part of the state inspired poems and intimate details of the Governor's personal life that are still discussed today. And finally, celebrated in anecdotes and verse, was the "marriage of the century" that came after his first wife died leaving him a widower at age 60. Getting remarried at age 62 was newsworthy, but when he suddenly announced he was marrying a 22 year old house-keeper who had been in his household for years, it created a scandal which rocked Portsmouth society and became the inspiration for a poem by Henry Wadsworth Longfellow.

Early in his reign as Governor, he and his family lived in a house in downtown Portsmouth. We do not know why he chose Big Island Pond for his first building project. Notwithstanding the beauty of the pond, it was in the interior of the state and forty-seven miles from Portsmouth and, although there was a lull in the Indian wars, the Abenaki Indians were still a potential threat. The virgin beauty of the island and the pond, and the abundance of fish and game the area offered, must have captivated him.

One half of the big island was given to the Hon Richard Saltenstall by the Proprietors of Haverhill for valuable services rendered to that town. On March 31, 1731 Saltenstall purchased the remainder for 30 shillings per acre. At the time the island was estimated to contain 200 acres and was called "Island Farm in Perch Pond." In 1734 Saltenstall sold the property to Jonathan and Peter Eastman and Peter Green. Wentworth purchased the property from them in 1741 and his heirs held it until 1780. It appears that the clearing of the land and the construction followed soon after and, judging by the research that has been done on the design and scope of the compound, this was no mere hunting camp in the woods.[24]

H. Tallant, a servant of Saltenstall, lived on the island beginning in 1731 and he seems to be the first recorded resident, but the location of his house is unknown. Some time after Jack and Lois Sieg completed their research there was another study done by Lillie Cleveland that focussed on the remains of Birch Farm.[25]

The Wentworths cleared the East End of the island for a garden and the high, corral-like stone walls that are still visible indicate that they kept livestock near the main house. They named the place Birch Farm on Islandy Pond and letters written by Lady Wentworth describe pleasant horseback rides to the farm. One can imagine the Wentworth family traveling in convoy from Portsmouth to their farm for a long summer weekend anticipating the quiet and charm of their private island after a busy week in Portsmouth. Undoubtedly there would have been a pair of carriages filled with servants and provisions with the boys and their parents riding as outriders for the convoy. When they reached the northeast corner of the pond they

---

[24] *Researches on Big Island Pond*, by Lois and Jack Sieg, 1978; Their important work contains copies of many of the original documents which detail the transfer of ownership of the big island beginning with its purchase from the Indians to the transfer to its present owners in 1909. Their report also contains drawings (roughly to scale) of the foundations for the main house and the servants house and the wash house and stone corral for the live-stock.
Original copies of this study can be read at the following locations:

Derry Library	N.H. State Library
East Derry Library	N.H. Historical Society, Concord
Hampstead Library	Derry Historical Society
Atkinson Library	Hampstead Historical Society
Derry News	

[25] *Benning Wentworth, Birch Farm on Islandy Pond* by Lillie Cleveland; This interesting report covered the political and social life of Benning Wentworth. She diagrammed the dwellings and outbuildings of the farm using the research of Lois and Jack Seig. She included photos of the foundations and thick stone walls of the corral. I found her research on Benning Wentworth to be quite accurate and I have adapted some of her research for this story.

crossed to the island over a wooden causeway which was the only access to the island at that time. There are signs that the workers tried to build a permanent stone causeway from the island to the mainland. This causeway began at a point on the island opposite the Emmert property where the land forms a point. They dragged stones out on the ice expecting them to sink and form a causeway with the spring thaw. It appears that the melting ice may have "rafted" the stones out of position and the project appears to have been abandoned. They had to settle for a boardwalk in the same location that enabled them to cross to the sandy point near the current location of the Emmert cottage. From there they walked to Drew Road in order to make their way to Hampstead. There are indications that they also had a barge at the extreme north end of the island that enabled them to ferry people and supplies from a dock located on the large sloping rock on the island to a landing on the shore.[26]

When one visits the original site of the Governor's summer mansion, ghosts of the past linger still. The heavy undergrowth and canopy of trees, cathedral-like, close off the outside world. Only the muted drone of the outboard motor intrudes upon the stillness of the place. The atmosphere imposes itself upon the visitor; conversation becomes muted as if one were in church. The existing foundations, now covered with poison ivory, appear to have supported two substantial buildings and two small outbuildings of some sort. Their location clearly suggests they were built to offer a view of the cliff and the body of water that was known as Perch Pond. Assuming the surface of the pond to be as much as 8 feet lower than it is today, an occupant of the house would have enjoyed a magnificent view from a promontory 40 to 50 feet above the pond. Having cleared that end of the island of trees, the location gave them a lovely panoramic view of the cliff and the Hampstead shore. Shallow draft rowboats and canoes were able to navigate between the two bodies of water that were joined by shallows and a marsh. In her chronicle that describes her family camping on the big island from 1878 to 1900,

---

[26] Author's note: The description of the two crossing points to the island is taken from conversations with Jack Sieg who originally got this information from Walter Stickney.

Elizabeth Schneider describes a picnic at Camp Blackstone (Sweeney's Point) that was attended by 60 guests who rowed over from what is now known as Sanborn Shores. Her account is the best evidence that people were able to go around the island by rowboat before the dam was built in 1878.

Benning Wentworth confounded friends and critics alike at a time when his political star shone brightest and his personal life was at its lowest ebb. His three sons had died relatively young and, on November 8, 1755, his wife Abigail died suddenly, a victim of a malady known as "The Dead Palsy."[27] When he was 62 years old, after living as a widower for two years, he was contemplating a personal decision that had the potential to destroy him politically. His proposal of marriage to a young woman named Molly Pitman had been rejected, and her subsequent marriage to a younger man must have deepened his mood.[28] He decided to make the house at Little Harbor his year-around home. There, in the 55-room mansion he had built overlooking the picturesque harbor, he continued to entertain foreign and domestic political notables. Still, he must have been lonely...sixty-two years old, living in a 55-room house with only the guarded conversation of servants to entertain him when important guests were not about. Subsequent gossip hinted that his life as a widower might not have been all that bad.

Martha Hilton had been part of his household since she was a child. Now, at age 22, her duties have been variously described as

---

[27] *Birch Farm on Islandy Pond*, Elizabeth Cleveland: (p.6) Taken from the Governor's orders to Gillman which was written by Theodore Atkinson, Secretary of State and brother-in-law to Benning: " His Excellency is quite incapacitated to think or transact business occasioned by the death of his lady who left him after about ten days illness of the Dead Palsy... The Governor is almost inconsolable."

[28] *Historic Houses of New England* by Mary H. Northend; "Lonely and discouraged, he offered himself in marriage to one Molly Pitman, who chose instead Richard Shortridge, a mechanic by trade. Doubtless through his instigation, because piqued at the indignity of her refusal, a press gang seized Shortridge and carried him away. He was sent from ship to ship, until a friendly officer listened to his sad tale and allowed him to escape and return home, to find his wife still true, although tempted by the allurements of wealth.

scullery maid, bar maid, and housekeeper.[29] The Wentworth family genealogy describes Martha Hilton quite well.[30] She was forty years younger than Benning Wentworth and may have been adopted by Abigail Wentworth before she died. She was apparently educated by the family and later took charge of operating the Wentworth mansion at Portsmouth. All sources seem to agree that Martha Hilton was a very sprightly, outgoing young woman who proved to be a charming hostess and a lady who had the knack of putting statesmen at ease in her company. Her critics said that, in her childhood, she had been a homeless waif wandering the streets of Portsmouth. Gossips hinted that she had been Wentworth's mistress during his first marriage.

One can speculate endlessly about what thoughts went through Benning Wentworth's head as he sat alone in his mansion and watched young Martha blossom into womanhood. The young girl described as a careless, laughing child, barefoot and carrying a pail of water, with a dress scarcely sufficient to cover her, is once said to have declared to an onlooker, "No matter how I look, I shall ride in my chariot yet." Who is to say that she did not tempt and encourage the events that followed?

On the occasion of the Governor's birthday an elaborate dinner was planned at the mansion at Little Harbor and a number of prominent people were invited. Among the guests was Reverend Arthur Brown of the Episcopal Church. At the conclusion of the elaborate dinner Benning gestured to a nearby servant who bent his head to receive a whispered instruction. Soon after he went on his errand, the beautiful Martha Hilton came into the room and stood silently by the fireplace, a vision in corn-colored silk and upswept hairstyle. The Governor rose and adjusted his waistcoat. He was a striking figure in his purple, gold-laced coat and his scarlet satin

---

[29] Author's note: The Wentworth file at the Portsmouth library contains a Boston Herald photograph of the Wentworth mansion at Little Harbor that bears the caption: "The House In Which Benning Wentworth Married His Bar Maid." There is a small pantry in the mansion in which they distilled rum.

[30] *Birch Farm at Islandy Pond*, by Elizabeth Cleveland; her description of Martha Hilton's relationship to the Wentworth family seems to best fit the facts.

breeches. His powdered wig was neatly tied with ribbons and a shower of ruffles fell from the sleeves of his waistcoat. He strode to Martha's side and she curtsied as he took her hand. As the mystified guests waited expectantly, he addressed Reverend Brown saying, "Sir, this is my birthday ...It shall likewise be my wedding day." And with a slight bow to the minister added.... "And you sir shall marry me." When the Reverend hesitated Wentworth's voice rose.... "Sir, you hesitate? As Chief Magistrate, I command you!".... And so, Martha Hilton became Lady Wentworth of Wentworth Hall. The assembled guests, many of them relatives, were unsure how to react, but realizing full well that they must show enthusiasm for the Governor's choice. It was one of the most stunning incidents of the 1700s and more than 100 years later, in 1871, Henry Wadsworth Longfellow immortalized the event with a poem:

LADY WENTWORTH

One hundred years ago, and something more,
In Queen Street, Portsmouth, at her tavern door,
Neat as a pin and blooming as a rose,
Stood Mistress Stavers in her furbelows,
Just as her cuckoo clock was striking nine.
Above her head, resplendent on the sign,
The portrait of the Earl of Halifax,
In scarlet coat and periwig of flax,
Surveyed at leisure all her varied charms
Her cap, her bodice, her white folded arms,
And half resolved, though he was past his prime,
And rather damaged by the lapse of time,
To fall down at her feet, and to declare
The passion that had driven him to despair.
For from his lofty station he had seen
Stavers, her husband, dressed in bottle green,
Drive his new Flying Stagecoach, four in hand,
And knew that he was far upon the way
To Ipswich and to Boston on the Bay!
Just then the meditations of the Earl
Were interrupted by a little girl,

Barefooted, ragged, with neglected hair,
Eyes full of laughter, neck and shoulders bare,
A thin slip of a girl, like a new moon,
Sure to be rounded into beauty soon,
A creature men would worship and adore,
Though now in mean habiliments she bore
A pail of water, dripping through the street,
And bathing, as she went, her naked feet.
It was a pretty picture, full of grace,...
The slender form, the delicate, thin face;
The swaying motion, as she hurried by;
The shining feet, the laughter in her eye,
That o'er her face in ripples gleamed and glanced,
As in her pail the shifting sunbeam danced:
And with uncommon feelings of delight
The Earl of Halifax beheld the sight.
Not so Dame Stavers, for he heard her say
These words, or thought he did, as plain as day:
"Oh Martha Hilton! Fie! How dare you go
About the town half dressed, and looking so!"
At which the gypsy laughed, and straight replied:
"No matter how I look; I yet shall ride
In my own chariot, Ma'am." And on the child
The Earl of Halifax benignly smiled,
As with her heavy burden she passed on,
Looked back, then turned the corner, and was gone.
What next, upon that memorable day,
Arrested his attention was a gay
And brilliant equipage, that flashed and spun,
The silver harness glittered in the sun,
Outriders with red jackets, lithe and lank,
Pounded the saddles as they rose and sank,
While all alone within the chariot sat
A portly person with three-cornered hat,
A crimson velvet coat, head high in the air,
Gold-headed cane, and nicely powdered hair,
And diamond buckles sparkling at his knees,
Dignified, stately, florid, much at ease,

Onward the pageant swept, and as it passed,
Fair Mistress Stavers courtesied low and fast;
For this was Governor Wentworth, driving down
To Little Harbor, just beyond the town,
Where his Great House stood looking out to sea,
A goodly place, where it was good to be.
It was a pleasant mansion, an abode
Near and yet hidden from the great high-road,
Sequestered among trees, a noble pile,
Baronial and colonial in its style;
Pandaean pipes, on which all winds that blew
Made mournful music the whole winter through.
Within, unwonted splendors met the eye,
Panels, and floors of oak, and tapestry;
Carved chimneypieces, where on the brazen dogs;
Doors opening into darkness unawares,
Mysterious passages, and flights of stairs;
And on the walls, in heavy gilded frames,
The ancestral Wentworths with Old-Scripture names
Such was the mansion where the great man dwelt,
A widower and childless; and he felt
The loneliness, the uncongenial gloom,
That like a presence haunted every room;
For though not given to weakness, he could feel
The pain of wounds, that ache because they heal.
The years came and the years went, ...seven in all
And passed in cloud and sunshine o'er the Hall;
The dawns their splendor through its chambers shed,
The sunsets flushed its western windows red;
The snow was on its roofs, the wind, the rain;
Its woodland were in leaf and bare again;
Moons waxed and waned, the lilacs bloomed and died,
In the broad river ebbed and flowed the tide,
Ships went to sea, and ships came home from sea,
And the slow years sailed by and ceased to be.
And all these years had Martha Hilton served
In the Great House, not wholly unobserved
By day, by night, the silver crescent grew,

Though hidden by clouds, her light still shining through;
A maid of all work, whether coarse or fine,
A servant who made service seem divine!
Through her each room was fair to look upon;
The mirrors glistened, and the brasses shone,
The very knocker on the outer door,
If she but passed, was brighter than before.
And now the ceaseless turning of the mill
Of time, that never for an hour stands still,
Ground out the Governor's sixtieth birthday,
And powdered his brown hair with silver-gray.
The robin, the forerunner of the spring,
The bluebird, with his jocund caroling,
The restless swallows building in the eaves,
The golden buttercups, the grass, the leaves,
The lilacs tossing in the winds of May,
All welcomed this majestic holiday!
He gave a splendid banquet, served on plate,
Such as became the Governor of the State,
Who represented England and the King,
And was magnificent in everything.
He had invited all his friends and peers,...
The Pepperels, the Langdons, and the Lears,
The Sparhawks, the Penhallows, and the rest;
For why repeat the name of every guest?
But I must mention one in bands and gown,
The rector there, the Reverend Arthur Brown
Of the Established Church; with smiling face
He sat beside the Governor and said grace;
And then the feast went on, as others do,
But ended as none other I e'er knew.
When they had drunk the King, with many a cheer,
The Governor whispered in a servant's ear,
Who disappeared, and presently there stood
Within the room, in perfect womanhood,
A maiden, modest and yet self-possessed,
Youthful and beautiful, and simply dressed,
Can this be Martha Hilton? It must be!

Yes, Martha Hilton, and no other she!
Dowered with the beauty of her twenty years,
How ladylike, how queen-like she appears;
The pale, thin crescent of the days gone by
Is Dian now in all her majesty!
Yet scarce a guest perceived that she was there,
Until the Governor, rising from his chair,
Played slightly with his ruffles, then looked down,
And said unto the Reverend Arthur Brown:
"This my birthday; it shall likewise be
My wedding-day; and you shall marry me!"
The listening guests were greatly mystified,
None more so than the rector, who replied:
"Marry you? Yes, that were a pleasant task,
Your Excellency; but to whom? I ask."
The Governor answered, to this lady here;"
And beckoned Martha Hilton to draw near.
She came and stood, all blushes, at his side.
The rector paused. The impatient Governor cried;
"This is the lady; do you hesitate?
Then I command you as Chief Magistrate."
The rector read the service loud and clear:
"Dearly beloved, we are gathered here,"
And so on to the end. At his command
On the fourth finger of her fair left hand
The Governor placed the ring; and that was all:
Martha was Lady Wentworth of the Hall!

To the chagrin of her critics, the new Lady Wentworth settled into her role as the First Lady of the State of New Hampshire and performed her duties admirably. She adapted quickly and was soon receiving and entertaining important personages from The Colonies as well as from abroad.

A much written escapade about Martha Hilton at Birch Farm reveals her as an independent and spirited woman. In most circles the incident would be passed off as a simple family disagreement, but since it involved the governor and his lady, the story has attained legendary status. There were enough eyewitnesses present to spread gossip about the incident and besides it has a ring of truth about it.

Local residents of Hampstead were honored by having the Governor and his lady in their midst, and they naturally were anxious to cultivate their friendship. One fine summer evening the Governor and his wife were invited to attend a local gala at the home of one of these neighbors. Martha, eager for some excitement, urged her husband to dress and escort her to the event. The Governor, his ardor for his new bride tempered somewhat by an attack of gout, refused to go and forbade her to attend as well. After the Governor was safely asleep, the headstrong Martha quietly dressed in her gown and slipped out of the house and walked over the wooden causeway to the mainland and joined the festivities in Hampstead. History does not give us the details as to how far she walked or what conveyance she used or, indeed, who might have given her a buggy ride back to the pond. She must have been a determined young lady.

Wentworth awoke to find himself alone in bed and, knowing where Martha had gone, he ordered the servants to lock the gate to the walled enclosure. He may have dropped off to sleep planning how he would chastise his bride when she returned and begged to be let into the house. Return she did, but Martha did not follow her husband's script. Finding herself locked out, she went to the shore of the pond where she took off her gown and her shoes and then emitted several piercing screams. Her screams roused the entire household and, when they found the dress and the shoes, a desperate search began directed by the distraught husband. In the confusion that followed, Martha slipped into the house in her undergarments, got into bed and promptly fell asleep. When the exhausted Governor finally stumbled into his bedroom he was greeted with the sight of his sleeping bride. With a sigh of exasperated relief, the exhausted man fell into bed, and one can imagine him thinking as he drifted off to sleep. "Why didn't I marry an older more sensible woman?"[31]

---

[31] *New Hampshire Folk Tales*, by Mrs. Eva A Speare, Mrs. Frederick J. Shepard of Derry and Miss Elizabeth P. Pope of Somersworth contributed a chapter to this book entitled, *A Tale of Island Pond:* In reference to this incident they offered a second version:

King George III assumed the throne after his father died in 1760. The youthful King soon exercised his power by relieving Wentworth as Surveyor of the King's Forests. The House of Lords underestimated opposition to the hated 1765 Stamp Act in their colonies, and the seeds for the American Revolution were already being sowed. Although Benning Wentworth continued to play his double role well, criticism began to swell in England as well as in the local community. It was apparent that he favored his Episcopalian friends in awarding many of his land grants and the ostentatious life style that he and his associates lived began to erode his popularity. Middle-class merchants throughout New Hampshire began to question his monarch-like powers and people in Concord and Derry were asking why all the power in the state was concentrated on the seacoast. Complaints concerning the Royal Governor began to reach the British Crown. Wentworth became lax in his communications with the King and his ministers, and he did not adequately counter the complaints of inaccuracies in the reporting of land grants, and the reported negligence in his duties as Surveyor of the Kings Forests.

When it became apparent that he was going to be ousted by The King, he once again used his political skill to allow him to exit with

---

Thoroughly alarmed, the sorry man called for lights and a hurried hunt began, but candles were flickering and pine torches penetrated the dark water too dimly to be of great assistance. Finally, in despair, the remorseful Governor turned toward the house. Deeply did he regret his anger; bitterly did he bemoan his stern orders. Only the morning could reveal the extent of the disaster cause by his sudden wrath. When the Governor returned thinly clad and shivering from his chilling exposure along the damp shore at the late hour, he found the doors of his house locked and was compelled to stand outside while a voice within demanded that he repent of his wrath and apologize for locking the gates in such a high handed manner. Glad to find his wife safe, and eager to gain the warmth of his bed again, the Governor humbled himself as a man must, when he finds himself so in the wrong to a Lady, and the doors were opened to his entreaty."

The Mrs. Shepard who contributed this story was a summer resident of Big Island Pond where she and her husband raised a family on Escumbuit Island. Her most famous son was Alan B. Shepard, renowned as America's First Man in Space.

pride intact. His nephew, John Wentworth, appealed to The Marquis of Rockingham to whom he was related. The Marquis arranged for Benning Wentworth to announce his voluntary retirement after having first extracted a promise from The Crown to appoint his nephew in his place. Once again Wentworth's ability to use his friends and contacts in England won the day. He resigned his office in 1766 and he died October 14, 1770.

His widow and son inherited his large estate which included the governor's mansion at Little Harbor, Birch Farm at Lake Wentworth, thousands of acres of prime New Hampshire land and substantial investments in Great Britain. Other family members were devastated to learn that they were not mentioned in his will. John Wentworth, who was rumored to be deeply in debt, is reported to have contested his uncle's will without success.

Martha recovered quickly from the loss of her husband. A mere two months after her husband's death, having rejected several marriage proposals, she married retired British Colonel Michael Wentworth. He was a so-called cousin of the new Royal Governor, John Wentworth. He had come to America from England when John was appointed Royal Governor, and he and John were roommates until their respective marriages. Mourning can quickly become boring, and the family apparently accepted marriage as an acceptable means of assuaging their grief. Michael Wentworth was a horseman and a high-liver, and is remembered for his considerable feat of riding from Boston to Portsmouth in a single day, having left Boston at 8 AM and arriving in Portsmouth at 6 o'clock that afternoon.

When George Washington's ship sailed into Little Harbor in 1789, Colonel Michael Wentworth and his Lady entertained him at the Little Harbor mansion. The Colonel died suddenly in 1795[32] and Lady Wentworth occupied the mansion with her married daughter until her death in 1805. The mansion at Little Harbor passed out of the family when her daughter departed for Europe in 1816. The Big

---

[32] *An Old Town By The Sea*: Author and date unknown; "The Colonel was young and handsome, and he gave Martha a good time and a baby. And in his final comments he said a very nice thing:"

"I've had my cake" said the Colonel, looking at Martha.... "and et it too."

Island Pond property remained in the family until Michael and Martha Wentworth sold it to Tristrum Dalton of Newburyport on May 22, 1780. During the next 119 years the island had a series of owners.[33] Then, on March 8, 1908, Governor's Island was sold by the heirs of the Little family to Arthur M. Emerson of Hampstead. At the turn of the century the north end of the island was clear-cut and there was a sawmill operating at that end of the island. The demarcation line between the pines and the hardwoods is still evident when one views the island from the pond or from the north shore. Finally, on September 1, 1909, the Governor's Island Company acquired the island from Mr. Emerson.

Had the Governor's Island Company not purchased the property, it is difficult to envision what the big island would look like today. It was regarded as having little value in the 1800s when a "Pest House" was maintained on the island. This was the terminology used to describe a special building used to quarantine people who had contracted smallpox or other contagious diseases. But what was merely blight on the area might have been a calamity! Mrs. Williams told me that the owners of Canobie Lake Park were negotiating to buy the island before The Big Island Pond Company bought it in 1909. Fortunately, the Lawrence woolen mill owners decided to develop Canobie Lake Amusement Park in its present location. Their motives were partly altruistic and partly mercenary. They imported cheap labor from Europe and provided them with low rent housing. They transported them to an amusement park they had built on electric trolley lines that they owned. The money spent by the workers on trolley fare and amusement park rides eventually paid for both the trolley lines and the amusement park. The arrangement suited everyone; the mill workers found the park a pleasant diversion from their jobs and the enterprise provided an investment opportunity for the mill owners. As for the residents of Big Island Pond, they can only sigh with nostalgia as they dream about what might have

---

[33] *Researches on Big Island Pond*, by Lois and Jack Sieg, (p.33) For a record of the multiple transfers of Governor's Island read their research which is available at the libraries previously listed.

been--an island paradise of bright lights and screaming, happy people only a short cruise from their boat dock.

Initially six individuals purchased the island from Mr. Emerson and formed the Governor's Island Company. With time eight additional island residents rented their lots from this company. Since they were classified as "tenants at will," and were unable to deduct their share of tax payments on their personal income taxes, they sought a change in the arrangement. Eventually the six original owners of the Governor's Island Company allowed the eight " renters" to purchase their proportionate share of the company.

Meanwhile Hampstead was attempting to tax the entire island as developed land. The town fathers decided that the 233 acres could be divided into 142 house lots with appropriate roads and attendant infrastructure, and that it should all be taxed as shore front property. Mrs. Mary Lou William's father, Mr. Edward V. French, success-fully blocked these efforts on two occasions by appearing before town authorities with photographs demonstrating that much of the land was swampland and wilderness. Had the towns succeeded in their efforts to tax the 233 acres as developed land, the Governor's Island Company would have been forced to develop the island or sell it to an outside developer. Despite the best of intentions, any attempt to develop the island would have overpopulated the pond and the quality of life would have been irretrievable degraded.

In the 1970's New Hampshire passed a law enabling farmers and owners of tree farms to classify their land under a "current use" category: the land could be taxed on the basis of its present use, not as though it were fully developed. However, persistent efforts to repeal this law made it clear to the shareholders of the Governor's Island Company that they would have to find a better solution.

In 1984, the company changed its name to the Governor's Island Association and laid out two acres around each of the 14 cottages that are currently taxed at the regular waterfront rate. They surren-dered forever the right to develop the other 205 acres by placing it under a conservation easement. The grantee of this easement was The Society for the Protection of New Hampshire Forests (SPNHF). This society was formed early in the 1900s to help to curb the "clear cutting" of forests in the White Mountain region. The 205 acres on the big island are, and have been for many years, a registered tree farm, which use is permitted under a conservation easement.

Bob French and Wally Williams arranged all this. It took seven years to do. Also, in 1984, the "Tenants at Will" were given an opportunity to buy a share of the new partnership and all but one did so. (That family moved away). So now all the residents of the island are on an equal footing.

Today life on the big island is reminiscent of a bygone era. All of the buildings on the island can still be accurately described as camps. Their individual histories are old and replete with pleasant memories. It is as if there has been a conscious effort to preserve the proprieties of parents, grandparents and great grandparents. These camps blend so well in their native settings that it is hard to imagine 14 dwellings in place on the island. The resident's acceptance of pine needles instead of lawns, natural rocks in place of concrete seawalls, and homes that share the forest reveals a common appreciation of the obvious. Since it is impossible to improve upon nature, why not enjoy it in the least intrusive manner possible?

The activities of people like Mr. French and other residents of Governor's Island have had an important effect on the quality of life at Big Island Pond. Combine their efforts with the work of Warren Kruschwitz, Herb Lippold, and the BIPC directors, and we can understand why the pond has retained much of its purity and unspoiled charm throughout most of this century. Even more important are the largely unheralded land conservation activities of Wally and Mary Lou Williams that are detailed in the final chapter of this book.

Among Mary Lou Williams' collection of papers there was a yellowed copy of a short story about Island Farm in Perch Pond. The nostalgic article about Governor's Island was designed to remind the people of Hampstead about the colorful history of the pond beginning with its most famous resident, Benning Wentworth. It concludes with a poem that Dr. George R. Bennette composed in 1900. The 100-year old poem has a nostalgic and whimsical air to it that is timeless:

LAKE WENTWORTH

On fair Lake Wentworth's silvery tide,
The water lilies blow.
The wild ducks through the waters glide
That close along its wooded side,
In rank profusion grow.

The smiling hills, that girt it round,
In softest beauty swell,
With shady grove, and sunny mound,
Where many a modest flower is found,
And many a ferny dell.

Its lapping water rippling flow
By soft green islands fair.
While glancing bird-forms come and go,
Through all the hours, to and fro,
Within the ambient air.

The Indian in his soft canoe,
Once glided on its waves,
Its wooded shores his warwhoop knew
As through the air his arrows flew,
The welcome of his braves.

How often on its glassy breast,
Wev'e pulled the laboring oar,
While floating echoes from the crest
Of Eagle Cliff, our lungs confessed
For all the listening shore.

From Pleasant Point by Marble's Cove,
We passed Old Gunner's Isle,
Through Peaty Bog to Chase's Grove
Are banks where finny legions rove,
The sportsmen to beguile.

100 ALFRED E. KAYWORTH

The Lone Pine stands in stately pride
Close by its gushing spring,
While Blackstone answers as a guide,
By which to reach Old Boston's side,
Twin Islands rocky ring.

By Escumbuit's wooded height,
We next will take our way,
Where Hundred Islands sylvan bright,
Lie sleeping in the evening light,
Reflected in the bay.

The Red Gate's toilsome Strait is passed,
With many a weary sigh,
Until we find ourselves at last,
Safe back again, with anchor cast,
Point Pleasant lying nigh.

And when the campfire's light,
We pass the time along,
And wake the voices of the night,
With song and jest, and laughter bright,
We'll sing this little song:

The moon runs high,
And the mists lie low,
And my spirit there
Is light and free,
As moonbeams fair on the greenwood tree.

When the moon runs low,
And the star fires glow,
As I list to the rippling water flow,
Oh! My heart is light,
As a bird in flight,
Ah! I love the quiet and dreary night.

Benning Wentworth, Royal Provincial Governor,
1741--1764

Birch Farm ruins, Governor's Island, circa 1900.

Chapter 5
THE HIDDEN NATION
1750--2000

The pond is a powerful magnet that draws its children unerringly back to its shores. It is very satisfying to watch middle aged campers return to the scene of their youthful adventures. Familiar scenes light eager faces and once again—they are children! One perceptive resident had a simple explanation for the lure of the pond:

> It is the only place that I know of where the entire family can enjoy the same activities without the kids constantly nagging to be allowed to go off someplace on their own.

A grandparent can experience no greater thrill than watching a son or a daughter teach a grandchild to dive off a dock or to get up on water skis for the first time. And, for the keen observer, there is the prospect of finding a flint arrowhead on a sandy shore. Such a discovery summons the image of a red skinned warrior drawing his bow on a deer taking water at a shoreline unmarked by signs of human habitation.

The history of the pond goes far beyond Benning Wentworth's decision to build a summer home on the big island in 1741. His celebrity draws our interest, but one is constrained to ask, "What about the others? Were there other people here when he arrived and what people preceded them? Numerous artifacts that date back as far as 7,000 years have been found around the pond. Who were the "Original People" and where did they go? *The Hidden Nation* reveals that the descendants of these people are still among us. It examines how *The Indigenous People* were assimilated by a dominant culture, and it reveals how their descendants came to be our neighbors and friends. Once part of the *Wabenaki Federation of Abenaki Nations*, their sovereign right to their land is gone, and their stone artifacts are mute reminders that their ancestors roamed the shores of Big Island Pond 10,000 years ago. Today, many of these Native American descendants are reclaiming their heritage and are learning to walk with pride in the knowledge that they carry the genes of a proud Ancient People. Through the publication of my book *Abenaki Warrior* in 1998, I developed friendships with a number of Native American descendants who have given me the fascinating details of their personal history that I share with you now.

The Original People had a great reverence for nature. They believed in a Creator whom they called The Great Spirit. Their beliefs were similar to our own Christian beliefs, but their legends included lesser spirits such as Glooscap and Odzihozo. These mythological beings were capable of performing superhuman deeds. Their mythology includes tales of evil spirits like Pomola who they believed lived at the summit of Mt. Katadyn in Maine. They believed that all things created by The Great Spirit were living things. Mountains, rivers, stones, and trees were considered living in an inanimate state, while the animals that The Creator provided for man's sustenance were viewed as animate beings. Even today Indians speak of Ndakinna (Our Land) with great reverence; they often refer to it as Mother Earth. In their heyday, many of their chiefs were noted for their oratory. The following eloquent address of Chief Seattle is a good example of the skillful way Indians used words and imagery to express their spirituality.

Address by Chief Seattle:

This we know. The earth does not belong to man;
man belongs to the earth. This we know.
All things are connected like the blood that unites one family.
All things are connected. Whatever befalls the earth,
befalls the sons of the earth. Man did not weave the web of life;
he is merely a strand in it. Whatever he does to the web,
he does to himself.
Every part of the earth is sacred to my people...
every shining pine needle, every sandy shore,
every light mist in the dark forest, every clearing...

and every winged creature is sacred to my people.
We are part of the earth and it is part of us.
The fragrant flowers are our sisters,
the deer and mighty eagle are our brothers;
The rocky peak, the fertile meadows,
all things are connected like the blood that unites a family.

These moving words by Chief Seattle fall strangely on the ear of modern man who is often reluctant to voice his spiritual thoughts. The Indian often thought and spoke in parables, and Chief Seattle's moving statement exemplifies the powerful oratory of his people. There is no doubt that the Indians shared our love for the pond and its physical surroundings. It is appropriate to examine their history, and it is important to learn how white prejudice forced them to assume white identities. Local Abenaki did not suddenly disappear, as one wipes clean a blackboard. There is a story to their disappearance, and the details of that story are fascinating. This chapter examines the history of a single Abenaki family and it reveals how they managed to "cross over" and become part of The Hidden Nation. Like many ethnic groups, modern Native Americans are defining themselves in new terms; they prefer the term Indian Nation because the term Nation reflects their goal to become *Independent Sovereign Nations*. In the United States and in Canada they are making some progress in that direction through legal action. Before scoffing at the notion of sovereignty for Native American groups, one should study the history of their treatment by the United States Government before rejecting the idea.

The Abenaki Indians resisted the takeover of their ancestral lands for 88 years despite the numerical superiority and advanced technology of the Europeans. Prior to contact by European fishermen in the late 1500's, the total Abenaki population was about 40,000. The smallpox, diphtheria, and influenza epidemics coming from these early contacts reduced their numbers to a mere 12,000 by the early 1600s. Fifty-six years after the Pilgrims established a foothold in the New World, their relationship with the Indians began to deteriorate. Disputes between the Indians and the Colonists over land sparked King Phillip's War that ended in the death of King Phillip (Chief Metacom) in a Narragansett swamp in 1677. This was followed by a series of wars between the Abenaki Indians of Maine, New Hampshire and Vermont that lasted until 1763.

1675—1677 KING PHILLIPS WAR. The war of the English Colonists and Wampenaug and Narragansett Indians of Massachusetts led by Chief Matacom:

1675—1697 King Williams War

1702—1713 Queen Ann's War (War of the Spanish Succession)

1722—1725 Governor Dummer's War with the Eastern Abenaki Indians.

1740—1748 King George's War (War of the Austrian Succession)

1755—1763 French and Indian War (The Seven Year War)

An analysis of these dates reveals that there were 36 years during which the settlers and the Indians were theoretically at peace. History reveals that both sides violated terms of the treaties. The whites built forts and garrison houses in Indian Territory in violation of treaties and Indian elders found it difficult to restrain hotheaded young braves seeking to retaliate. The miracle is that 3,000 to 4,000 Abenaki warriors were able to hold off vastly superior forces for 88 years. The answer undoubtedly lies in motivation; the Abenaki Indians were fighting to preserve their way of life. Another factor was the ability of the Indians to strike without warning and then disappear into their natural element—the forest.

The Abenaki ability to adapt to changing conditions and to blend with their surroundings served them well in times of peace. Many of them adapted easily to the white lifestyle. They made wonderful guides for surveyors and hunters and they were willing and skillful workers in the lumber camps and as crewmen aboard fishing boats. Their natural artisan skills allowed them to become carpenters, stone masons, boat builders and some of them even became missionaries.

When the peace was shattered, as it often was, by some overt act by either side, Indians and whites suddenly found themselves figuratively staring into the muzzles of guns in the hands of former friends. In the famous 1725 "Marathon Battle" that took place at Saco Pond in Fryeburg, Maine between Lovewell's 44 rangers and 60 to 80 Pigwacket Indians, former friends shouted jibes and insults at each other during the six hour battle. In the midst of the fight Chief Paugus and Chamberlain went to a brook to clean guns fouled by excessive firing. The two had known each other well in peaceful times. They were both reloading their guns when they spotted each other. Chief Paugus is reported to have exclaimed:

"Me kill you quick!" Chamberlain's response was a terse, "Maybe not!" Chamberlain was able to prime his later model musket more quickly by tilting the gun to pour powder through the touch-hole into the pan. He finished priming his gun and shot Paugus dead just as he was raising his own musket to fire.

By the end of the Seven-Year War in 1763, the Abenaki will to resist the growing power of the Europeans had been broken. Indian raids on Colonial settlements gave way to Colonial forays into Indian Territory as the balance of power shifted to the English. Roger's Rangers fell upon the French mission village in Saint Francis and killed indiscriminately. In the end, the Indians were left with only two options: The first and most popular choice was to move to Canada and live in one of the settlements created for them there by the French. Or they could choose to conceal their Indian heritage and learn to live like the white man. A large number of Abenaki people chose the latter course and, like chameleons, successfully blended into the white culture. They assumed English names and identities and began to raise children who were never told that they were Indian. Many people of European heritage lived out their lives in Maine, New Hampshire and Vermont unaware that many of their neighbors and friends were descendants of Native Americans. In only 88 years a people whose heritage went back 12,000 years was conquered, and Abenaki men and women were reduced to being second-class citizens beholden to whites for their livelihood.

One must understand the nature of the Abenaki to understand why Indians living outside official government reservations have been unable to achieve sovereign status. Much of the problem lies in the traditional independent nature of the individual tribes. The Indians were organized into loosely allied small bands that engaged in intertribal feuds prior to the arrival of the white man. Their custom of moving from place to place to take advantage of available food supply led the Colonists to believe that they were nomadic people who lacked a well-defined culture. The Indians did not understand the white man's concept of property rights and the transfer of property for consideration. They thought of Mother Earth as a gigantic Turtle Island floating in a universe established by the Creator of All Things. They could not understand the concept of man owning part of Mother Earth. In their eyes man could not own the earth since all living creatures of the earth, including man, were the children of Mother Earth. There was much doubt among English and French Historians whether Indian leaders really understood the complicated terms of the treaties that they agreed to sign.

The French Canadians skillfully used the Indians as pawns in their confrontation with the English. They assigned Jesuit missionaries to every major Abenaki village in Northern New England whose mission was to covert the natives to Catholicism. They adopted the customs and lifestyle of the Indians and learned to speak their language. The Indians, who embraced the rituals and pageantry of Catholicism, respected the Jesuits. When Canadian authorities urged the Jesuits to incite the Indians against the Colonists some resisted the pressure, but others viewed it as vindication of their personal militancy. But when the French finally wrote off their war with the English, they left their Abenaki allies holding the bag. With their numbers decimated by white man's diseases, and the cream of their youth sacrificed in endless raids and battles, the final tragedy was the burning of their villages and the murder of their elders, women and children. History books that examine the series of wars between the Abenaki Indians and the English Colonists fail to answer one of the most intriguing questions about the period. How did these two different cultures get along during times of peace? Also--when overwhelming European power and technology ended the so-called "Indian menace", what happened to the vanquished?

Measured in the context of the 12,000 year history of the Abenaki people, their near extinction as a race happened as if the candle illuminating their history had been snuffed out in an instant. But, like other lost cultures, the Abenaki people refused to be discarded as irrelevant. Today, a ripple of interest in Native American culture and irrelevant. Today, a ripple of interest in Native American culture and spiritualism has become a groundswell that one day may become an outpouring of the human quest for personal peace and meaning in a complicated world. The impact of movies like "Dances with Wolves" shows that the general population is beginning to question previous portrayals of the Indians. Indeed, increasing numbers of Americans are beginning to compare their own traditional values with the simple beliefs of Native Americans who have a reverence for the entire physical world about them. The scramble for material wealth has not brought individual fulfillment. Material goals attained through sacrifice and hard work turn out to be hollow shells of disillusionment. As people search for spiritual fulfillment, the spiritualism of Native Americans seems increasingly attractive.

The large number of books that chronicle events during that period might lead one to conclude that, at the close of the French and Indian War, New England had wiped out the "Red Menace". Today, there are 12,000 Abenaki descendants living in Maine, New Hampshire and Vermont after having their numbers reduced to 1,000 at the time of The Revolutionary War. The United States Government currently recognizes the Penobscot, the Passamaquaddy and the Maliseet Abenaki who live on reservations in Northern Maine, and there are seven Maliseet reservations in New Brunswick and Quebec. However, there are thousands of Abenaki descendants living in Maine, New Hampshire and Vermont who have not been officially recognized by our government and are therefore not entitled to any of the benefits received by reservation Indians. In the aftermath of the Indian wars, our government rounded up all known Indians in New England and transported them in wagons to reservations in Canada. Many of the passengers on these wagons slipped away from the wagon train and made their way back to familiar territory where they had lived all their lives. These people adopted English names and customs in order to be accepted as white. By hiding their identity, and by adapting the ways of the white man, they were able to avoid deportation and extinction as a race.

In trying to call attention to the plight of indigenous people who have been overwhelmed by more advanced cultures, there is a tendency to overstate the arrogance and greed of the dominant society while portraying all the victims as good and noble. In reality the English were not all bad and the Indians were not all good. In truth, the Indians did many things to hasten the demise of their own race. Their main weakness came from their tradition of living in small independent bands carefully guarding their independence from other tribes and nations. Had they formed a League of American Indian Nations to take a stand against the earliest Colonial expansion, they may have been able to clear the continent of European invaders. But one must realize that the Indians, like any society, had their share of incompetent leaders who were motivated by greed, jealousy and hubris. Some of these leaders sold vast tracts of land to the Colonists in exchange for personal gifts with little permanent value.

In 1646 two Indian representatives of Chief Passaconaway signed a contract with the English that transferred land north of Haverhill that measured 14 miles to a side (196 sq. miles). The purchase price was 3 pounds, 10 shillings (about 7 American dollars) plus other trinkets and items of food. On the face of it one has to wonder; did the English really believe that they were acting ethically in this exchange? If an adult persuades a 5-year old child to give him the $100 bill he holds in his tiny hand in exchange for a piece of candy, is that an ethical transaction?

Still, the Indian hurt his cause in other ways. Often their hotheaded young braves broke treaties that had been signed by their Indian elders in solemn ceremonies. Many became uncontrollable under the influence of alcohol and committed atrocities. The Colonists complained about the Indians "not fighting fair." The guerilla type attacks by the Indians terrified the Colonists who failed to understand that this was really the only advantage their weaker adversary had in an uneven contest. The main tactical error of the Indians was to take sides in the war between the English and the French. Both the English and the French skillfully exploited this lack of unity, and the Indians were the inevitable losers in this power struggle between the two European powers.

Among the unexpected benefits that came with the publication of *Abenaki Warrior* in the spring of 1998, were the friendships I made with members of the Native American community. Christine Dube, in particular, became a rich source of information about the Native American population that lives in our midst. Her personal experience is not only interesting, but she spent much of her life in the Big

Indian descendant who was delivered by a veterinarian in a log cabin in Alna, Maine in 1913. Her family name was Drew. Details about Christine's father are limited; he was French and Micmac Indian and he was Catholic. He disappeared from the screen of Christine's memory at an early age; the details of her family come from the Drew side of the family. Most long-time residents of the pond know where Drew Road and Drew Brook are located. Drew Road begins just below the Fire Station that is located at the intersection of Warner Hill Road and Island Pond Road. At the bottom of a steep grade it meets North Island Pond Road and crosses Drew Brook that runs in a southerly direction to where it enters the pond between Germantown and Howard's Grove. On the left side, 100 yards beyond the brook, an old farmhouse and barn have lined the road as long as I can remember. Drew Road and Drew Brook were named for the people who owned this farm from the 1700s into the 1800s and this chapter examines how Abenaki people came to this farm and how they became known as the Drew family.

In the mid-1700s an Englishman named Drew lived at this site. His search for a wife took him to Boston where he paid off the bond of an indentured woman and brought her back to his homestead. Sometime after they had settled near the north shore of what was then called Lake Wentworth, he suddenly became ill and died. A wandering Abenaki Indian chanced upon the woman as she was digging a grave for her deceased husband. The solitary woman accepted his offer of help and together they finished the sad job. He stayed on to help the woman with chores around the farm and, as winter approached, the woman, recognizing her predicament, invited the man to stay. In the natural course of events that followed, the woman found herself pregnant in the spring.

This man already had a family, and his Indian wife eventually learned of his whereabouts from another Abenaki who had seen him at the Drew farm. Christine explained that the restraints and traditions of marriage that we know today were not shared by Indians of that period and the Jesuits who lived among the Abenaki Indians had done their best to discourage the practice of polygamy. When the man's family showed up at the farmhouse it was not at all unusual that they were invited to stay. As time went by, it was apparent that the Englishwoman and the Indian's real wife were compatible and the Englishwoman and the Indian's real wife were compatible and eventually they became a family unit. When they learned that they needed to apply for a deed of ownership for what was now their joint property, they decided to use the name Drew as their family name. This was a common tactic used by Indians who decided to hide their Abenaki identity in order to survive. Thus, through curious but legal means, this Abenaki family managed to cross over the race line and attain a new identity as white Americans. It strikes one as ironic that the Indigenous People of this land had to resort to subterfuge in order to attain legal status in their own country.

In about 1875 two of the Drew boys drove their buggy to Haverhill and returned with two English girls who had agreed to marry them. They built houses on each side of the Drew Road for their new brides but after a dispute one of them moved away. The remaining brother was the great grandfather of Christine's mother. I interviewed Christine's mother at her tiny apartment in Derry. I found Lorna still sharp and very independent at 85. Understandably, after experiencing a lifetime of prejudice, she was somewhat reluctant to discuss her Indian background. Nevertheless, she gave me several fascinating glimpses into her early life. In about 1910 her father got a job bossing a crew of lumberjacks in Alna, Maine. He and his wife were assigned to a small log cabin at the camp, and that is where Lorna was born and spent her early years. Her mother told her that the camp did not have a regular doctor, and that the camp veterinarian had delivered her. She had a harrowing memory of being alone in the log cabin with her mother and a pack of wolves scratching at the door. They had no refrigeration and the men hung game they killed from the limbs of trees to keep it cold and out of the reach of animal predators. The smell of the meat drove the hungry wolves to frenzy. They kept launching themselves off the roof of the cabin in a vain attempt to bring down the hanging game.

She showed me a picture of a large dog she called Charlie. He appeared to be a mixture of St. Bernard and husky and he looked huge. One day, as she was playing alone near the cookhouse, a drunken Frenchman attempted to molest her. Charlie responded to her screams and attacked and killed the man. Lorna says that, when the lumberjacks came back from the woods and learned what had happened, they dragged the dead man out into the woods and left him to the animals.

Christine's grandfather on her mother's side was born in 1873; his full name was Elbridge Chesley Drew. All of her ancestors on her mothers side had Abenaki roots with some English mixed in. The English had introduced the Church of England to the strain and the family considered itself Episcopalian. A strapping 6" 4," he was a Maine lumberjack in his youth and he later became a farmer. After farming the family property on Drew Road he moved to Sandown for awhile, but he was eventually drawn back to the site of the Drew family's origin. He bought land that fronted on Gulf Road and backed up on Island Pond Road. He farmed this land until the early 60s. Her grandfather was a very pragmatic man. He refused to teach her how to speak Abenaki:

> The Abenaki language is for old men, and a young girl can get into trouble hanging around with old men. Besides, you better learn to speak the language of the man who signs your pay check.

She remembers when she was 13 years old sun bathing in a two piece bathing suit, smoking a cigarette and listening to rock music. Grandpa marched up and raised her by her long hair and marched her in to her mother. The reason for his anger was unexpected. It had nothing to do with the cigarette, the skimpy bathing suit or even the modern rock music. As he held her in front of her mother he declared with conviction:

> If you want this child to grow up to marry someone other that a black person, you better see to it that she stays out of the sun." [34]

---

[34] Author's note: Many of the southern blacks that were transported to Canada by northern Abolitionists during the Civil War married Narragansett and Wampenaug Indians. Their benefactors did not accept them as equals and it was natural for them to intermarry with the Indians who were also considered racially inferior to the whites.

His personal experience with prejudice against Blacks, Hispanics and Indians had taught him that it was a lot easier to get along as a white man in a white man's world. Demeaned by the reality of his origin, he was still pragmatic enough to know how to avoid the spotlight of prejudice in order to keep meat on the table.

Lorna met a Cherokee man and she and her daughter went to live on a Cherokee Reservation in North Carolina. Christine was called Honey Flower when she was a child and had always been called Honey around the house. But when it came time for her to go to school Lorna registered her as Christine Drew, and she forgot to tell her daughter about the change. It took some time for Honey to learn to respond when her teacher called her by her new Christian name.

Mother and daughter ended up near another Indian reservation in Michigan when Christine was in her early teens. It was there that she had her first experience with prejudice. They had two girl basketball teams at her school; one was made up entirely of white girls and Christine's team was composed of Black, Hispanic and Indian girls. She knew some of her friends were Black and some were Hispanic, but it had never really occurred to her that she was anything other than white. Awareness came unexpectedly through an idle comment she made to a friend about going out for a certain school activity:

"You can't do that Christine; that activity is only for white people" her friend told her.

An early romantic experience came in Michigan in the form of a friendship with a young white boy. One day the boy's mother revealed herself to Christine: "Its OK for you and John to be friends, but you know that it can't go beyond that because you're Indian." At that moment the reality of her heritage began to sink in. The Minister of the Methodist Church she was attending bred purebred dogs as a hobby. One of his females accidentally had puppies by an off-breed dog. Christine loved dogs and went to his house to pick up the puppy that he had promised her. When she arrived, he was in the process of chloroforming the remaining puppies in the litter. Suddenly the Indian beliefs that were deep in her consciousness surfaced and her strenuous objection to the needless killing of the puppies was the beginnings of her estrangement from the Christian

Church. From that point forward she began to revert to the spirituality of her Abenaki forefathers, and it was the beginning of her determination to embrace her heritage and to walk with pride in the traditions of her people.

She was a teenager in the turbulent 60s and she saw plenty of evidence of unrest in America; some of the things she saw on television added fuel to her awakening. About that time a Mexican man somewhat older than she, in the time honored custom of his people, sent a relative to Lorna asking permission to court her daughter. Lorna's reaction was a perfect example of how people regard themselves in the pecking order of American society. She responded quickly and decisively; she immediately made plans to return to her father's farm in New Hampshire where she hoped that Christine would meet a boy of her own background. More succinctly, her reaction was; "She ain't gonna marry no Mexican."

Christine did return to her grandfather's farm on Gulf Road and, when she was 17 years old, she wed a local man. They had a son and lived in a waterfront house on Big Island Pond for five years. The details of the failed marriage are not relevant here, but there is a clue in remarks made by Christine. Apparently her husband did not share her pride in her Indian ancestry and he asked her to hide her Indian heritage from his friends. Young and inexperienced, she ended up with only her freedom and her young son.

Today, at age 50, she lives in Methuen and works for an outside contractor to nursing homes administering respiratory care to nursing home patients. In less than a year she expects to earn her LPN. Many years ago Kukukuo (the owl) replaced Honey Flower as her Indian name. According to Indian legend the owl comes to assist a stricken person and to arrange for his or her passage to the Spirit World; the owl is said to be the last being to speak a dying person's name. Her Native American friends nod knowingly and say,

Christine, you have come around to your Indian name. You were meant to take care of the dying and ease their passage to The Spirit World, and now—you are fulfilling your destiny.

She is on a committee that is raising money to place a beautiful bronze sculpture of The Indian Maiden on the corner of Pawtucket Boulevard and Varnum Avenue overlooking the Merrimac River. The sculpture is a symbol for the contributions that have been made to our society by all women of the world. The project is being developed through the cooperative efforts of the Indian Maiden Monument Committee, the Department of Environmental Management, the Massachusetts States Park System, the City of Lowell and Lowell General Hospital. The world-renowned artist Mico Kaufman sculpted this striking 7-foot bronze statue of an Indian woman performing a traditional smudging ceremony. A number of his sculptures are displayed in Lowell and Tewksbury, Massachusetts including the Wamesit Indian on Route 28 in North Tewksbury. Committee members have worked tirelessly without personal compensation to raise the $150,000 needed to pay for this project. Tax deductible donations to this project can be mailed to:

Becky (Soft Talker) Jackson
18B Mill Road
Kingston, NH 03848

Today, after many years as a single mother, Christine is free to pursue her personal interests. The experienced observer may see her heritage in her coloring or perhaps her hair but, unless she is dressed in ceremonial regalia, she appears to be a typical middle class American woman. Her friends find her to be humorous, intelligent and very much a fun person to be with. She is knowledgeable about public affairs and politics and she will surprise you with her understanding of the investments in her 401K retirement fund. She gives talks on Native American culture to schools and civic organizations and is a well adjusted, upbeat person. Having grown up in the area, and having enjoyed her home on the Hampstead shore, she still misses the pond and her childhood haunts. She is proud of her Abenaki roots, and she tries to be true to her heritage. She routinely offers a small prayer for the living creatures that are sacrificed to provide the food she brings home from the grocery store and she offers an apology to the living grass as she prepares to cut it. She also believes that when one is well fed it is proper to throw a bit of food to the little people: the birds, the fairies, the trolls and the gnomes. She is proud of her Abenaki heritage, and she is confident about the survival of her people. With a mischievous glint in her eye she cautions:

For 10,000 years the Abenaki were known as the *People of the Dawn*, so don't forget that when the last Abenaki is gone, the sun will rise no more.

THE CHASE FAMILY

The Chase name and Big Island Pond fit together like mom and apple pie; so closely are they identified. The family has occupied the tract of land that extends from the shore of the pond out to Island Pond Road ever since The British Crown granted it to an ancestor in the 1700s. In 1934, after being a frequent guest of the Korb and Minzner families since 1928, I finally found a place where I could be independent. The camping area that we called Hobo Lodge was located up on the hill behind the dance hall. The cows up at the farm provided my daily pint of milk that I bought from Ruth Chase at the store by the icehouse. She had black hair, gathered at the back of her head, and I can remember her features as if I had seen her yesterday. Her husband Willie was a thin man with an unruly shock of brown hair that topped a lined face. Herbert was mostly bald, he appeared to be well fed and I remember him smiling a lot and that he was kind of shy. I was a fourteen years old kid in a bathing suit and they were the adults who ran the store. They had a gas pump at the shore and they used to deliver ice and milk around the pond in a rowboat powered by a small outboard engine. Ten years later, as I steamed in a Navy task force off the coast of Japan, I used to daydream and yearn for those idyllic days at the pond. An indelible image of those days stays with me and, although the individuals are gone, the names Chase and Big Island Pond remain almost synonymous to me.

Bill Chase and his wife Claire are now the elders of the family. Bill is retired and lives on the shore of the pond where he has spent his entire life. Although he doesn't realize it, his memory holds the details of many interesting stories about the pond. Every day his front window frames a view that his family has enjoyed for more than 250 years. There is a certain fascination that comes with exploring the memory of people like Bill to bring together stories about the pond. Often the information seems to have little value until fragments of information from different sources suddenly come together to produce a fascinating story. That is how it happened with the Chase family.

The Chase property may have come from the original Mason Land Grants that were awarded by Mason himself before he died. The King of England granted a huge portion of New Hampshire and Vermont to Mason as a reward for his service to the English Crown. Mason made smaller grants of this land to Englishmen who were willing to risk their lives to settle these lands. The offer of free land may have been given with a certain proviso: "I am awarding you a grant of land in the province of New Hampshire. Be advised that there are hostile Indians in the area, but if you and your family can make improvements to this land in the form of a house and cultivated fields, the land is yours to keep." By using proxies to settle portions of his huge grant, Mason would have seen the value of his remaining land steadily increase its value.

In 1741 Benning Wentworth was appointed Royal Provincial Governor of the State of New Hampshire. In 1746 he persuaded his cronies to buy up the remaining Mason Land Grants for 100 pounds per share. In a politically astute move, he and his friends declared that the land grants that had already been made to the Chase family and others was unaffected by this purchase. During his term as governor of the state he awarded over 200 townships to friends and political allies. The recipients of these townships routinely deeded back 500 acres of prime land to Wentworth and his friends. Between supplying tall pine masts for the King's navy and his land deals, Wentworth became a very wealthy man.

During the winter of 1998-99 I had a letter from Tim Chase in which he told how much he had enjoyed reading *Abenaki Warrior*. Having been brought up on the pond, he had a natural love of nature as well as a keen interest in the history of his family at Big Island Pond. In one of my letters to him I mentioned my research of the Drew family. In his response he mentioned that his great grandmother's maiden name was Naomi Drew! I was immediately struck by the implications of this information and made it a priority for further research. After all, the Chase and Drew families had lived less two miles from each other in the 1800s.

When I arrived at the pond in June of 1999 I had some medical problems that needed attention and I was temporarily diverted. After surgery to clear a blocked carotid artery and other medical procedures, I found myself feeling as well as a 79-year old man can feel, and I was delighted to have Christine Dube (my Abenaki friend) up for a visit. She had made me a beautiful buckskin medicine bag to put around my neck. The bead design on the front depicts the pond, Escumbuit Island, a pine tree and the rising sun. After she performed an Indian smudging ceremony on my person and gave me the medicine bag to drive out the bad spirits, we retired to the deck to sit in the sun and sip a glass of wine. As I sat there, moved by her thoughtfulness and at peace with the world, I had a phone call from my doctor who wanted to know how I was feeling. When I described the scene and the smudging ceremony, the doctor said, "Well, it sounds like you are in good hands; I am enjoying my copy of *Abenaki Warrior* and I wish you well." As I hung up I thought to myself, "That doctor must think I am a real whacko!"

I decided that it might be a good time to bring up the subject of Naomi Drew. Christine's mother Lorna could not recall a Naomi in the family history, but she said that she might have used a different name. Although her birth and marriage records listed her as Naomi, she may have adopted a Christian name. She added that the Iroquois meaning of Naomi is "Heaven Shaker." Indian legend depicts Naomi as a large woman with big feet who stamps around heaven during thunderstorms to create thunder. Then Christine said: "I have been told all my life that we are related to the Chase family and I know that my mother was brought up by my great aunt who lived over at Chase's Grove."

Both Bill Chase and Christine Dube recall this woman's name was Olive Thomas and that her maiden name was Drew. She lived in a house on the shore next to Whitney's Grove. As we investigated further, it turned out that Olive Thomas had a sister named Naomi Drew who went by the name of Mary and sometimes by Madge. She married Charles Chase and they lived at the farm on Island Pond Road. She was Bill Chase's grandmother. She and her husband eventually became estranged and she refused to have anything to do with her husband. Apparently despondent over the separation, Charles hung himself from one of the crossbeams of the barn on

Island Pond Road. His oldest son Arthur and his brother found the body hanging in the barn and Arthur cut it down hoping to revive his father. Bill says that the authorities took a dim view of his action; apparently they wanted evidence at the scene to be left undisturbed so that they could conduct their investigation properly. They seemed unable to understand the perfectly normal reaction of a son who was merely trying to save his father's life.

My immediate concern was the effect this news would have on Bill Chase and his family. I found that he was quite interested in these new facts about his family, but I had the impression that he was not very surprised by my revelation about his grandmother. He commented:

"I like to read about my family history, but I'm not one to spend a lot of time digging into it."

He agreed that it was an interesting story and he had no objection to me writing about it. Additional evidence came from young Bill Chase who told me that his grandmother, Ruth Chase, told me that some of their ancestors were Indian.

The Chase family has another link to an important historical figure. They are related to Hannah Duston. There is a large society in Haverhill for the descendants of Hannah Duston, the famous 17th Century frontier woman who was carried into captivity by the Indians in 1696. Abenaki Indians forced Hannah and a girl named Mary Neff to carry loot taken from her own home to a small island in the Merrimac River north of Manchester. The Indians planned to take her to Canada where they planned to deliver her to the French in exchange for a bounty. Instead, during the night, she and two other white captives killed and scalped 2 adult male Indians and 10 assorted women and children and used their canoes to make their way back to Haverhill. Given up for dead by her family, she and her two companions arrived in Haverhill carrying the scalps of the dead Indians in a piece of linen that had been looted from her own farm. She was hailed as a heroine in all the Colonies and was given a cash reward by the council in Boston. Statues in Haverhill, Massachusetts and Boscowen, New Hampshire memorialize her deed.[35]

The story of how the Chase and Drew families became part of the process of the assimilation of the Abenaki Indians is a fascinating part of Colonial folklore. Today, Native Americans everywhere are researching their roots and openly embracing their proud heritage. Three hundred years ago they might have had the white man lined up in the sights of their musket, but ultimately they survived by learning to blend with the dominant culture. This is the strength of America. It is the exclusiveness of inbred societies that weakens nations. The strength of a nation comes from the diversity of its people.

---

[35] *Abenaki Warrior* by Alfred E Kayworth: (Pages 112-118) Six pages are devoted to Hannah Duston's abduction by Indians and the details of her miraculous escape from captivity.

By His HONOUR

SPENCER PHIPS, Esq;

Lieutenant-Governour and Commander in Chief, in and over His Majesty's Province of the *Massachusetts-Bay* in *New-England*.

A PROCLAMATION.

WHEREAS the Tribe of *Penobscot* Indians have repeatedly in a perfidious Manner acted contrary to their solemn Submission unto His Majesty long since made and frequently renewed ;

I **have therefore, at the Desire of the House of Representatives, with the Advice of His Majesty's Council, thought fit to issue this Proclamation, and to declare the** Penobscot **Tribe of Indians to be Enemies, Rebels and Traitors to His Majesty** King *GEORGE* the Second : **And I do hereby require His Majesty's Subjects of** this **Province to embrace all Opportunities of pursuing, captivating, killing and de- stroying all and every of the aforesaid Indians.**

AND WHEREAS the General Court of this Province have voted that a Bounty or Incouragement be granted and allowed to be paid out of the Publick Treasury, to the marching Forces that shall have been employed for the Defence of the *Eastern* and *Western* Frontiers, from the *First* to the *Twenty-fifth* of this Instant *November* ;

I **have thought fit to publish the same ; and I do hereby Promise, That there shall be paid out of the Province-Treasury to all and any of the said Forces, over and** above their **Bounty upon Inlistment, their Wages and Subsistence, the Premiums or Bounty following, viz.**

For every Male *Penobscot* Indian above the Age of Twelve Years, that shall be taken within the Time aforesaid and brought to *Boston, Fifty Pounds.*

For every Scalp of a Male *Penobscot* Indian above the Age aforesaid, brought in as Evidence of their being killed as aforesaid, *Forty Pounds.*

For every Female *Penobscot* Indian taken and brought in as aforesaid, and for every Male Indian Prisoner under the Age of Twelve Years, taken and brought in as aforesaid, *Twenty-five Pounds.*

For every Scalp of such Female Indian or Male Indian under the Age of Twelve Years, that shall be killed and brought in as Evidence of their being killed as aforesaid, *Twenty Pounds.*

Given at the Council-Chamber in *Boston*, this Third Day of *November* 1 7 5 5, and in the Twenty-ninth Year of the Reign of our Sovereign Lord *GEORGE* the Second, by the Grace of GOD of *Great-Britain, France* and *Ireland*, KING, Defender of the Faith, &c.

By His Honour's Command,

J. Willard, Secr.

S. Phips.

GOD Save the KING.

BOSTON: Printed by *John Draper*, Printer to His Honour the Lieutenant-Governour and Council. 1755.

1756 bounty notice for Indians--dead or alive.

The author with Christine Dube, Abenaki,
and Roland Giraud, Micmac

Chapter 6
THE FIRST CAMPERS
1878--1900

I n the late 1800's there were 11 farms that bordered the pond and shared its shoreline. The man-made cove, where the damn is located, was "the lower pasture" for the Stickney family. The adjacent property, which was owned by the Chase family, fronted on Island Pond Road and went all the way back to the pond. After the Civil War the existing rail lines did not come close to the pond and it could only be reached by horse drawn conveyance or on foot. The farmers had rowboats for fishing and recreation, but people from the cities were slow to discover the charm of the pond. In the years that followed the end of the Civil War it remained the private domain of the families who lived around the pond. By a remarkable stroke of good fortune we can enjoy a fascinating chronicle about how, in 1878, a group of men from Lawrence discovered the joy of camping out at Big Island Pond.

The two women who wrote these chronicles are as interesting as the stories they left us, and it is appropriate that we acknowledge them in the lead-in to their story.[36]

Elizabeth Schneider was 78 years old in 1963 when she wrote about her childhood memories of Big Island Pond from the 1878 to

---

[36] Author's note: Mrs. Mary Lou Williams extensive collection of papers yielded the initial clue in the form of a 15 pages of material typed by Elizabeth Schneider in 1963. When I pressed Mary Lou Williams for details she referred me to Arthur Sweeney in Freeport, Maine. His wife Edith in turn passed me on to Mr. Franz Schneider in Marblehead, Massachusetts who was working on a chronicle of his father's life. It is his grandmother and his aunt who wrote the material presented in this chapter.

1900 era. Some of the details came from a chronicle that her mother (also named Elizabeth) had written for the Schneider family in 1921.

America is a land built by immigrants, and the marriage of Franz Schneider and Elizabeth Sweeney in 1884 was typical of the era. She was the only daughter of an Irishman named Patrick Sweeney. The son of Irish immigrants, he became a successful landlord, merchant, publisher and politician in Lawrence. Franz Schneider was an Austrian clock maker who arrived in American penniless in 1876. He founded the Schneider Jewelry business in Lawrence, MA and became a millionaire when a million dollars was a lot of money. The camping adventure he began with his friend Joe Sweeney evolved naturally into a courtship of Joe's sister Elizabeth at Big Island Pond.

The chronicles of mother and daughter begin with excerpts from a family journal written by Elizabeth Schneider in 1921 in which she describes some of her experiences at Big Island Pond. Her description of her courtship by Franz Schneider at the pond sets the mood for the entire chapter. Her comments about her daughter confirm what seems apparent in the daughter's work; she was a skilled and practiced writer. The daughter never married. She was 78 years old when she typed her child hood recollections of the pond. She had an eye for detail and a talent for description that is apparent in her writing. We are indebted to both women for their contributions.

The 1921 Chronicle of Elizabeth Schneider (mother):

In the summer of 1882 Mr. Schneider became acquainted in a business way with my brothers, John and Joe, and was a welcome visitor at the camp. He used to drive a smart little nag, Sukey, harnessed to a high-topped buggy, and he was always ready on summer afternoons to take a fellow camper up to Island Pond, which was a great accommodation in those days when there were no electric cars to transport one part of the way, and a regular livery outfit was considered an extravagance.

At that time I was in the West visiting relatives in Chicago, Wisconsin and Ohio. During that time, Mr. Schneider had become quite a favorite among the campers. There had been a good deal of visiting between the campers and the people over in Hampstead and I happened to be present on the one day when the campers invited all their friends and acquaintances in Hampstead. Old and young, rather more attractive than the average, they came, mostly in boats from the Hampstead shore, and they brought generous basket-lunches, which were supplemented by coffee, light drinks and substantials from the camp larder. Very good pictures were taken of the crowd by Owen Kenefick, and most of them can readily be identified even after the lapse of years.

I returned from the West in November of 1882 and soon afterward met Mr. Schneider on Essex Street when I was coming from skating with my brother Joe, as related above. The summer of 1883 saw a renewal of camp life, and a party was formed to go up to a picnic similar to those of the year before. Mr. Schneider was to take some over the road in a large "carry-all"(wagon) with a span of horses which he drove himself. I went with my brother Peter, Owen Kenefick, and others, in the "carry-all." It was a beautiful day. All the Hampstead people, mostly the same who attended the year before, came over to the camp, and a jolly time was had. I remember that we walked around the island (on a margin of beach which existed at that time on account of the low water) from the "ruins"...a favorite spot...which we reached by a good road through the woods. Somehow Mr. Schneider seemed to be at my elbow all day, especially in going over the rough places on the walk. It was near dark when we reluctantly had to think of going home. When we got to Hampstead we waited still later at Mr. Nichol's house for some of the young folks who were still out in the untrustworthy boats on the pond. Charles De Courey was in charge of one party, and when there seemed to be some danger of his boat sinking, he made what they called a "catamaran" with a better boat, and brought all safe to shore. Some of the mothers, especially Mrs. Smith of Haverhill, mother of Sue, Alice and Kate, were much worried at the delay of their daughters in arriving. We started off in the darkness with Mr. Schneider driving the span, and Owen Kenefick and I in the back seat. Mr. Schneider was quite nervous over driving in the dark, and did not enjoy the pleasantries of Owen who was slightly affected by Mr.

Nichols' hard cider, and was really funny about an enormous bug (June bug) that was buzzing about.

After that, Mr. Schneider and I met frequently. He soon after accomplished the great feat of taking father and mother to camp for a Sunday. He expected me to go, but as I was not regularly invited, I never thought of going. Soon after that, I went with him one afternoon for a call at camp, and then it began to be a regular thing for us to go "buggy riding" almost any pleasant afternoon. In the fall of 1883 we became engaged, though nothing was said about it, and I simply transferred a plain gold ring which I wore to my engagement finger. The idea of marrying a man of a different nationality to my own appealed to me, especially one who had had such a varied experience. He had the old world idea of something besides just money-making, an idea of mingling simple, outdoor pleasures with the daily grind, a care-free fashion of taking life at one's own valuation, not slavishly following the conventional rule. It meant a turning from the old way in which I had been brought up and the entering upon a freer life, more in accordance with the freedom of thought which I was developing. I became interested in the German language, studied it by myself, and learned something of German literature and customs. I also got acquainted with Austria, of which I knew even less than of Germany, and a whole new world seemed to open up to me. The daily drives out into the country continued as an afternoon pastime. We generally drove to a farm of a German couple we knew, had a walk in the woods, and then a simple supper with coffee, and the drive home.

In a later passage of her chronicle Elizabeth described the academic achievements of her daughter in the following way:[37]

---

[37] Authors note: Elizabeth Schneider never married. Her mother suggests she had problems with her health, but she was 78 years old when she wrote her story and she lived another 20 years. They also had a son named Franz. His son, Franz Schneider of Marbelhead, MA, furnished me with material for this chapter. He is currently writing a chronicle of the life of his father. The senior Franz had a remarkable career that spanned eight decades; he was 105 years old when he

"In 1906 and 1909 Elizabeth and Franz had graduated from their respective colleges. Although they had both done well at school, their mental development had been very different. Elizabeth had been rather precocious. She learned to read at the age of three, and was always poring over books. From the age of seven she wrote stories and verses. At Abbot Academy she was for four years editor of the school magazine, "The Abbot Courant", and for three successive years she was chosen for the Draper Reading. Her activities at Vassar were limited by ill health, but she got the highest rank, (A), in every course she took, was editor of the "Vassarion", won the Shakespeare Prize, was elected to Phi Beta Kappa, and was chosen to speak at commencement, being excused, however, from doing so because of her health."

Camp Blackstone
By Elizabeth Schneider-1963 (daughter)

In the 1870s, few people thought of camping out in the woods, simply for the pleasure of camping. City men, who went on hunting or fishing expeditions, occasionally were forced to construct a rude shelter in the wilderness and spend a night or two there; it sounded very romantic and exciting to the folks at home, but it was only incidental to the pursuit of game. Camping in tents was associated chiefly with the Armed Forces, and the Civil War was still too close to make anything of that sort seem very attractive. In 1878, however, a young law student in Lawrence, Moses Ames, heard about the idea of camping for pleasure, and decided to try it. He invited my Uncle Joe and two other young men to make a camping trip with him to Island Pond, in Derry, New Hampshire. For some reason Uncle Joe could not go so he passed on the invitation to his younger brother Arthur, then a student at Harvard Medical School. "Mose" drove the equipage, carrying along a tent, some horse blankets and a few cooking utensils. In those days Derry was thickly

---

died.

populated with Chases. One branch of the family owned a picnic grove on the shores of Island Pond. Mose Ames left his horse and wagon at the Chase's barn and hired some rowboats with which to explore the pond. In any other part of the country, Island Pond would have been called a lake. It contained a number of small islands and one very large island covered several hundred acres. When Mose Ames's party rowed along the shores of the big island they discovered a pretty cove in which was a fine, sandy beach. This beach later was found to be the best beach on the pond, in fact, the only good one. The young men pitched their camp in a woodland dell that opened off the beach and settled down for the night. Unluckily a heavy thunderstorm poured torrents of rain into the woodland glade. They had to get up and dig trenches to let the water run off. In the morning one youth was alarmingly spotted with red and was feared to be breaking out with measles or chicken pox or scarlet fever, until the campers realized that the spots came from the red blanket in which he had been sleeping during the night. Spreading their blankets in the sun to dry, they went prospecting for a better location. They discovered it almost immediately on a little knoll at one side of the beach.

This was afterward acknowledged to be the most desirable campsite on the pond. The bathing beach was on one side; on the other side, a rocky point of the island jutted out into the water, to give a wide view of almost two-thirds of the pond.[38] The boys stayed a week there, and enjoyed immensely the unique sensation of living in the woods, Uncle Arthur was so pleased with this experience that he interested his three brothers in camping. The next summer they, with some of their friends, got a camping outfit and pitched their tent on the site occupied the year before by Mose Ames' party. They had a glorious time. As most of the group was made up of lawyers or law students, they named the place Camp Blackstone. It was characteristic of Mose Ames that he never went

---

[38] Author's note: Ted Williams's camp is located at the site of this original camp. There was an original Camp Blackstone cookhouse that featured picturesque "gingerbread trim" that Mrs. Williams had planned to use for her children's playhouse, but Hurricane Carol demolished the building in 1954.

camping again, although he sometimes visited camp for a day. Satisfied with having tried the new pastime, he turned to something more conventional.

For five summers, mothers, brothers and their friends enjoyed Camp Blackstone. One summer a young photographer from Lawrence joined the party and took many pictures of the campers. As a child I used to pore over these photographs picking out my uncles and their friends. Uncle Arthur brought several fellow students from Harvard Medical School including a dark handsome Cuban named Dr. Jova (pronounced Hova), but most of the men were lawyers, like Uncle John and Uncle Joe. One friend, Charlie D became a well-known judge. Although mother referred to them as "the boys" they were mostly in their twenties except for mother's youngest brother Peter, still in his teens and his cousin George who lived in Lowell. Peter enjoyed camp so much that he once spent his entire vacation there without once going home.

The photographs showed the tent in which they all slept. They built an open stone fireplace for cooking and constructed a dining table under the pines with seats made of planks nailed to trees. Uncle Arthur, who was handy at carpentry, made a floor for the tent and outdoor tables and chairs, and even improvised hammocks of barrel staves. They had no regular camping costumes—they simply went barefoot with their trousers rolled up to their knees and their shirts open at the neck, without collar or tie; they all wore white linen caps. Some of the photographs show two fashionable young ladies who were invited to spend a day at camp. They posed in one of the sailboats and in the outdoor dining room. Their elegance in such a place seems comical to modern eyes. They wore tight-fitting bodices with long sleeves and gauzy fichus, and elaborately draped silk or satin skirts, and picture hats loaded with ostrich plumes. One even brought a tiny poodle that she held in her lap or carried in her arms. No one saw anything incongruous in such attire out in the woods.

An old colored man named Francois and his white wife, a German, kept a tavern on the mainland directly across from the rocky point that was included in Blackstone Camp. Francois[39] was a good cook and the campers depended upon him for frequent substantial meals; the rest of the time they experimented with the simpler foods. They once tried to cook baked beans, but did not know that the beans should be soaked over night before cooking. When the full pot was put upon the fire, the beans began to swell. They lifted the cover right off the pot and were sprinkled all over the camp. The boys never tried to bake beans again.

Although the camp was in Derry, the bathing beach was in Hampstead, as the big island was divided between the two townships and Hampstead village was much nearer the big island than was the town of Derry. The boys used to row around the island to the Hampstead shore and walk up a grassy lane to the one long street, in order to get their provisions. They soon became acquainted with many of the Hampstead people and with summer boarders who came to Hampstead from Haverhill. When the Hampstead folk had a church social or a picnic, they invited the campers who gladly sang for their supper. They formed a rousing chorus of tenors and baritones; a few like Uncle Arthur and Dr. Jova sang bass. In return, the boys invited their new friends to Blackstone Camp. The village people were so curious about this novel way of life that there was a constant stream of visitors. Often picnic parties were organized and on two occasions over sixty guests came in boats with generous basket luncheons, and spent the day at camp. On one of these occasions Uncle Arthur met a beautiful girl of sixteen who, with her mother and sister, was a summer guest from Haverhill. Seven or eight years later, after she had graduated from Bradford Academy, and Uncle Arthur had become a full-fledged doctor, they were married and 'lived happily every after."

My mother used to go to camp frequently with friends from Lawrence and once, chaperoned by a cousin's young wife, she spent a night in Chases's farmhouse. It was not to be thought of that a girl would "camp out" and sleep in a tent. Mother does not appear in any

---

[39] Author's note: In the chapter entitled "Stories of the Pond" I speculate that Francois may have been runaway slave from the south who came to the area via the Underground Railroad.

of the camp photographs. That summer of 1882 she spent with cousins in Wisconsin. In her absence, however, my father had become acquainted with her brother who invited him to some of their big parties at camp. He was enchanted with the place and with the whole idea of living close to nature. He used to drive a smart little nag, harnessed to a high-topped buggy, and he was always ready on a summer afternoon to take a fellow camper up to Island Pond. This was a great accommodation in those days, when there were no electric cars to transport one over part of the way, and of course no automobiles. A regular livery outfit was considered an extravagance.

When mother finally returned from the West, she found father firmly established as a family friend. In the summer of 1883 it soon began to be a regular thing to go buggy-riding with father almost any pleasant afternoon, usually to make a call at camp and in the fall of 1883 they became engaged. So their romance, like Uncle Arthur, might be said to have originated at Blackstone Camp. Mother always thought that Uncle Joe was interested in the granddaughter of a Hampstead family and that only his sudden death prevented the blossoming of a third camp romance. Uncle Joe, the law-partner of his elder brother John died at the age of twenty eight as a result of, what was then called, "quick consumption." A neglected cold developed into pneumonia, which left him with tuberculosis of the lungs. Uncle Arthur, still in medical school, took Uncle Joe to Aiken, South Carolina, but Uncle Joe lived there only six weeks, dying exactly three months after he had been taken ill. Surely this sort of disaster would have been prevented in our day. Uncle Joe was considered the "flower of the family". He must have been a singularly lovable person. Blackstone Camp without him was unthinkable and for twelve years it was deserted.

When my grandfather died, my bachelor uncle (mother's youngest brother) gave up his work in Chicago and came to Lawrence to live with grandmother and to take charge of grandfather's estate. He managed to combine these duties with frequent journeys to Europe and to the Orient as well as on this continent. After his return from Japan in 1897 he decided to revive Blackstone Camp. He bought three tents and other camping equipment, and spent much of the summer there, entertaining an occasional man friend or a group of boys in our family--usually my brother, my cousin Arthur, a second cousin from Cambridge, and one of my Austrian cousins. Camp was not then supposed to be suitable place for persons, young or old of the other sex. The boys enjoyed the life hugely, but they complained about Uncle Peter's cooking. My brother declared that he gave them ham and eggs for breakfast, eggs and ham for midday dinner, and ham and eggs for supper.

Late that first summer, Uncle Peter defied precedent by inviting my mother and my Lawrence aunt to visit camp for three days, each bringing a daughter with her. Mother could not go because of other engagements, but my aunt took her eldest daughter, my six-year-old cousin Louise and me. The result was, for me, three days of sheer delight. Of course we girls thought it great fun to live in tents. The largest tent, a double canvas with a wooden floor, crowned the knoll where the original tent had stood nearly twenty years earlier. The cots were ranged on one side, and on the other side Uncle Peter had built a long rack where we hung our clothes. On the upright tent pole at one end was fastened a kerosene lamp with a reflector. On the pole at the other end was hung a small looking glass with a pincushion dangling beneath it. There was no need of screens of mosquito netting, for in those happy days before the dams were built in the Spicket River, (the outlet of Island Pond), there were no mosquitoes. An army of daddy-long-legs always congregated along the ridge pole of the big tent, and Louise and I used to look up at them fearfully as we lay in bed, squealing with alarm whenever one dropped. We were both afraid of spiders. The dining room was smaller, but it too had a double canvas and a wooden floor. It contained a deal table, and folding chairs with a small ice chest the top of which we often used as a seat at table. The kitchen tent was still smaller, without a cover, and with an earthen floor. The oil stove, which Uncle Peter allowed no one else to touch, stood opposite the door, and the pots and plans were hung on nails in roughly made wooden racks on each side.

We children played mostly on the long bathing beach, and collected brush for a bonfire there one night. My only out-door bathing had been in salt water at seaside resorts, and I was pleased to find the lake water so much warmer than the ocean. I wore the usual bathing suit for little girls—a sailor blouse trimmed with braid, and a full skirt that completely covered my bloomers, which in turn covered my knees. I wore no stocking, so I did not conform exactly to the code of the day. It is amusing to remember Louise in the water, wearing a long-sleeved high-necked button-down-the-front, gray flannel nightgown in place of a bathing suit. The dear little girl used to stand around sedately with the water up to her chin. When I urged her to jump and splash and frolic with me she would reply quietly: " No, I like this way." It is a commentary on the lives of little girls in the nineties that she had no bathing suit and never dreamed of romping in the water or attempting to swim. Later, she and her sisters became marvelous swimmers and even taught the sport. Louise, while a teacher at a girl's camp in Newfound Lake, N.H. once swam four miles without stopping, on a chilly morning in September. Her nieces, at the age of six, not only swam, but would joyously dive into forty feet of water when they were permitted to do so, and my nieces were equally daring at that age.

In those days we were the only people on the big, densely wooded island and there were no permanent camps on the pond at all. Its beauty was absolutely unspoiled. A sturdy old birch tree at the very tip of our rocky point hung low over the water and then reared itself to the perpendicular. The curve of its trunk became my favorite seat, with the water rippling below me, the foliage rustling overhead and a wide view across the lake, north, west and south. Louise found a seat beside me on the same tree, not so far out, and the next summer my chum, Blanche, succeeded her there, but I really enjoyed the birch tree most when I was alone, simply dreaming.

The summer of 1898 at camp was altogether different. It was no long a male paradise; Uncle Peter admitted the whole family. Mother laughed to scorn her brother's idea that women could not be trusted with his possibly explosive oil stove. Consequently, they were no longer restricted to a diet of ham and eggs. But the greatest change was due to the fact that we were all riding bicycles that summer. We wheeled from our house to the Lawrence railway station and boarded a train for Canobie Lake (formerly called Policy Pond by the farmers) checking our bicycles in the freight car at ten cents a piece, then rode about six miles through North Salem to the Francois house, and from there crossed by boat to our big island. My brother already knew how to row, and the rest of us were learning. Mother and Father and Sophia, our hired girl, enjoyed the swimming, and we all thought that living in tents was something special. Our night clothes and bathing suits were packed in bundles tied to our handle bars, and as our baggage was necessarily limited, we stayed only two or three days over week-ends or holidays.

We now began to call the big island: "Governor's Island" because mother told us that it had once belonged to Benning Wentworth, New Hampshire's first-and-last royal governor.[40] When the little settlement that is now Hampstead petitioned to be set off from Haverhill, Governor Wentworth, in granting it a charter, named the village after the English town of Hampstead, where he had lived in his youth while studying law. In the English Hampstead he used to see women doing the weekly wash at a sheet of water called Wash Pond, so he gave the same name to a small pond near the American Hampstead. The name of this pond, by the way, has been changed to Sunset Lake.

When the governor took possession of our big island, he built a causeway to it across the narrowest part of the pond, which was also the nearest to Hampstead and had the land at that end of the island cleared for farming. Long before Camp Blackstone was thought of, the farmhouse had burned to the ground. Only the massive brick chimney was left, the large cellar hole and the huge, flat stones of the doorsteps.[41] The chimney was notched with fireplaces and with a deep, arched alcove, which we decided must have been a closet.

---

[40] Author's note: Benning Wentworth retired and was replaced by his nephew, John Wentworth, in 1748.

[41] Author's note: The photo of the chimney shown at the end of this chapter was taken when the surrounding trees were clear-cut. A few scattered broken bricks mark the site where the chimney once stood. During the depression my old mentor and friend, Otto Minzner, laboriously collected the fallen bricks and transported them by rowboat to the north shore near Howard's Grove and built a new chimney that stands today. This chimney is commonplace in every way except for one thing, the well-traveled bricks are now about 260 years old.

Stonewalls, in the woods, marked former pastures and the open land around the ruins was overgrown with juniper bushes and blackberry vines. Every summer we made several excursions to the "ruins" following a dim and doubtful path through the woods and coming back to camp with pails and cans full of blackberries.

Every September Uncle Pete had to use his two wooden tent floors as rafts, on which the tents and camp furniture were piled to be towed to the mainland and stored in the barn of a neighboring farmer. He finally decided to have cabins take the place of tents. His first building--which was also the first building on the island since Governor Wentworth's day--was the little cookhouse. It must have been built in the fall of 1898, because in pictures of us at camp the following January, the cookhouse was there, but still unpainted. On that winter day, Uncle Peter, his artist friend, Louis Norton, my brother, my cousin Arthur and I had a hearty dinner in Mrs. Francois' hospitable old house. (Mrs. Francois now being a widow), after which we crossed on the ice to Governor's Island. The thick ice made strange cracking noises which alarmed me. Then we walked to the ruins with some difficulty as the crusted snow had obliterated the path. I was further alarmed by huge tracks in the snow around the ruins; they looked like footprints of a bear. My uncle thought it was more likely that a dog had made the tracks, which had later been enlarged by the melting of the snow.

The summer of 1899 was recorded in great detail in my diary. There were innumerable visits to the camp. The pond was still unspoiled and lovely; the water was so low that we rarely saw a mosquito, and we could walk along the shore of the island picking flowers--all of which pleasures were taken from us later by the building of the Arlington Mills dams in the Spicket River. I did not mention, in 1899, the erection of our dining-house, a sort of open-air pavilion, which Uncle Peter built I think the following year. In 1899 we still ate in the tent, although by now we boasted a sleeping house and a cookhouse.

My chum, Blanche, stayed at camp with us over Independence Day. I remember that Uncle Peter, in a dashing new golf suit and cap of brown and orange plaid, entertained a large party of Lawrence friends with mother's help. On the Fourth our family and Blanche rowed to Hampstead to attend a great celebration of the town's bicentennial or sesquicentennial, I have forgotten which. I remember having luncheon and ice cream with our Hampstead friends in a grove that bordered Wash Pond. It was a hot, wearisome affair, and we children were glad to get back to our own beloved island. I recorded in my journal a day when my brother caught two big pickerel. We ate one at camp and carried the other home; it measured twenty inches.

July fourth, 1900 saw us all at camp again, with Blanche. I described the place as greatly improved, the dining house built, all the houses painted a woodsy green, and graceful rustic benches between the trees in front. (Uncle Joe's coachman made these benches, of wild grapevines and of white birch logs). We had bonfires and fireworks for our celebration. Blanche and I, aged fifteen and almost fifteen, spent much of our time building a castle with a moat and a village and a steepled church on the bathing beach and a parochial residence, school and convent, connected by avenues of tiny maple seedlings, hardly and inch high. We explored the lake by rowboat and picked water lilies and reveled in the bathing. "I sat in the sturdy birch tree that hangs from the steepest rock on the point over the water and it was splendid to feel it toss and bound and leap in the wind, shake out its branches and glossy green leaves and then, with a long shudder, grow motionless again."

Later in the summer we all went to camp with at least half a dozen friends on several occasions. Once, Mother and I walked along the shore of the island and found a mountain holly tree with its red berries, and also found some deer grass, or meadow beauty. "Blanche and I spent an afternoon on the beach building a splendid palace in the wet sand. We made terraces and gardens and winding avenues lined with maple trees and great walls guarding all, with watch towers looking out to sea and over the plain." If I saw two girls of that age amusing themselves in such a fashion today, I would suspect them of being feeble-minded.

At the turn of the century there began to be more talk about summer camping. Permanent camps were being built at sightly spots along the shores of our pond and on a few of the small islands. There were even three or four, besides ours, on Governor's Island. My oldest uncle, with his five children, found it inconvenient to be obliged to take turns with others of the family in staying at Uncle

Peter' camp, so he built a camp on a high point at the other side of our bathing beach. My cousins called it Black Birch Lodge. In many ways it was more comfortable and attractive than Uncle Peter's camp, but we always loved Blacksktone, regardless of its inconvenience. We had felt that we were getting "soft" when we changed from tents to houses, and we tried to live as if we were still in tents.

How well we succeeded in doing this may be judged by the comment of a young Swiss girl who visited us during the summer of 1915. She asked us all to sign a message written to her mother on one of our homemade--or rather, camp-made-birch-bark postal cards. We noticed that she had told her mother, in French, how much she was enjoying our camp, "where one lived in the forest like savage red-skins."(peaux rouges).

One of the first permanent camps on the pond was built on the small island of Escumbuit by Colonel Shepard, who had a big house in East Derry. Escumbuit was supposed to have been one of the stopping places of Hannah Dustin's Indian captors, after their raid on Haverhill. It was marked for us permanently by the Shepard's two-story cottage, which was bright yellow with a bright red roof. We often saw the large Colonel and his three small boys, but it was many years before Mrs. Shepard or any other women of the family appeared at camp. When the boys were at college, they often came to Black Birch Lodge to see my younger cousins. The oldest and the youngest of the three Shepard brothers went to M.I.T. and belonged to my brother's fraternity. The middle boy, Bartlett, went to Dartmouth, I think, and years later became the father of our first astronaut, Alan Shepard.

We had always dreaded the thought of Governor's Island being cut over. I don't remember the date when the owner of the island, a bearded old gentleman in Newburyport, decided that the timber could wait no longer. My two uncles combined with four other owners of permanent camps to buy the whole island.[42] Then they arranged with the timber company to leave a fringe of pines along the winding shores and also a grove of trees around each of the

---

[42] Author's note: According to Wally Williams this group bought the island in 1909.

camps. Anyone who wished to buy a campsite and build was also obliged to buy a share of the island. The owners built good roads across the island and to their various camps and inserted a bridge in the causeway to that boats could circumnavigate the island without having to be dragged over the causeway.

It seems to me that the golden age of Blackstone Camp was the time when my brother and I had our school and college friends visit us there. Although camping was gradually becoming popular, not one of the many young people who were our guests had any personal experience of such a primitive way of life. We played all sort of games and sang all sort of songs, new and old; we cooked and washed dishes, made beds and cleaned house; we did errands for mother on the mainland getting superlative berry pies from a farmer's wife who specialized in puff pastry; we searched out all the nooks and corners of the lake, discovering hidden bays and landing on lonely picturesque little islands, rowing up Bond's brook which emptied into our pond and rowing down the Spicket river to the first dam; we had swimming races and rowing races and the boys always proved their stamina by swimming across the pond from Chase's Grove to our boat landing--about three-quarters of a mile. In Hampstead, we climbed the steeple of the Town Hall (which had originally been a church) in order to read Paul Revere's name on the big bell of his manufacture, accompanied by the solemn words:

> The living to the church I call,
> And to the grave I summon all.

Instead of going on foot for provisions, my Abbott Academy friends and I used to row to Chase's and speed down the rough country roads on our bicycles to the General Store in North Salem. We felt very camp-like, with our collar-less shirtwaist open at the neck and our sleeves rolled above the elbow.

Elizabeth Schneider was an excellent storyteller. The fact that she made the effort to leave us the legacy of her experience hints that she may have hoped that her writing might be read long after she had passed on. In these few pages she offers us a window into the past with nostalgia that only she could create. We are indebted to her for her contribution.

Becky (Soft Talker) Jackson, Apache, Comanche, Navajo,
and Chippewa, Kingston, New Hampshire.

Black and white rendition of Ella Pearson's water color of Shepard cottage on Escumbuit Island, circa 1898.

Chapter 7
THE THREE TOWNS
1719--2000

E ach of the three towns, whose boundaries touch parts of Big Island Pond, had its unique difficulties achieving township status. The common theme they shared in seeking to become townships was a desire to run their own affairs. The decision to go it alone was usually painful and, like many divorces, the process was often acrimonious. Indeed, when the town of Atkinson separated from Plaistow, anger and resentments rose to such a high degree that some townspeople went about armed in order to defend themselves from possible harm by persons on the other side of the many rancorous disputes. It serves no useful purpose to describe all of the details of these spin-offs in the scope of a single chapter. Like most failed marriages, the decision to go it alone was seldom accomplished without rancor. Big Island Pond is a part of Atkinson, Derry and Hampstead and it shares their history. Although the pond remains our focus, the transition of each of these towns from pre-colonial status to their incorporation as townships is an important part of local history.

This chapter examines the events leading to their incorporation as townships and their development through the Revolutionary and Civil wars into the early 20th Century. It does not address all of the political, educational, and religious events that occurred during this period. Excellent books in the respective libraries of each of these towns cover every detail of their development up to the present day. The village-like character of each of these towns makes a positive contribution to the rural ambience of the entire area.

The Town of Derry

The first settlers in Derry, New Hampshire were Scotch Presbyterians who were seeking religious freedom. In 1612 they migrated to the small port city of Derry in Northern Ireland to escape persecution by the Anglican Church of England. In Ireland they encountered renewed opposition by Irish Catholics who considered them invaders of their land. When Derry was granted to the City of London for colonization, its inhabitants built a wall around the city and renamed it Londonderry. In 1688 they successfully resisted the siege of the armies sent by King James II to conquer Ireland. When King William succeeded James II, he gave a tax-exempt status to those who had defended Londonderry. When some of them decided to migrate to The New World, they carried this tax-exempt status with them. Many of the homesteads of the first settlers of Nutfield (Derry, NH) were called "tax exempt farms." These people were exempt from taxes levied by the British Crown on Colonial landowners.

In August 1718 five sailing ships entered Boston Harbor loaded with Scotch Presbyterian refugees from Ireland. Sixteen families sailed further north to Casco Bay in Maine and other families decided to settle in Boston. The rest decided to follow wherever their spiritual leader, the Reverend James MacGregor, chose to lead them. Quartered aboard ships frozen in the ice of Boston Harbor, their provisions ran out and the Massachusetts Council had to vote special funds to buy food to enable them to survive the harsh winter. Reverend James MacGregor, in his first sermon in the New World, reminded his flock why they had suffered the hardships of the long ocean voyage to the New World:

We came to avoid oppression and cruel bondage; To shun persecution and designed ruin; To withdraw from the communion of idolaters; To have an opportunity of worshipping God according to the dictates of conscience and the rule of his inspired word.

With the spring thaw, the bulk of the immigrants sailed up the Merrimac River to the small town of Haverhill located on the

Merrimac River. After securing the ships in Haverhill the men explored the territory to the north beyond Big Island Pond. The ancient Indian trail they followed led through Atkinson and passed close by the southwest side of Big Island Pond and followed what is now known as Gulf Road to its juncture with Island Pond Road. Near Beaver Lake they found an area where there was a profusion of butternut, chestnut and walnut trees. It is not surprising that they decided to name their settlement Nutfield. Several Derry business enterprises still use this name in one form or another to identify with the original name of the settlement.

A plaque on a rock near the north shore of Beaver Lake marks the spot where Reverend MacGregor preached his first sermon to his followers on April 11, 1719. During the next two years his followers built the first Presbyterian Church in America. Each family was given a 60-acre homestead with 500 feet of frontage on West Bound Brook. In spite of being close to starvation on their ice-bound ships the previous winter, they had resisted the impulse to eat the seed potatoes they carried with them. They now planted these white Irish potatoes to provide a store for the coming winter.

The treaty ending *Queen Ann's War* had been signed in 1713 so, theoretically, the newcomers were safe from Indian attacks. They did not realize at the time that they faced new wars beginning with *Governor Dummer's War with the Eastern Abenaki Indians* that began in 1722. The 15 years of peace that began in 1725 was disturbed by the outbreak of *King George's War* that lasted from 1740 to 1748. The following 7 years of peace was interrupted by the onset of *The French and Indian Wars* which lasted from 1755 until 1763. One would think that a people who had endured persecution in England and then Ireland for so many years could expect to live in peace. Now they faced a new threat that would have them living in the "eye of the storm" for the next 50 years.

Wary of Indian raids by renegade bands during periods of so-called peace, they decided to build two garrison houses to shelter them in the case of surprise attacks. One of these houses was built near the junction of Lane and Floyd Road in East Derry and the other at 24 Thornton Street, Derry Village. By the standards of the period they were in an extremely vulnerable position as regards to the Indian threat. The modern garrison type house is similar to the structures. The second story was wider that the ground floor creating an overhang on all sides of the house. Holes were cut in the floor of the overhang that enabled the defenders to fire down on Indian attackers. The design offered the means to retaliate against anyone who might be attempting to chop through an entrance door, or trying to set fire to the outer wall. It was a very effective means of defense if the defenders were well supplied with food and water. History records many episodes in which the besieged were able to fend off attackers until reinforcements arrived. Still, given the advanced location of their settlement, simple logic begs some further explanation for their seeming immunity to Indian attack.

The reason for their charmed status was surprisingly simple; they had a protector in the person of the Colonial Governor of Canada, the Marquis de Vaudreuil. He and the Reverend MacGregor had been college classmates and apparently they had stayed in touch after their college days. Canadian authorities through resident Jesuit missionaries effectively controlled the Abenaki Indians of Maine, New Hampshire and Vermont. Some of these missionaries refused to respond to Canadian pressure urging them to keep the Indians stirred up against the paleface. Others were very effective in persuading their converts to take up the tomahawk against the English. The Marquis de Vaudreuil instructed the Jesuit missionaries who were living with the Indians to advise them that these were a different people than the English. They pointed out the obvious differences; the local settlers ate a root they called the potato and they made cloth from a plant which they wove into cloth. Even their manner of speaking (their accent) was different from the English. A measure of their success in convincing the Indians rests in the fact that Derry was never attacked in the Indian wars that followed.[43]

---

[43] *Abenaki Warrior*, by: Alfred E Kayworth. During my research for this historical novel that was published by Branden Publishing Company of Brookline Village, MA, I was puzzled by seeming contradictions. Noting the dates of incorporation of Derryfield and Derry I couldn't understand how the town had escaped Indian raids. In the course of my research for this book I discovered the connection between the Reverend MacGregor and the Marquis de Vaudreuil.

In 1722 the community of Nutfield was incorporated as Londonderry, undoubtedly because of the nostalgia they had for their former home in Ireland. All immigrants tend to carry some of the best of their former lives with them to their new home. The Scots brought flaxseed that they planted alongside their Irish potatoes. Soon they were harvesting flax fiber that they wove into the same fine linen they had produced in Ireland. Having achieved their religious freedom, they were now beginning to become a hard working community with an identity of their own.

In Sept 28, 1748 the town purchased a seal to stamp all of their finished linen goods identifying it as "Londonderry Linen" in order to distinguish it from fraudulent imitators. The measure of its quality comes from the historic fact that both George Washington and Thomas Jefferson were known to wear shirts stamped with the trademark, "Londonderry Linen."

On June 12, 1804 the New Hampshire Legislature authorized the construction of the Londonderry Turnpike. This Concord to Boston toll road opened the isolated township to commerce and to outsiders. When the Frenchman Lafayette visited the Adams Female Academy in June 1825, his visit was undoubtedly facilitated by the convenience of this new highway. During his visit Lafayette is said to have spent two hours pondering the mysteries of the collection of stone structures we now know as America's Stonehenge. A brass button of the type worn by French military men was recovered at the site and is on display in their small museum. Derry sent many men off to fight in the Revolutionary War, but was fortunate to suffer only one casualty. Lt. McCary was killed in the battle of Bennington.

On March 21, 1827 the New Hampshire Legislature approved a petition submitted by 295 residents that divided Londonderry into two parts; the new township that was created was called Derry. The people living in the eastern part of town apparently wanted to distinguish themselves from the rest of the town by name and by philosophy.

Among the many new industries that came to the area was a gristmill located at the East End of Beaver Lake. A "falling mill" was established at Adams Pond and another company named Hazen & Underhill manufactured axes and edging instruments. In addition there was a hat shop, two carding mills, two blacksmith shops and a shingle mill. For years East Derry was the business center of the area. In about 1810, Adams & Redfield, began to import salt, molasses and rum from Boston and became a very prosperous enterprise. Their goods were shipped from Boston to Lowell by way of the Middlesex Canal and then up the Merrimac River to a landing below Thornton's Ferry where they were unloaded and brought overland through Litchfield to the store in East Derry. In 1849 the Manchester to Lawrence Railroad began operation. The total cost for the land and depot that was built to serve this railroad was $1,600. The station agent was paid $1.50 a day--the passenger train conductor got $70 per month--a brake man pulled down $1.25 per day, but the highest paid employee was the railroad master mechanic who earned $100 per month! In 1887 the Boston & Maine Railroad took over this railroad.

During the Civil War news from the battlefronts came by way of the telegraph office at the railroad depot. Townspeople gathered there daily to learn if there was any news from the southern battlefields. Twenty-four Derry men fell during this war and 128 received honorable discharges. It is likely that some Derry men joined units in other parts of the state, but these 24 are the only ones recorded.

The footwear of the new settlers soon wore out in the rugged terrain of their new environment, but they quickly adapted the Indian moccasin to their own use. Later shoe making became a cottage industry in the area and almost every family farm had a "ten footer." This was a small building set off from the main house in which they made shoes by hand.[44]

---

[44] Author's note: In 1947 I bought a lot on the North Island Pond Road next to the Dillon place. In addition to a small broken down building with a caved in roof, there was a small 8X10 foot outbuilding that I fixed up for a tool shed. Mrs. Dillon told me that farmers made shoes in this building before the Civil War. Amidst the rubble inside was a small wooden box shaped like a shoe shine box and in it were metal laths for different shoes sizes, and square cut nails for nailing soles to shoes. These items may date back to the Revolutionary War. They are still in my possession on Escumbuit Island.

During the winter, when there were no fields to tend, people worked in these shops and they could typically produce a six-pair case of shoes each day. The end of the Civil War marked the beginning of the shoe making industry in Derry and, by 1899, W.S. & R.W. Pillsbury had organized a shop that began to manufacture shoes with machine tools. By 1904 they were producing 4,500 pairs of shoes a day and Derry had become a part of the Industrial Revolution. In 1874 James Coburn built a barrel factory that manufactured 100,000 barrels a year with work force of 150 people.

Out of the variety of mills that were built, one of the more interesting was the Taylor Saw Mill on Island Pond Road. Before the Civil War it was operated as an up-and-down saw mill, but after the war it was converted to a circular saw. The maximum width of boards cut by a circular saw is limited by the width of the blade from the edge of its central shaft to the tips of the cutting teeth. The up and down saw was a mechanical device which operated a straight saw as if were a six-foot, two-man saw. These saws produced boards much wider than could be produced by the circular saw, but the cutting rate was much slower.[45] In 1939 Ernest K. Ballard bought the property and installed an old up and down saw he had found under a barn in Sandown, NH. He overcame many problems, and through his ingenuity and persistence that included having parts handmade, he finally got the mill operating. The State of New Hampshire acquired the mill after his death and they began to operate it for public viewing twice a year.

In 1873-74 the Nasua & Rochester Railroad began operations and Hubbard Station on Warner Hill Road was named for the family who had previously owned the property. This railroad was later taken over by the Boston & Maine Railroad and some Lawrence people

---

[45] Author's note: The lot I bought in 1947 next to the Dillon place on North Island Pond road had an old 12x16 foot broken down building that I rebuilt. The plaster taken off of the wooden lathes was filled with horsehair and the ceiling beams were hand-hewn. All the nails were hand-made. The boards that formed the wainscoting for the walls were single piece pine boards measuring 24 inches in width--cut by an up and down saw. I believe this building is of Revolutionary War vintage. This building that I restored to serve me for a few years still stands today.

used to travel to the pond by taking a train into Haverhill and then on to Hampstead. The rail bed headed west from the north limits of Hampstead to Nasua and there was a stop at Hubbard's station on Warner Hill Road. One of the earliest families at the pond was the Korbs of Germantown. They used to come up to the pond carrying supplies for the weekend and get off at Hubbard Station and walk down to the north shore. They also took the electric trolley from Lawrence to Canobie Lake where they got off at the junction of Rt. 111 and Rt. 28. That station was on the West Side of Rt.28 near the present market. From there they walked the rest of the way to the pond carrying their supplies.

By 1900 the population of Derry had grown to 3,500 and they had moved into the machine age. By then the town had three large shoe factories and Derry Village even boasted a sewage system. The underground pipes collected all sorts of waste along Broadway and discharged it into Beaver Brook! The City of Derry had entered the Twentieth Century and it would never look back.

The Town of Hampstead

The land that makes up the Town of Hampstead was originally a part of the Massachusetts Bay Colony. The heavily forested character of the area earned it the name Timberlane. After the English Crown settled the boundary dispute between Massachusetts and the newly established Royal New Hampshire Colony in 1741, Timberlane became part of the New Hampshire Province. As early as 1733 Timberlane residents were making the long trip to Haverhill by carriage to attend church services. In time Haverhill authorities granted them permission to build their own log meeting house in which they were able to hold church services. Initially the services were conducted by visiting preachers from nearby towns as well as by local lay ministers. The History of Rockingham County reveals that a man named Ford was the first white man to live in the town prior to 1728. In the same year a man named Emerson settled in the south end of the town. He later bought the big island which he sold to Benning Wentworth in 1741. Prior to the arrival of these two pioneers the Hampstead area had been the exclusive home of Abenaki Indians

The Abenaki Indian population of the Maritimes and the territories of Maine, New Hampshire and Vermont may have been as high as 45,000 before contact with the white man. Early contacts with European fishermen in the 1500s brought epidemics of smallpox, typhus and other diseases that decimated their population. In the decade before the Pilgrims arrived there were three epidemics which took a heavy toll of the Indians. These Aboriginal People had no previous contact with Europeans in their 10,000-year history and they had not developed any natural resistance to white man's diseases. It is estimated that the population of the Eastern Abenaki Indians of Maine fell from 20,000 to 5.000 as a result of these epidemics. The literal translation of Abenaki is *People of the Dawn* and is derived from their belief that each day the sun rose first on the original people of Maine and New Hampshire. The *Abenaki Indian Nation* was made up of loosely affiliated tribes whose tribal names reflected their physical surroundings.

After the early 1660s epidemics wiped out 80% of the Indians in Haverhill, Chief Passaconaway relocated the survivors to Concord, New Hampshire. Passaconaway was an important Sagamore who was the leader of all of the small bands of Indians that lived on the Merrimac River between the Atlantic Ocean and what is now Concord, New Hampshire. He and his Chief's Council with the advice of their tribal Shaman, concluded that this plague-ridden area was to be avoided. This may explain why Passaconaway subsequently sold a strip of land that extended 7 miles east and west beginning in Haverhill and 14 miles to the north. This large tract of land was deeded to the white settlers for approximately $7.50 in cash plus other food and trinkets. It is quite possible that the Indians believed that they were unloading cursed land on the unwary settlers.

The numbers of Indian artifacts discovered in the Sanborn Shores area of the pond suggest that Indians had a village there. Crowell's Grove on the eastern side of Sunset Lake has also yielded artifacts. The Williams family of Governor's Island have a collection of arrowheads that were found on the island and Jack Seig found a beautifully crafted stone knife below the dam at the outlet to the Spicket River. When white men came to the Hampstead area they found the bleached bones of Indians lying on the ground of their abandoned villages. Plagues had so decimated their numbers that the weakened survivors fled the area forsaking their traditional Indian burial ceremonies in their haste to escape.

Timberlane residents presented a township petition to Governor Benning Wentworth in 1746 and on January 19, 1749 their petition was finally approved. It is likely that negotiations between Wentworth's representatives and the townspeople delayed the decision. The chapter describing Benning Wentworth's tenure as Royal Provincial Governor of New Hampshire describes how the governor used these township grants to accumulate his personal wealth. Many of the townships awarded by the governor were named after his relatives and friends at his request. In this case he asked that the new township be named after the small village of Hampstead in England where he made his headquarters during his many trips to that country. The governor's proclivity for naming places was captured in a poem written by G R Bennette in 1899:

WASH POND

In far off Merry England
Close by old London Town,
With Finchley bridge upon the right,
And Hampstead looking down,
There used to be a little lake
With watery arches few,
Where wandering geese fed on the slugs
That in its waters grew.

Where early cocks at rosy morn,
His merry clarion blows,
The women from the palace came
To wash the royal clothes;
And when their morning work was done
And all the clothes were sloshed,
They brought the royal carriage down
From mud stains to be washed.

When Benning Wentworth went abroad,
To counsel with the Crown,

He took his nightly lodging there
Near by in Hampstead town,
And every morning he would walk
Close by the washing place,
The cunning rascal dearly loved
A pretty woman's face!

He soon came back to Portsmouth town,
And then he came this way
And when he saw our lovely lake
He straightway thus did say:
Good-sooth, it is the very place
To bring your clothes and slosh,
And wash the sheep, and water cows,
And so he named it Wash.

The water nymphs that in it dwelt.
To guard its secret springs,
Who loved its sylvan Indian name
That still about it clings,
In deep disgust, their duty lift
Regardless of their bond.
And so 'tis called unto this day,
Just homely, plain Wash Pond.

The venerable history of the Hampstead Town Hall is an integral part of the history of the town of Hampstead. After its completion in 1747, it was used for ninety years as the town meeting house and as the place of worship for the Congregational Church. When the church moved to another location in 1837, the building continued to be used for town meetings. The framework of the building was built with hand-hewn white oak timbers that were shaped to 8" and 10" cross section. The sills, framing uprights and plates at the top were joined together with mortise and tenon joints using wooden pegs to secure them. The board sheathing and clapboards were cut with a shiplap joint designed to provide a tight fit over the adjacent piece and the various nails and spikes used were hand wrought in local shops.

The original interior had a complex seating arrangement with enclosed pews behind which were built simple plank seats. Winding staircases led to elevated galleries that were also fitted with plank seating. The town's people were segregated by class, and were identified as squires, yeomen, and laymen. Preferential seating was sold to the highest bidder, as was the lesser plank seating in the back of the room and the galleries.

When renovations were made in 1792, they added a belfry tower and a porch. The corner posts of this belfry tower are made from hand-hewn 14x16 white oak. The bell deck is 48 feet above the ground and is capped with an octagonal spire that rises another 50 feet. The weathervane installed on the top of the steeple in 1793 eventually decayed and, in 1882, it was replaced by a new gold weathervane.

The 1856 renovations were extensive. The galleries were taken out and a second story was added. Outhouses were installed on the first and second floors; one assumes that a visit to the second floor must have been a drafty experience.

A Governor's island resident decided that a church with a belfry ought to have a bell. Mr. Thomas Huse told the minister that he would pay for the bell if the minister would go to Brookfield, Massachusetts and arrange for its delivery. The bell arrived under cover of darkness and was temporarily hung between oak trees in the front yard of a Main Street residence. Virtually the whole town responded to the early morning toll of the huge bell. But their enthusiasm was somewhat muted by the somber message on the surface of the bell: "The living to the church I call, and to the grave I summon all." The bell also bears the following inscription: "Presented by Thomas Huse, Esq. 1809." On its other surface it is inscribed with the trademark: "Revere, Boston" The bell was cast by the son of Paul Revere who left his father's employ to set up his own business. The 1,212-pound bell cost $600, and was given to the town and to the church by Mr. Huse to be used by them forever.

In 1906 the town selectmen voted to discontinue the long established practice of ringing the bell at one minute after midnight on the 4th of July. Four enterprising boys concealed themselves under the floor of the building on July 3rd and gained entrance to the building through a trap door that had been left open. After climbing to the belfry tower, they tied one end of a long length of fine wire to the clapper of the bell and dropped the remainder over the side of the building to the ground. Having retrieved the end of the wire they lay in a field and waited until midnight. At 12:01 they began to pull on the wire and ring the bell. One of the selectmen who lived nearby came with his lantern to investigate, but when his search of the building revealed nothing amiss, he returned to his home hoping to get back to sleep. No sooner was he in his bed than the bell began to ring again. After several repetitions of this game, he finally gave up and stayed in his bed. Whether he managed to get back to sleep we do not know; but we doubt it!

One of the pranksters was Ike Randall and this episode and the entire account of the history of the Hampstead Town Hall was taken from the interesting and more detailed article, *The Old Meeting House History*, 1745--1995, written by his son, Maurice Randall.

In 1758 the Town of Kingston brought suit against Hampstead claiming that Amesbury Peak, a small section in the eastern part of Hampstead, belonged to Kingston. This dispute between the two towns lasted for eight years until Governor Wentworth concluded a settlement by granting Kingston a compensatory tract of land on the Connecticut River. His power to grant land located near the New Hampshire-Vermont border to settle this dispute demonstrates the awesome powers Wentworth enjoyed as Provincial Governor. The new township was named Unity to commemorate the settlement that was finally signed by both towns in 1776.

The early settlers of Hampstead were resourceful people. They had to build their own houses, make their own shoes and tailor their own clothes. Later, water wheels built on local streams furnished power to a myriad of small industries including saw mills, grist mills and cider presses. Mr. Pressey installed a lumber mill that supplied building material to local carpenters as well as boxes to the woolen mills and shoe factories of Salem and Haverhill. During one period more than 100 men and women brought home shoe stock from Haverhill to manufacture shoes in their little home workshops that were called "ten footers". In the early 1800s felt and beaver hats were manufactured in the town, and women in Hampstead and surrounding town made money by weaving palm leaf hats at home for the Ordway family of West Hampstead. At one time they were producing as many as 40,000 hats a year. In 1850 a shoe factory built by Smith & Brickett burned down and a year later it burned again. Later William Emerson & Son manufactured shoes at their factory at Shop Pond. Apparently, there was a strong local market for hand-wrought nails in the late 1700s. Entrepreneurs, working in small home shops, produced 600,000 nails of various sizes in 1791 and 1792.

Before the rail lines arrived there was a great deal of wagon commerce that moved through the town. The first known road to be built in Hampstead entered the south end of town from Plaistow and followed a northerly route on the present Central Avenue and ran by the west side of Angle Pond and north to Chester. It was built to transport the King's pine trees that were destined to become masts on ships of the British Royal Navy. This unusually wide road, that has since been abandoned, was called "12-Rod-Road". Ox-drawn wagons traveling from Concord to Newburyport and Salem were a daily sight in the early days. In winter, when the crude roads were impassable to normal traffic, ox-drawn sleds transported loads of potash, charcoal, and other farm products. This slow mode of transportation created a demand for "Ordinaries." a term used to describe the taverns that were used by the wagon masters as "stopovers." The best known of these taverns was Hutchens Tavern, later called Harriman's Tavern. In 1775 this tavern was the rallying point where Captain Hezekiah Hutchens mustered 61 men to defend the colony against English tyranny. The 35 Hampstead men, who were part of this group, shouldered their muskets and followed Hutchens to Bunker Hill to help make history. In the years that followed, 142 Hampstead men left their peaceful little town to oppose the British at historic sites like Trenton, Bennington, Saratoga and Ticonderoga.

The arrival of the railroad sparked a boom in the local economy. It gave local dairy farmers a way to get their milk to market. H.P. Hood made a daily milk run through Sandown, Hampstead, Atkinson and Haverhill to Boston and the railroad enabled local lumber mills to broaden their markets. At one time "Ike" Randall made a very interesting presentation to the Hampstead Historical Society that is reproduced in its entirety in the town history. Prominent among his various anecdotes about the railroads are two episodes that are worth repeating here:

Before the First World War Ike and Raymond Stevens used to operate a one-man handcar that had two wheels on one side and an idler wheel that ran on the opposite rail. They sat on either side of a board placed across the seat and pumped the car from Nashua to Fremont filling the box signals with kerosene along the route. In 1911 two strangers arrived at the West Hampstead depot on the 5 o'clock train. Under the cover of darkness they broke into the handcar storage building and lit a fire in the stove to keep warm until midnight. They then walked over to the shoe factory and held up the watchman using a shotgun they had found with the handcar. They apparently thought the safe held cash earmarked to pay the workers the following day but, after blowing the safe, they were rewarded with only few handfuls of change. They walked back to West Hampstead and made their get-a-way on the stolen handcar. They pumped it all the way to the Windham Station where they abandoned it. Ike Randall's story reminds one of the old black and white movies that we used to view at local theatres for a ten-cent admission in the early 1930s.

In 1866 one hundred and ten blue clad Hampstead men traveled south to fight against General Lee's men in gray. In the war of 1812, thirty-eight local men set aside their plows and their carpenter's tools to answer the call to arms. All of the twenty-five men who went to Europe in World War One made it safely back to their hometown. A mere twenty three years later one hundred and fourteen sons of these veterans returned to fight World War Two. This time, the town was not so fortunate; three townsmen failed to return. All of the young men who fought in Korea came back.

In 1814 the renowned lawyer, statesman and orator Danial Webster was summoned from Portsmouth to defend a young local man who challenged the right of the authorities to draft him into military service. The trial took place in the old meeting house and people came from far and wide to see the famous orator in action and his performance disappointed none among them.

To view the white building today with its bell tower and the splendid golden weathervane atop the soaring steeple, one is moved to ponder the events of history over which it has presided. Our debt of gratitude to the young men who never returned to lift their faces to this golden symbol of Colonial America must endure always.

The Town of Atkinson

Atkinson was still a part of the town of Plaistow when Governor Wentworth finally approved the petition making Hampstead a town. Plaistow had already been partitioned from the City of Haverhill at an earlier date. Haverhill had originally been called Pentucket and the Pentucket Indians who had originally lived there had moved north to Concord to escape the pestilence they believed resided there. When the Pilgrims arrived in the early 1600s, the material advantages of their more advanced society were a boon to the Aboriginal Indians who already lived here. However, the benefit of the metal axes, knives, pots and pans and muskets was diminished by the devastating effect the white man's diseases had on the Indians. Pennacook Indian folklore describes Haverhill as an area of pestilence and disease. After several years in which 80% of the native population was felled by these plagues, Chief Passaconaway abandoned Haverhill and led his tribe northward to a new home in the Concord area. When early settlers ventured to the Sanborn Shore area of the pond they found the sun-bleached bones of Indians lying on the ground of their abandoned village. Survivors of the plague, too weak to bury the dead, had fled from those evil spirits they thought to have destroyed their people.

Atkinson continued to be a stopping place for other Indian bands traveling the well established trails which criss-crossed all of New England. They often stopped to camp and rest at Big Oak or at Indian Rock. Indian Rock is near the Pope Road Recreation Area and the Big Oak is said to have been behind the home of Robert Kachanian on Main Street. Another stopping-place was said to have been in the Conley's Grove area. The Pawtucket trail out of Lowell ran in a northeasterly direction to Conley's Grove where it crossed over to the Big Island via the small islands at its southern end then transited the marshy area between the island and the mainland at the north end of the island. In the absence of a dam, the water level in the pond was much lower than its present level. The dam built by

Mathew Taylor to control water flow to mills on the Spickett River raised the level of the lake to what it is today.

In 1640 some Ipswich and Newbury pioneers moved to Pentucket (Haverhill) where they settled on lands owned by the Pentucket Indians whose famous leader was Chief Passaconaway. He was the most amenable of all the Indian chiefs and he did his utmost to accommodate the white man's insatiable thirst for land. Throughout the Indian border wars, which lasted for more than 80 years, the Pennacook Indians under his control were the most peaceful of all the New England Indian tribes. Although the respected Passaconaway lived to be 100 years old, his negotiations bought him little more than time and his tribe eventually relinquished all of their land to the newcomers. Passaconaway lived out his life on a small island in the Merrimac River.

With the threat of war with the colonists looming in 1642, Passaconnaway sent two representatives to the Pentuckett settlers with a message of peace. Passaquo and SaggaHew, acting on behalf of Passaconaway, agreed to give up a large tract of land that extended from Haverhill 14 miles to the north. This conciliatory gesture failed to satisfy the Colonist's thirst for more and more wilderness land. The text of this land deal is quoted here using the language and spelling from the original deed:

> Know all men by these presents, that wee Passaquo and SaggaHew with ye consent of Passaconnaway: have sold unto ye inhabitants of Pentuckett all ye land wee have in Pentuckett; that is eight myles in length from ye little Rivver in Pentuckett Westward; six myles in length from ye aforesaid Rivver Eastward, with ye ileand and ye rivver that ye ileand stand in as far in length as ye land lyes by as formerly expressed: that is, fourteen myles in length: And Wee ye said Passaquo and SaggaHew with ye consent of Passaconnaway, have sold unto ye inhabitants all ye right that wee or any of us have in ye said ground and lleand and River: And wee warrent it against all or any other Indeans whatsoever unto ye said Inhabitants of Pentuckett, and to their heirs and assignes forever Dated ye fifteenth day of November Ann Dom 1642.

The agreed payment for the land was three pounds and ten shillings (roughly seven American dollars), and the transaction included beads, food, and other things valued by the Indians. Little wonder where the expression "Yankee Trader" came from. The English wrote the names of the two Passaconaway representatives on the agreement and the two Indians drew the crude outline of a bow and arrow to seal the agreement. By affixing their "totems" to this agreement, and by accepting seven dollars and other trinkets in payment, these two representatives of Passaconnaway transferred 196 square miles of land that included Big Island Pond within its boundaries.

Haverhill continued to be the target of raiding parties made up of Canadians and Indians over whom Passaconnaway had no control. They had to construct several garrison houses to protect their residents against marauding Indian bands, but Atkinson residents lived too far away to use these garrisons as a refuge. During Indian raids local residents assembled at the Clement home (the present American Legion Farm) and waited for the danger to subside.

A neighbor of the Clement family named John Robie built his house in about 1676. A veteran of the Indian wars, he and his wife Mary had seven children, but she died shortly after the birth of their youngest child. John continued to live at Robie Hill with his seven children, the oldest of whom was eleven years old. In 1691, reacting to the news that an Indian raiding party was moving against Haverhill, he took his seven children to the Clement house for safety. He decided to return to the house with his son Ichabod to retrieve family valuables. Indians hidden at the site of the present Holy Angels Church killed John and took Ichabod to Canada where he was ransomed to the French. A grandfather who lived in Hampton, New Hampshire later bought his freedom from the French.

Benjamin Richards built the first frame house in Atkinson in 1727. It was built during a short lull in the long series of wars with the Indians. Ben Richards went out of his way to befriend the Indians. He often left his door unlocked at night and in the morning he and his wife occasionally found Indians asleep in front of their eight-foot fireplace. Family legends describe him engaging in a friendly shooting contest with the Indians. The Indians gave him a powder horn as a token of their respect for his marksmanship. At the age of eighty-seven he was still able to mount a horse without using stirrups with a broad-axe in his hand.

The long dispute between Massachusetts and New Hampshire over the proper location of the border between the two states was finally settled in 1740. Although the English Crown wanted the settlers to resolve their dispute, arguments by both sides eventually had to be submitted to the King for final resolution. New Hampshire was represented in England by the wily John Tomlinson, who later performed meritorious service for Benning Wentworth. Tomlinson demeaned the Massachusetts Colony labeling it, "The vast, opulent, over-grown province of Massachusetts" while describing New Hampshire as "The poor little, loyal, distressed, Province of New Hampshire." When the boundary was finally established, New Hampshire ended up with territory measuring 50 miles by 14 miles that the state had not even bargained for. The citizens of The Royal Province of Massachusetts, after losing more than 700 square miles of land they considered their rightful territory, were furious and refused to share the cost of surveying the new lines. One year after the boundary settlement, the bankrupt merchant, Benning Wentworth, was named Royal Provincial Governor of the State of New Hampshire. He accumulated his wealth by extracting fees and land from the more than 200 townships he granted during his tenure. In less than twenty years he acquired 100,000 acres of land and became a millionaire.

In 1749 a charter was granted to the township of Plaistow, the boundaries of which included Atkinson. Following his customary practice, Governor Wentworth set aside a portion of the land now known as Providence Hill for himself. This choice piece of land, known for its wild turkeys, was later given to his nephew Theodore Atkinson. The residents of this so called "West Side," frustrated by being isolated and ignored by powerful political figures in Plaistow, voted in 1766 to separate themselves from Plaistow. After a great deal of political infighting the township was finally granted on September 3, 1767. The people decided to name their new township Newcastle, but when they learned that this name had already been incorporated, they decided to name their community in honor of Colonel Theodore Atkinson. He had been given the large tract of land on Providence hill that the townspeople had originally deeded to Benning Wentworth. During the lengthy deliberations one group petitioned to have their area annexed to the Town of Hampstead, and ironically, after the Atkinson Township was granted, another group petitioned to be reunited with Plaistow. The discord has a familiar ring to those people with long experience in town politics.

In the early years the residents of Atkinson were mostly "Gentleman Farmers." Those who had done particularly well in the community earned the title of "Esquire."Before reaching this esteemed status, people were called merely "Yoemen" or "Husbandmen."

It was inevitable that the town would attract various tradesmen whose services were required by its residents. There were coopers, black smiths, housewrights, and joiners and, of course, entrepreneurs emerged to open inns and build gristmills. A sawmill was built on Island Pond road and Paul Heald operated a black and white smith shop in the same area. Richard Heald explained that his grandfather gave the business the black and white label to advertise that he worked in both metal and wood. James Merrill was granted a permit to operate a tavern on the Old Londonderry Road, and a brick kiln was built at the boundary of Plaistow and Atkinson. French's store may certainly have been the first business of its type established in Atkinson.

In 1768 the first meetinghouse was built by subscription of "those who are a minto." Freely interpreted, this means that it was built by those who wished to contribute to the cost without penalizing those who did not wish to contribute. Church services were held in the meetinghouse and, after a motion were approved at an 1811 town meeting, other ministers were allowed to preach. Eventually Baptists, Methodists, Congregationalists and Universalists shared the building on Sundays and the number of worship days allotted to each sect was based on the proportion of the town taxes that were paid by their members.

The town pound of Atkinson still stands prominently on the East Side of Route 121. This stone structure built to hold stray cattle, dogs and other animals was built in 1787. The original road passed to the east of the pound. The early pound-keepers were nearby residents. A short entry in the September 9, 1805 town records reveals the following notice:

Taken up in the enclosure of the subscriber on the night of the fourth, inst. a dark chestnut or brown mare with a small star in her forehead supposed to be about 5 or 6 years old, trots all. The owner may have the said mare by proving property and paying charges.

Signed, Jonathan Page

Ninety-seven Atkinson men signed the Association Test prepared by the State Committee of Safety during the Revolutionary War. This test was designed to determine loyalty to the colonies. The men who signed this test vowed as follows:

We do hereby solemnly engage and promise that we will do to the utmost of our power, at the risk of our lives and fortunes, with arms oppose the hostile proceedings of the British fleets and armies against the United American Colonies.

In September of 1775, the Atkinson Selectmen certified this oath by making a separate declaration:

That all males 21 years of age and upwards belonging to Atkinson in ye aforesaid State (Lunaticks, Ideots & Negroes excepted) have freely and voluntarily subscribed their respective names to the foregoing declaration.

One hundred and twenty-eight townsmen served during the nine years of this conflict. Men normally volunteered for a single campaign or even for a particular battle. When a campaign or battle was completed, they were free to return to their village. Each town was given a quota and it became a common practice to offer bonuses to individuals enticing them to fight "one more campaign," or "one more battle." Special committees were named to solicit the service of young men from neighboring towns in an effort to fill the quotas that had been assigned to their own village.

Nathaniel Peabody of Atkinson was involved in one of the earliest acts of colonial rebellion. Governor John Wentworth commissioned him Lt. Colonel in the New Hampshire Militia and the King of England approved his appointment.

In the period leading to the Revolutionary War the English were worried about the security of their munitions depots. As tensions grew between the Colonies and the monarchy, England made plans to reinforce these depots. Fort William Henry at Newcastle, New Hampshire served as one of these weapons depots. Apprised of these plans, Boston patriots sent a rider to New Hampshire to warn the northern settlers of the British plan to reinforce Fort William Henry. Peabody was one of the leaders of a raid on the Newcastle fort.

He and his men disguised themselves as Indians and overwhelmed the English captain and his five guards. The munitions they captured were distributed and hidden in various caches in New England in preparation for the coming revolution against English authority. From the British point of view the citizens of Atkinson were committing treason by concealing The Crown's property.

There is the story of Joseph Chandler who went off to fight in the Revolution and did not return to Atkinson for seven years. Either he enjoyed fighting, or perhaps the inducements offered by the recruiters for "one more campaign" were irresistible. When he finally returned to Atkinson his wife happened to be sweeping out the house. Startled by the dirty, unkempt man on her doorstep, she proceeded to beat him about the head with her broom until he finally identified himself as her husband.

The forty men who fought in the Civil War are listed on the monument on Dow Common. George Parson Dow was awarded the Congressional Medal of Honor for meritorious service in that conflict. Sergeant Dow and his men had become separated from his regiment in the battle of Richmond, and his exploits in leading his men to rejoin their regiment are told in great detail in *Atkinson Then and Now*. Of the forty Atkinson men who volunteered to serve in this War of the Rebellion seven failed to return to their peaceful little village.

Alonzo McNeil, who was born in Atkinson, served in the Twentieth Infantry Regiment of the Maine Volunteers. Following the Civil War, he stayed in service and served in General Custer's regiment during the Battle of the Little Big Horn where the famous general fought his last stand. History reports he was caught slightly drunk the night before the big battle and he was assigned to the guardhouse where he remained during the battle in which Custer and all his men were wiped out. Lucky Alonzo!

The Richards family tradition lists Frank Richards as the youngest northern soldier to take part in the Civil War. It is difficult to imagine this mere boy, twelve years old, serving as a drummer for Company K.

The large granite boulder that bears the names of the twenty World War One veterans has an asterisk beside the names of two men that failed to return. The town has since named Leroy Avenue and Maurice Avenue in honor of Leroy Rivers and Maurice Given who fell in France during that war. There is an honor role displayed on the lawn of the Atkinson Congregation Church that bears the names of eighteen men who fought in World War Two and the Korean War.

On a cold, snowy December 4, 1888 William C. Todd dedicated a memorial to the Atkinson men who served in the Civil War. His remarks could well serve to immortalize the names of all young Atkinson men who, throughout its history, willingly served their people, their town and their country:

I now present to the town a soldier's monument, a granite shaft with the names of the forty who went from here to war. I am happier to give it than the town can be to receive it. It is but a small token of my regard for the place of my birth and the soldiers. No class deserves better to be remembered than those who have risked their lives for their country; yet the town records do not record who went to war and, in a few years, no list of them could have been given. Some sleep in unknown graves with no stone to mark their resting-place. I felt then that their names should be engraved on stone, and placed where their names could be daily read and kept in remembrance. And I am sure they will not be forgotten, for they were part of one of the grandest event in the history of our nation, the abolition of slavery and the preservation of our Union.

First Hampstead Meeting House, 1748--2000.

Atkinson Town Pound, Rt 121, circa 1785.

Chapter 8
TALES OF THE POND
1692--2000

The millennia is virtually upon us and in a few years local residents of the pond will be referring to events that occurred in the 1900s with the same nostalgia with which we presently view the 1800s. In the last few paragraphs of Elizabeth Schneider's chronicle she described the changes that began to occur in 1900. By then the women of her family were being allowed to join the men at the pond, and she mentioned that camping was slowly becoming a popular pastime. She told how her two uncles and four of their friends got together to buy the big island, and that one of the first permanent camps was the one built by Colonel Shepard on Escumbuit Island.

Up to that time those who wished to explore the pond did so with rowboats and canoes. The only sound of their activity on the pond was the splash of the oars, the creak of oarlocks and the happy shouts of people having fun. Up to that time no one had ever heard of noise pollution. One hundred years of progress have improved our lives immeasurably, but along with the automobile, refrigerator, television and the supermarket came outboard motors and jet skis. No one can deny the joy of skiing behind a fast boat or skimming the water on a waverunner, but these advances in sports craft came with a price. Strangely, in spite of these advances in watercraft, traffic on the pond today is lighter than it was back in the 1960s. Thanks in large part to the residents who form the BIPC, the quality of life on the pond remains unchanged.

Every longtime resident has his favorite folk tale or anecdote about the pond that he can be persuaded to relate over a casual beer or cocktail. Indeed, in the days before radio and television, important event were passed to succeeding generations in this way. Only when one begins to research and collect stories about Big Island Pond does it become clear that the pond and the surrounding communities offer an unusual collection of historic personalities, colorful episodes, unsolved mysteries, ancient legends and nostalgia. As we enter the 2nd millennia it seems appropriate to record this collage of stories that might otherwise be recalled only in the minds of a departed generation.

The Legend of Lover's Leap

Fifty years ago a fascinating article about Big Island Pond appeared in the August 3, 1949 issue of the Haverhill Gazette. The header for the article was "Story of Amesbury Lovers Hampstead Tragedy Recalled". The climatic scene in this 17th Century drama took place on the cliff in Pine Acres. When the article was originally published it attracted interest in Hampstead, but most people on the pond never heard the strange tale. Tom Gregsak of Big Island Pond Realty revived the story in a 1975 newsletter that he mailed to potential clients. Much of the historical information in his newsletter came from Jack and Lois Seig's research, but his short paragraph about the tragedy on the cliff came from this 1949 Haverhill Gazette story. Richard A Jones, a director of the pond association, has a copy of the original article. He ran across the yellowed clipping quite by accident when he cleaned out an old desk that was left at the camp he bought in 1967. He built the current home that presently sits atop the cliff in Pine Acres. A retired airline pilot for American Airlines, his interests run to antique cars, archeology, ancient mysteries and history. He was fascinated with the legend of the cliff for years, but the tale of a young couple's flight from witchcraft charges and their subsequent suicide pact appeared to be little more than unsubstantiated myth. Now he held in his hand the details of a tragedy that had taken place virtually at his doorstep more than 300 years ago. As he read the story it was almost as if ghosts from the past were sending him an ethereal message:

Please tell our story! We were young and in love and were unjustly condemned. At this place we chose to be one through eternity.

It is through Dick Jones' discovery of a 50-year old newspaper article that the details of this compelling 17th Century tragedy are revealed. It is a tale of superstition, injustice, love, adventure, despair and sadness.

The picturesque cliff that guards the narrows that give way to Sanborn Shores, Sunset Brook and Point Pleasant has challenged the imagination of residents for years. It has been called Eagles Cliff, Lover's Leap, Suicide Ledge and Wellman's Ledge and it is arguable the most famous landmark on the pond. Notwithstanding the fame of ghosts of the past like Benning Wentworth and the legendary Chief Escumbuit, the climatic event that gave the cliff its name strikes a deep responsive chord. The manner in which the story became public information is a story within itself.

In the afternoon of August 9, 1901, a Boston visitor to the pond named John Williams launched his rowboat and rowed to a spot opposite the cliff where he baited and dropped his line over the side. Later, warned by the dark clouds of an advancing thunderstorm, he set aside his fishing pole and decided to row to the base of the cliff to take shelter in one of the two shallow caves located there. The water was substantially lower than its present level. The base of the 30-foot cliff revealed a shallow cave that offered temporary protection from the storm. As he waited for the skies to clear, he noticed that loose stones had formed a pile of rubble that extended above the water line part way up the rock wall. As he idly poked at this loose aggregate with the blade of his oar, he uncovered what appeared to be a book or a journal wedged into a crack in the wall. Yellow with age, it appeared to have been protected from the elements in its niche at the back of the cave. He identified it immediately as a diary or handwritten journal. He noted that the first entry was dated January 1st and that the final entry was dated--August 16, 1692. One can only imagine his reaction to the handwritten date. It must have occurred to him that the diary he held in his hand was 209 years old. And, as he read the handwritten words, he must have been filled with an urgency to tell someone about his find. Somehow, 48 years passed before the Haverhill Gazette picked up the story and printed it in 1949.

The entire episode arose out of an emotional frenzy generated by children. In 1692 an impressionable group of Salem, Massachusetts teenaged girls, exposed to the dark tales of voodoo and witchcraft told to them by a black servant from the West Indies, began to literally act out her tales of the occult. Encouraged by Cotton Mather, the Puritan preacher who saw signs of evil everywhere, these twisted teenagers claimed they could identify witches. They falsely accused a crippled, pipe smoking black woman who had an illegitimate half-caste son. The woman was tortured and forced to admit that she had harmed the girls. The girls acted out pain and paralysis that they claimed had been caused by the accused woman. This strange union of teenage frivolity and religious intolerance combined to produce the greatest farcical evil this country has ever witnessed. Before sanity could be restored, dozens of innocent people were hanged and one man was pressed to death under a pile of stones. And seventeen years later, when two of the young conspirators confessed that they had been faking, not a voice was raised to call for their punishment. It was a grave miscarriage of justice.

The madness began in Salem, Massachusetts when a group of young girls went to the home of Reverend Samuel Parris to hear his West Indies servant tell stories about African voodoo and witches. Elizabeth Parris and Abegail Williams, aged nine and eleven, repeated the stories to friends and some of the impressionable girls began to act out the maid's scary tales of voodoo and spell casting. They began to throw books and writhe on the floor and eventually involved over fifteen of their friends in the delusion. From this innocent beginning the teenage frenzy quickly spread to surrounding communities. The madness that consumed the communities of Andover, Amesbury and Salem, Massachusetts during this period defies logic. In almost every case the accusers were children with twisted, imaginations who turned their pretended powers against individuals in their community with whom they had petty differences. Inexplicably, the Reverend Cotton Mather, famous Boston fire and brimstone preacher aided and abetted their poisonous reign of terror. This was the same preacher who engineered the hanging of Hannah Duston's sister for having lost two newborn children that were born out of wedlock. She was unable to prove to the court that the infants had died of natural causes. (In this judicial farce, Cotton Mather and his hand-picked panel of jurors tried and sentenced her to death by hanging.)

The first six months of 1692 witnessed the spectacle of the witchcraft trials in Salem, Massachusetts. During that period 19 people were hanged at a place called Gallows Hill and another condemned man was pressed to death under a pile of stones. Sensible people who counseled caution and attempted to protect the accused were themselves accused of being witches. Sympathetic teenagers in Andover quickly embraced the new craze. In the words of Marion L. Sterkey, the Devil took over Andover and the village was paralyzed with terror. At the crisis of the delusion, the worse and the best, the old and the young might be charged at any hour of witchcraft and convicted on the most preposterous evidence. During this period Colonel Bradstreet, a magistrate in Andover, signed 40 warrants against witches in his town. When he refused to sign any more warrants the youngsters accused him of witchcraft, and he and his wife fled the village. His accusers hung his dog for witchcraft during his absence.

The dates in the long lost journal at Big Island Pond and the story it told fit the tenor of the times perfectly. The terror and despair of the young couple became understandable as the details in the diary unfolded. Hannah[46] was the niece of Susannah Martin of Amesbury who had been accused and convicted of witchcraft. The Gazette article mentioned that descendants of one of her accusers later lived in Hampstead. When Hannah condemned her aunt's accusers as liars they immediately branded her a witch. She was then confined by the authorities and was awaiting trial. Recognizing the danger he would face by condemning her accusers, her boyfriend, Richard, immediately began to make plans to rescue his sweetheart. One morning a guard discovered that the girl had been released and, when they were unable to locate the couple, they knew that they had fled the town of Amesbury together. They knew they could not seek refuge in nearby towns because of the nature of the girl's "crime," and citizens of the

---

[46] Author's note: Unfortunately, the Haverhill Gazette article did not give the names of the two people who left the journal. People do not always identify themselves when making notes in a diary, but in order to improve the readability of the story I have assigned the names Hannah and Richard to the young couple.

town buzzed with speculation over the fate that awaited them in Indian country.

In this era French and Indian raids were a constant threat to the border settlements and some of the citizens had abandoned their homesteads and returned to Boston. The most serious Indian attacks still lay ahead, including the raid in which Hannah Duston was taken captive in 1697, followed by the violent 1708 raid in which Chief Escumbuit was wounded. In the face of the pillage, murder, arson and kidnapping by their French and Indian adversaries, one has to wonder why the citizenry would turn on their own in such a demented way. In the immediate exhilaration that came with their reunion and freedom from persecution, the spirits of the young couple must have soared, but eventually they were forced to face the stark reality of the new danger they faced. In the following paragraphs the Haverhill Gazette article describes how the young couple survived in the wilds, and it speculates on the likely fate of the ill-fated couple.

Haverhill Gazette
August 3, 1949

The writer of the old book tells with great fullness how he rescued the niece and described their wanderings in the wilderness. He had carefully planned the rescue. Knowing there would be no safety for them in any of the settlements so long as the witchcraft frenzy continued he had prepared as thoroughly as possible for the long journey. Together they entered the dark forest, trusting in God that in some way they might find safety, but preferring death rather than separation or the continued suspicion and persecution of the settlers.

In a few days their stock of food became exhausted and they were compelled to subsist on wild berries. They came to a place where a friendly Indian lived, but they dared not stop there; later, arriving at the wigwam of another Indian, under a great oak, nearly famished as they approached, they were given some coarse food, which greatly refreshed them, but they dared not tarry, and wandered on. They were suspicious of the old Indian and felt they were being watched and surrounded.

They turned in various ways, but the same feeling continued that the Indians were determined upon their destruction. At length, they came upon a high rocky point, overlooking a deep lake. On one side was a swamp, on the other an arm of the lake. Nearly exhausted, they sat down there. The last page in the book, written there on the rock, records:

We have been talking together of the past, of the present situation and of the future. We are not sorry for what we have done. It is the best we could do. May God forgive our friends and neighbors for their cruelty. Providence has not guided us to a place of safety. God knows best, but we are resigned. It is hard to die, but we will die together. We are determined that if the Indians come upon us, we will leap from the rocks into the dark, deep waters and die in each other's arms.

The account is brought to an end with a conclusion that this is exactly what happened, as there is no evidence that the couple could have met any other fate. Before they made the fatal leap, they cached the diary, perhaps hoping that it would be preserved to posterity, as actually happened.

Germantown
1928

I got my first glimpse of Big Island Pond in 1928. I spent a weekend with the Korb family at their camp in Germantown. Roland Korb and I attended gym classes at the Turnverein on Park Street in Lawrence and the family invited me to their camp for a weekend. Emil Korb owned a German bakery on Chestnut Street in Lawrence and was one of the first campers on the pond. He was married to the former Louis Minzner whose family had property next to Howards Grove. Emil got the camping bug from his wife's family. The train they boarded in Lawrence went through Haverhill to Hampstead then headed west where it discharged the campers at Hubbard Station on Warner Hill Road before going on to Nashua. From there they walked down to their camp carrying their supplies. Other people took the electric trolley from Lawrence to a station at the intersection of Routes 28 and 111. The owners of Canobie Lake Park constructed this line in about 1893 to transport people to the site of their new amusement park. The spur on Route 28 was a branch off that line. In those days people were willing to walk four miles to get to the pond. By 1928 the automobile became the preferred means of transportation, and the exodus from the cities began.

The Roaring Twenties ushered in a wave of prosperity that came on the heels of the American doughboy's victory over the Kaiser's Army and their 1918 welcome home parade down Broadway in New York City. Like most Americans in the summer of 1928, Mr. Korb continued to let the good times roll oblivious to the economic problems that loomed ahead. I remember several weekend visits to the Korb camp with eight year old Roland Korb and his family. At that time his two older brothers seemed like young gods; Herb later graduated from M.I.T. and Emil attended the U S Naval Academy. One September weekend Mr. Korb organized a Schlachtfest for his male friends. They butchered a hog and made weiswurst, blutwurst and lebenwurst and we had spare ribs and pork chops, sauerkraut, rye bread and a variety of kuchen from the Korb Bakery. I was wide-eyed the entire, glorious weekend. The men were boisterous, but good-natured; they drank beer and schnaps(whiskey), and they sang wonderful German songs. Less than a year after that carefree weekend the 1929 stock market crash signaled the onset of the worse depression of the 20th Century. Ten years later, as German panzer columns rolled through Poland and Czechoslovakia virtually unopposed, America slowly began to build its war machine to prepare for the coming war with Hitler and his "Nazi Supermen."

Campers at the pond were still using iceboxes in those days and many of them bought their ice at Chase's Grove. When the ice froze to a thickness of about 18 inches the Chase boys and their helpers were out cutting ice for their icehouse. It was located to the right of the beach as viewed from the pond. The men hand-cut a narrow channel through the ice to an adjustable ramp at the front of the icehouse. After cutting out a large square of ice the men sawed it into pieces that measured about 2x5 feet. The individual pieces were floated to the ramp and slid up into the icehouse where successive layers were insulated with sawdust. Bill Chase described how they got the pieces of ice up the ramp. A crude harness that fit over the end of a slab of ice was attached to a rope that passed through a pulley at the top of the ramp. The rope was then passed through a ground level pulley and tied to a horse. Bill laughed when he recalled what it was like to ride on the horse's back:

> When I was a kid they would put me on the horse's back and I thought I was controlling the horse, but he knew his job better than I did. He moved when he felt a strain on the line and stopped when the ice was up the ramp. I was just along for the ride.

Many people came by boat throughout the summer to pick up chunks of ice to cool their perishables and the Chase family also made ice deliveries by boat. There were numerous icehouses around the pond in those days. They cut ice in the channel between Escumbuit Island and the shore and stored it in an icehouse that was located near Herman Heinrich's camp. As a young boy I remember Fred and Otto Minzner cutting ice for their uncle Al Minzner next to Howard's Grove and storing it in an icehouse adjacent to their back camp. This ice was used to cool a metal-lined "icebox" in which they stored their perishables during the summer. I can vividly remember hot August days made bearable with lemonade cooled by ice cut from the pond the previous January.

The mundane details of food shopping and food preparation were time consuming in those days. Al and Emma Minzner were year-round residents at the pond. They grew much of the food they ate in a large garden they tended between the back camp and North Island Pond Road. As a 15-year-old boy I anticipated and loved the ritual of Saturday night. No teenager had better role models than Otto and Fred and Walter Minzner. They were older than Roland and me by about 10 years. They celebrated their adult status by quaffing a cool beer on Saturday night while Roland and I watched thoroughly impressed.

Someone would say: "I'm getting hungry; I wonder if the beans are ready?"

Footstep on the porch would signal the arrival of supper and a beaming Uncle Al would walk in bearing a steaming crock of baked beans.

"They've been cooking for two days," he'd announce grinning at our anticipation. The crock of beans was the feature event, and the supporting cast was the liverwurst, fresh German rye bread and fresh tomatoes and cucumbers from the garden. Then came streusel and blueberry kuchen for desert. No eating experience has ever topped those Saturday night feasts marked by good-natured banter in the company of the Minzner boys.

In the years preceding my introduction to Big Island Pond, the brothers and their friends had a fife and drum corp. Given the appropriate military attire of the Revolutionary War, they could have added color and gaiety to any public event. Instead they entertained the locals with old time tunes like Londonderry Air, a tune that was made for the shrill, keening sound of the fife and the rat-a-tat-tat of the drum. Having learned to play an accordion and later a guitar, I suddenly found myself a student of the fife.

Otto Minzner taught me how to play some of the classic old English and Scotch marching songs such as "Where, oh where has my bonny blue boy gone. He's gone to join the King..." The sounds coming out of that part of the pond in the early spring and late fall must have sounded weird.

I saw an unforgettable example of the resourcefulness and unity of the Germans during my first visit with my friend Roland Korb. In the spring of 1928 we paddled a canoe down the shore to Howard's Grove to visit Roland's cousins. When we arrived we saw a gang of men moving a camp from its site on the shore to a new location behind the camp owned by Al and Emma Minzner. The owners did not own the property on which the camp was located and circumstances demanded that they move it or lose it.

A weekend crew of friends managed to slide two large timbers under the structure after it had been jacked up by a series of large mechanical screw jacks. They threw a heavy line around the base of the camp and used manual labor to haul on the block and tackle that would slowly inch the building to its new location. Lacking modern hydraulic jacks, horses and oxen to supply the necessary power, this determined group of men still managed to haul that building the length of a football field and place it on a new foundation over a single weekend. When work for the day was completed they celebrated with a shot of schnaps chased with a cool beer. Nothing stopped these men when they focussed on a project.

The Entrepreneur

An early day's inconvenience at the pond was the lack of refrigeration. Campers had to carry all of their supplies in to the pond and it was difficult to keep milk, meat and vegetables from spoiling. Indians had time-tested methods of preserving food. Their principal occupation was food gathering and they learned how to preserve surplus food. In the spring they dried salmon, shad and sturgeon by drying it on racks built above fires that they kept going constantly on the banks of the Merrimac River. They dried corn and squash and blueberries and stored them in birchbark containers in their wigwams and longhouses. The surplus meat from their winter hunts was cut into strips and dried on racks built above their fires. Their pemmican was a mixture of dried chopped meat, nuts and dried berries mixed with animal fat. Pemmican and reconstituted parched corn sustained them on long trips.

During the 1920s the Chase family delivered ice and milk around the pond in one of their boats, but it wasn't until 1935 that a young entrepreneur named Al Teischmeier began to really cash in on the demand. He was a high school student when he started, and he continued to expand his business during his four years in college. A Harvard football player named Vern Struck helped him out for a couple of summers. The business was so lucrative that he continued to operate it while he attended graduate school. He said that he made more money at that summer job than he made fresh out of Harvard Business School. Now retired, he and his wife Ann still spend part of each summer at the pond. When I interviewed him in September 1999 I found him to have almost total recall and I was amazed to learn the complexity of the business he created in 1935.

He got his ice from an icehouse that was located in the right-of-way opposite the south end of Escumbuit Island. The 300-pound bars if ice were about 5 feet long and 2 feet wide. He had to dig them out of the sawdust and break them into manageable pieces before he washed them off and slid them down the ramp to his boat. Every morning an H P Hood truck would make a delivery to his camp that was located on the north shore near Germantown. A Lawrence bakery also delivered goods to his dock. Soon he was selling cakes and doughnuts and he began to deliver ice cream on Sunday. He made a deal with a Chinese Restaurant in Lawrence and Thursday became Chinese takeout day at the pond. He even made a deal with Rutter's Laundry in Lawrence to provide laundry service by boat. Business got so darn good that he had to add another boat. In true American tradition Al Teischmeier had found a way to make money by filling a consumer need. Roland Korb ran the route for a couple of years after the war. He said that the dirt roads leading into the pond were so bad that regular milkmen refused to make deliveries to residents of the lake. He used to have a standard order on Friday afternoon to drop a piece of ice into the ice boxes of certain camps so people would have a cool place for their perishables when they arrived at camp for the weekend

People loved the convenience. There was a special novelty in hearing a child call out, "Mom, the milk man is here!" Instead of the normal delivery to the side or the back door she might go out to help dock the boat. Nevertheless, most senior ladies will say without hesitation that the single best addition to camp was the electric refrigerator. The refrigerator and the family car changed everything. The housewife was able to store a week supply of food in her refrigerator and the automobile made it simple to replenish the larder.

Ten Minutes to Eternity

One of the traits of youth is an undeniable sense of immortality. It is the certainty that if death pays a visit it will be to someone else's doorstep. It is part of the nature of the young to believe that is so. Shortly after the end of World War II the pond witnessed such an event. We had driven up to the pond on a beautiful March day hoping to see the ice go out. When we arrived, we were greeted with the magical scene of open water; the ice had broken up and the jumbled corn ice was being wind-driven to the big island by a southwesterly breeze. Roland had brought along Peggy Monihan and Elaine Stoehrer and Bubsy Allen had arrived in a separate car. I drove up alone and joined the group. We were in high spirits, buoyed by the thought of another summer at the pond.

Roland said, "Lets throw the sailboat in and take a sail," and with the optimism of youth it seemed like a great idea. Five of us set out on a long starboard tack in a snipe that was designed for a skipper and a single crewmember. We were dressed in jackets and sweaters to shield us from the cold gusty wind. We made a port tack and settled onto a course that would take us the length of the pond. It was exhilarating to be out in the open air with friends after the long, confining winter. When the gust of wind put our starboard rail under, we didn't have a chance to recover. In a matter of seconds the cockpit filled with water and suddenly we found ourselves in the frigid water. Startled shouts gave way to a dead silence. The hull had just enough buoyancy to support the weight of the two girls and, although they were soaked through, they were spared the chill of the water. I am sure that the severity of our situation registered on each of us at that moment. The frightened eyes of the others mirrored the panic I felt. The air temperature was about 50, and we were alone in near freezing water in the middle of the pond. There was no prospect of rescue from shore. On that March day in 1947 the pond was deserted except for us! The reality of our dilemma chilled me to the bone. I thought--we're gonna die out here! Then I got angry! How could we have not seen the danger? How could we have been so stupid? Roland wanted to swim for shore but after I gauged the distance to Dixon's Grove in the frigid water I said:

You'll never make it, the wind is carrying us towards the big island. Let's stay with the boat and kick with our legs to keep it moving in that direction.

We made slow headway towards the island absorbed in our private thoughts as we concentrated on the task at hand. We were in ice water and, despite our physical activity, hypothermia was slowly but surely claiming our bodies. The girls were able to do little more than sit and wait. Under normal circumstances we would have gone under the boat and lowered the sails to reduce the sea anchor effect, but the freezing water closed that option. When our movement stopped completely, we realized that the tip of the mast was on the bottom and we were stuck about 100 yards from shore. It was a moment of pure truth: go for it now or die! The girls were temporarily safe, but

Peggy couldn't swim and Elaine opted to stay with her. The sandy beach looked tantalizingly close, but I was numb with cold and I knew that it would take everything I had to make it to shore. Normally there is safety in numbers, but now it came down to individual survival. I was conscious of the others swimming to my right, and I knew that if one of my companions faltered I would have to go on. When I finally got to shallow water I crawled up onto the sand and collapsed. I lay there for 5 to 10 minutes, and then I raised my head and saw the others on the beach to my right. The girls sat wordlessly on the upturned snipe watching intently. I finally managed to get up and stumble to a nearby camp where, in the urgency of the moment, I broke a pane of glass to get inside. I took a pull from a half bottle of whiskey I found in the kitchen and found a set of keys hanging on a nail. My immediate concern was for the girls so I took the keys and gained access to the boathouse where I found a rowboat. After I brought the two girls to shore I saw that Roland and Bubsy were sufficiently recovered to make it to the camp. We were a somber group; I think we were all suffering some degree of shock. Elaine and I were in the best shape, so we rowed across the pond to retrieve one of the cars from Germantown. We drove around the pond onto the island and picked up the others. There was virtually no discussion about our narrow escape as we separated and headed for home in three separate cars. I went to bed at eight o'clock that night and woke up at ten the following day and I slept twelve hours the next night. In the years that followed, despite numerous contacts, we never discussed the events of that day. Shaken by our near fatal encounter, we instinctively pushed the experience into the deepest recess of our mind. On that cold March day in 1947, we stared into the abyss and fate decreed--not now!

The Way Station

An old building on North Island Pond Road guarded its secret well since before the Civil War. Old timers in the area referred to the ancient house as "The Nigger Lady's place." The people who used that term during the 1930's saw nothing racist in the way they described the property. Standard terminology in those days referred to African Americans as Colored People, or Negroes and of course they used the N-word. In my own lifetime I have seen these terms superseded by the term Black People and recently African American and People of Color have come into vogue. As a boy, I assumed that a colored woman had lived in that house. In the process of researching this book I came across evidence that this old house may have been a Way Station for the Underground Railway that was used to transport runaway slaves before the Civil War.

Elizabeth Schneider's chronicle describing early camping adventures of her family on the big island from 1878 to 1900 referred to this house and its occupants. She wrote that a Negro man named Francois and his German wife operated a tavern and a restaurant there. When the Sweeney boys grew tired of their own cooking, they often went there for a home cooked meal. Later in her journal she wrote that, after Francois died, the German woman continued to operate the establishment by herself. As late as 1950 the occupants sold penny candy to children from a small store they had in the house. A few years back, this rather ordinary looking house was dismantled and carried off in a truck. Some of the hand-cut beams and wide boards from this old house were used to restore an historic house down in Connecticut. By combining the information from Elizabeth Schneider's chronicle with the childhood memories of Virginia Krauklin, one forms a plausible theory about the house and its original occupants.

Back in the 1940s Virginia (Meier) Krauklin was friendly with children who lived in the house and she often went there to play. The children showed her a secret hiding place built into the vertical matchboard wainscoting that extended half way up the wall of the kitchen. The space was sufficiently large enough to conceal documents. Virginia added that she would never have noticed this hiding place had her friends not revealed it to her. And this was not the only curious feature of the house that they were anxious to display. It was the strange arrangement of the cellar that impressed itself upon the young mind of Virginia Meir. The cellar was divided into what she described as stalls or cubicles. When she commented on the odd partitioning of the cellar they told her that the house had once been used to hide run-a-way slaves. The cubicles were provided to allow some measure of privacy for individual families or for male and female runaways. They may have been required to remain hidden for several days before arrangements were made to transport them at night to the next Way Station.

During the Civil War there was a clandestine organization that concealed and transported escaping slaves to freedom in Canada. The occupants claimed that this house had been used as a Way Station for the Underground Railroad. The chapter on America's Stonehenge examines reports by other writers that the stone caves on that site also served as a Way Station. The proximity of this house to that site lends credence to the theory that local people were deeply involved in this clandestine operation. Books on the subject mention that many of the slaves made friends at the various stops in their flight to the north and that some of them stayed and were absorbed by the local community. Francois, the black man of Elizabeth Schneider's time, may very well have been an escaped slave who befriended and married a local German girl. They were the couple who operated this house as a tavern in the late 1800s. The known dates neatly fit the theory. A 25 or 30 year old black youth fleeing north during the Civil War would have been about 60 or 65 at the time of his death in the year 1900.

The Brothel-1915

North Island Pond Road seems to have had a rather lurid history. According to Maurice Randall, back in the early 1900s, there was some strange activity in the area of Rockingham Road. This access road to the pond is situated between Germantown Road and Collette's Grove Road. Maury's history of Hampstead was published in 1999 in time for the 250th celebration. Like his father before him he has recently been named the town historian. An associate of his father told Maury that, back in the early 1900s, North Island Pond Road was a popular Saturday night hangout for some of the more adventurous youths of the town. That was the place to go on a Saturday night if you were looking for action.

An old frame house that once stood on property now owned by Alfred Teichmeier provided the setting for an interested story about early life on the pond. It was a simple structure built on cedar posts that had a staircase to a second floor-sleeping loft. The establishment was known as the Rockingham Hotel and the present dirt road that leads to this building is presently called Rockingham Road. At one time the hotel took in boarders but, according to this account, the present proprietor had discovered new ways of making money. A scenic carriage path that came down from the main road ran along the shore behind the so-called hotel.

The old-timer said that the woman who owned the house used to sit out in back of the house and wave at people passing behind the hotel. Since she weighed about 300 pounds, it may be more accurate to say she reclined in her back yard. But the spectacle of a 300-pound woman waving at strangers from her back yard is only a teaser because, hidden under the ample folds of her tent-like dress, was a gallon jug of liquor. Furthermore, this fat lady entertained an inordinate number of visitors--and they were all men!

The old timer proceeded to recall a particular Saturday night when he and three other Hampstead youths were out looking for excitement. In the era before World War I, a young man got a job after graduating from high school and he usually lived at home with his parents. But this Saturday night, after paying mom for room and board, these young thrill seekers had cash in their pockets and they were looking for action. Fortified by a few beers at a local tavern they decided to pay the fat lady a visit. Undaunted by the long walk (It was still the horse and buggy era) they walked into the fat lady's yard in a festive mood. After an effusive greeting she got down to business:

"What can I do for you boys?" and with a gesture towards her hidden supply, "Got some mighty fine stuff here!"

After she cached the few bills the boys gave her within her voluminous bosom, she poured out two pints from her jug and said:

"Let's go in the house and get some water from the hand-pump. Ya don't want to drink that stuff straight."

Inside the house the guys finally got a glimpse of what had really brought them to Laverne's house:

"That's Dorene over there on the sofa and the skinny one over there in the corner is Ellie" said Laverne sweeping her ample arm in the direction of her girls. "Ain't these boys nice to come by on a Saturday night to visit us way out here in the country?"

As the whiskey flowed, Laverne steered the conversation towards the business at hand. About the time two of the men headed up to the second floor with their young "hostesses," a third member of the party bolted for the yard holding his hand over his mouth to hold down the "good stuff" that Laverne had sold them.

With the assurance that comes from being the only eyewitness, the teller of the story claimed he was alone in the living room with Laverne when the raid began. "Open up, it's the police!" came the cry from outside and the pounding on the door seemed to shake the entire house. Laverne suddenly found herself alone as her guest bolted out the kitchen door to the yard. Collecting his sick companion, he crouched and watched intently as one of their friends emerged feet first from a second story window and hung to the window sill for a moment before dropping to the ground. By the time the second lover made his escape and joined them, Laverne had opened her door to the police demanding to know what was going on. As they made their way back to town they were a study in contrasting emotions. The sick one kept saying, "I'll never do that again, another couldn't stop laughing at the spectacle of his two half-dressed companions climbing out of a second story window, and the two big spenders grumbled all the way home about unrequited love. Presumably, the four young men grew up to be upstanding members of their community, sworn to keep their secret for the rest of their lives.

Hobo Lodge-1934

By the end of The Roaring Twenties people began to explore the world beyond the ethnic neighborhoods of the city. As more and more people bought automobiles, they unerringly headed for the seashore and the country in their time off. The "Big Band" era was in full swing and the dance halls located at lakes and ponds were a strong draw for city-bound people. Big Island Pond featured two dance halls; one was built on the shore at Conley's Grove and the one at Chases Grove is still active. Working class people were able to afford the cost of the mass-produced automobile and people were no longer limited to electric trolleys. Big Island Pond with its scenic beauty and its dance halls became a big draw.

The woods in back of the second row of camps at Chases held an impressive assortment of tents owned by people who did not have the wherewithal to own a permanent camp. The people who called this camping area Hobo Lodge were mostly blue collar workers from the Lawrence area who relished the opportunity to spend their weekends at the pond without busting their budget. Many of these people eventually found the means to purchase their own camp. They were hard working, fun loving, honest people.

I used to hitch hike up to the pond from my home in Methuen carrying little more that my tooth brush and my bathing suit and a few canned items from our pantry. I usually arrived with about 50 cents in my pocket and I often managed to stay at the pond for a full week. I managed through the generosity of the tent people in Hobo Lodge. There was always someone ready to offer me a sandwich at noon or an invitation to a cookout in the evening, and I never spent the night without a tent over my head. In the two summers that I spent camping in Hobo Lodge I never experienced any fights or drunks or behavior that a 15 year old boy should not be exposed to.

Large ballrooms were springing up all over America. Locally we had the Canobie Lake Ballroom and the Crystal Ballroom in Shawsheen Village. Further afield was the Totem Pole Ballroom down towards Boston and our radio brought us the music of the big bands from glamorous places like the Trianon and Aragon ballrooms in Chicago. We listened to live radio broadcasts of Glenn Miller's band from Catalina Island off the coast of California. But there was nothing like getting a dance with a local girl who you had met down at the beach at Chases. Most of the young people who attended these dances were singles and it took a lot of courage to walk over to a covey of girls and ask for a dance. It was a long walk back to the boy's section if you were turned down. There was little drinking and no drugs in those days. It was a different time.

The Assignation-1946

A story about the pond that refuses to die, is an intriguing tale about a member of a prominent family who was involved in a clandestine affair with a woman who was not his wife. Many men in his situation might have settled for a stolen moment in a hotel room or in the back seat of a parked car, but not this guy. He had money and he was going to do it his way. One can almost see him rubbing his hands in anticipation as he made his plans for the secret trysting place that he had in mind. In about 1946 he bought a cottage on a small island near Escumbuit Island that was accessible only by boat. Apparently his attorney, the realtor and his mistress were the only ones who knew that he had acquired the property. The anticipation must have been delicious as he completed plans to take over his secret hideaway. Secrets are more fun if they can be safely shared, but that was no problem for this guy. What a crazy idea the girl friend thought; what a wonderful crazy idea!

It was a perfect setup! It was so easy! The deception worked like a charm. Urgent business in New York was actually cover for a trip to the pond. A sales meeting in Chicago turned out to be an idyllic week on Fantasy Island. As summer gave way to fall they enjoyed the pageant of changing colors and their retreat seemed even more secure as neighbors on the shore closed their camps for the season.

"What a shame" she said "Soon the pond will freeze over and we have nothing but dreary hotels to look forward to until next summer. I wish it would never end."

He looked at her and grinned:

"Hey babe, I have news for you. When the ice freezes over we can drive right out here on the ice and park beside our very own island. I have a case of whisky in the closet and plenty of wood for the stove; we'll be as snug as two bugs in a rug" Wide eyed, she looked at him and said, "Honey, I should have known you think of everything." It looked as though love would conquer all.

He was up there every week testing the ice. When people at his office complained about the cold weather he would declare, "Waddaya talkin about? This is great weather!" When the great day came at last, they laughed like two school kids as they drove out on the ice and began to unload supplies for the weekend. Later, with a fire blazing in the fireplace, they stood at the window and laughed at the magic of their situation.

"You know what honey, I want a snapshot of your Cadillac sitting there on the ice to remind me of this weekend. Let's go to bed now-- don't forget you promised to get up to feed the fire." Later as they drifted near sleep in their warm bed she murmured, "Honey, you deserve to be rich because you're smarter than everyone else."

He got up first and, after visiting the bathroom, he stumbled out to the living room to put some more wood on the fire. He was relaxed and still sleepy. He rubbed his eyes as he strolled over to the window to check the weather. His face blanched and his knees sagged...a jagged, dark hole marked the spot where his Caddy was parked the night before! For a long breathless moment he stood there, and then he walked unsteadily to the bedroom door where he leaned against the jam and said:

" Wake up Honey--we've got a problem!"

There are a number of old timers on the pond that will attest to this tale, and some will even name names. According to them the man had to go out and buy a new Cadillac to conceal the loss from his family. One can only imagine the consternation of his family when they ran across the deed to his hideaway after he died. As far as I know the car is still at the bottom of the pond.

The Sailors

There had been snipe sailing races at the pond before World War Two, but the heyday for snipe competition came after the war. The North Cove Yacht Club still stands next to Collette's Grove, but they no longer sponsor sailing regattas. There were a few sailing members in the club, but most of the sailors had camps on the pond. At the peak of enthusiasm for sailing a fleet of 15 snipes could often be seen driving hard for a single marker. The races normally were started in front of the yacht club and they sailed a triangular course. The typical course had a marker set at the approach to the channel between Escumbuit Island and the mainland and a second marker between Escumbuit Island and the Big Island. They normally sailed the course twice on Saturday and twice on Sunday. In the first race they might leave the markers to port and then change the course slightly by leaving the markers to starboard for the second race. The competition was spirited and there were times when tempers flared. Sailboat racing by its very nature is rife with official protests over things like failure to yield to an overtaking boat when approaching a buoy or failure to yield the right away in a crossing situation. Bruised egos were not confined to competing skippers. Husband and wife teams were rare due to the stresses inherent between skipper and crew. The crew rarely got the whisker pole out fast enough for his or her demanding skipper and it was the rare crewman who didn't think he could choose a better course than his skipper.

By the early 1950s technology was beginning to take over the sport, and ordinary sailors began to win regattas with superior equipment built of fiberglass with self-bailing hulls. It is the nature of man to seek better ways to compete against other men. Lacking the funds to buy the expensive equipment that the modern sport demanded, it became too expensive for some people to compete. Some of the early sailing whizzes left the pond for any number of reasons and today we are left with the sight of the occasional lone snipe tacking across the pond. The snipe races did not necessarily mark a better era; it is simply that, like Whitney's steamboat, the image of 15 boats heeling before a stiff breeze lent an unforgettable charm to the local scene. Perhaps more important, was the bonding between crew and skipper. Fathers and sons who survived the pressure of competition shared something precious. Recently I met Mark and Lillie Cleveland who share the camp at the East End of the island with other heirs of Bill Flanders. As I expressed my admiration for Bill as a competitor and friend, my mind's eye suddenly transformed the small boy who had crewed for him back in 1951 into the man sitting before me. It surprised me and saddened me somewhat to realize how many times the pond has iced over since I sailed against Bill and his grandson. My eyes wide with recognition, I exclaimed, "You were the boy who crewed for him" and he nodded and smiled and the memory pleased him. Later, as I climbed the knoll to my camp on Escumbuit Island I thought...my grandchildren need memories like that.

A Sobering Experience-1952

One lazy August afternoon I was sailing my snipe between Conley's Grove and Escumbuit Island. Fred Minzner, was handling the jib and we found ourselves almost completely becalmed in the protected cove. About 100 yards from shore a group of swimmers appeared to be searching for something in the water. People lined the shore staring intently at the group in the water. I called to the swimmers as we approached to find out what was going on. One of their friends was missing and they were searching for him. We approached the shore where people were waving to get our attention. They were frustrated.

"They're looking in the wrong place; he didn't go down there; he went down in the area you just came from."

We doubled back and when those on shore indicated we were over the spot, Fred took the tiller and I went over the side in about 12 feet of water. The water was clear and as I approached the bottom I saw a male form in blue jeans laying face down on the bottom. I needed air, but a jolt of adrenaline drove me downward to where I reached and grabbed his hair with my left hand and pushed hard off the bottom and stroked for the surface with my right arm. My lungs burned for oxygen and when I reached the surface I took a deep breath. I pulled his head above the surface and when I heard a chilling gurgling sound I shouted, "He's alive!" I took him in a cross-chest-carry and paddled over to the boat--the alcohol smell was strong--he was not breathing; he had been under water for at least 20 minutes. Fred held him while I crawled back into the boat and we then pulled the limp form up onto the forward deck of the sailboat. We slowly paddled our way to shore knowing that we were too late.

They had come up to the pond from Boston for an outing. They were young, they seemed invincible and they had been drinking--a bad combination. Their carefree outing at the pond had turned to tragedy. Now the gaiety was gone and some were crying. Their stunned faces reflected stark disbelief. It was a painful to witness. We were like intruders at a stranger's wake and, in the context of that moment, our condolences were meaningless. We sensed their need to grieve the loss of their friend privately. Shaken by the experience, we sailed back to our camp in silence. It was a melancholy ending to a beautiful August afternoon at Big Island Pond.

Taylor Saw Mill

At a dip and a turn on Island Pond Road a mile north of the pond, the State owned Taylor Saw Mill offers a glimpse of a bygone era to passing motorists. Robert Taylor brought this property in 1799 and by 1805 he was operating an up and down saw mill very similar in design and appearance to the present structure. This mill cut large diameter pine logs with an up-and-down saw until it was converted to a modern sawmill sometime after the end of the Civil War. Faced with the need to cut logs faster and cheaper, and with a dwindling supply of large diameter pine trees, Taylor sold the old equipment for scrap. Records indicate that he also operated a gristmill on this site.

When Ernest R. Ballard bought the property in 1939 he wanted to recreate the original up and down saw mill that had once been there. There was no commercial advantage in doing so unless he expected to create a tourist attraction for profit. We believe he may have merely been motivated by a sense of nostalgia, and his drive to accomplish his dream demonstrated a remarkable strength of purpose. After searching all over New England for a used saw, the unexpected happened. He learned that a man named Dan Hoit in Sandown had a used up and down saw under his barn. He bought the equipment "as is" and the $180 he paid for the old saw turned out to be a small part of the final cost. It took almost two years for he and his wife to locate necessary missing parts and put the equipment in working order. Finally they had a working up and down saw. The next challenge they faced was to locate a replica of the original wooden water wheel that had supplied power to the original saw. New or even used models did not exist and the cost of building one from scratch was beyond their budget. The Fitz Water Wheel Company of Hanover, Pennsylvania sold them a steel model that was six feet wide and twelve feet in diameter at a cost of $3,000. The 1800-pound water wheel with its 40 buckets was finally mounted in the dam serviceway and coupled to the saw.

One can only imagine the eagerness and pride with which the Ballards watched the first pine log advance towards the mechanically driven two-man handsaw. Long before the invention of power driven saws, planks had been laboriously sawed by hand. The log was supported in a cradle that bridged a deep pit in the ground. The long saw was pulled downward by the pitman and upward by the man above. Although the pitman had the easier pull he was on the receiving end of all the falling sawdust. The water wheel's mechanical linkage to the saw took the place of the muscular arms of two strong men.

The saw they built could cut a 12-foot long log with a diameter up to 28 inches. The carriage fed the log to the saw at the rate of about 3/8-inch per stroke and was able to deliver about 60 strokes per minute. Records indicate that saws built in the hey day of up and down saw mills could accept logs up to 38 feet in length and could handle widths in excess of 30". Many old New England farmhouses had single-piece-pine wainscoting that measured 30 inches or more from the floor. The modern circular saw cuts much faster, but the maximum width of its cut is limited by the height of the blade above the carriage on which the log rests. To cut a 30" wide board one would need a circular saw with a diameter in excess of five feet.

In 1954 this mill and 85 acres were donated to the State of New Hampshire, and today the Division of Resources Development manages the property. A number of years ago the state used to operate the mill for public viewing, but they had to discontinue the demonstrations when the water wheel deteriorated beyond repair. The computer firm NEL-TECH-LABS of Manchester is currently building a new wooden water wheel that should have the mill operating in The New Millennia. Gary Nelson Stapleford, President and CEO has taken on the design, expense and execution of this formidable project that will restore the historic landmark. At the middle of December 1999, the dam and spillway had been repaired and an esthetically charming oak water wheel was in place. By the spring of 2000, local residents may catch a glimpse of a scene from a bygone age as they travel on Island Pond Road. If they are lucky they may see pine boards being cut as they were 200 years ago. The Taylor Mill is a part of the 85-acre Ballard State Forest.

Stickney's Folly?

In 1958 some old timers around the pond thought that Walter Stickney had gone off the deep end. In those days the cove at the dam was a swamp. The narrow entrance to this cove was the original outlet of the pond. In 1878 Maxwell Taylor built an earth and timber dam to control the flow of water to his mill at Cowbell Corner and to supply water to four other mills downstream. About 1900 the Arlington Mills in Methuen, Massachusetts bought the water rights from Taylor to control the water they needed for their mills. They replaced Taylor's earth and timber dam with the present stone structure. In 1958 Walter Stickney bought the rights from Arlington Mills when Lawrence woolen mills moved to the Carolinas. The Big Island Pond Corporation acquired the rights in 1978 when Warren Kruswitz organized the Big Island Pond Association and purchased the water rights from Stickney.

The lower pastures of the Stickney property backed up on this swamp.[47] By 1950 available waterfront property at the pond was dwindling and Mr. Stickney came up with an idea to sell more camp lots. Noting that most of the available frontage on the pond was taken, he decided to create that which no longer existed. With typical Yankee foresight he had bought the water rights for the pond so he could put his plan into effect without outside interference. In the fall of 1950 he opened his dam and allowed the water level in the pond to drop to its lowest level. He brought heavy equipment in to dredge the cove to a 7 to 8 foot depth. By using the muck from the swamp to raise the level of the shoreline he accomplished two things. He created a picturesque cove navigable by small boats, and he turned the surrounding land into premium house lots. When he began, residents on the pond scoffed at the idea of buying camp lots in a swamp, but Walter Stickney knew what he was doing, and the picturesque cove he created remains a testimony to his ingenuity.

---

[47] *Abenaki Warrior*, by Alfred E Kayworth: (p 21) The Indian residents of Escumbuit Island had a garden in the low-lying ground where the dam cove is now located. In this garden they grew squash, beans, corn and tobacco. There was no dam and the crops were easily watered with water carried in birch bark pails from the small brook that meandered through the garden.

Cave at base of Eagle's Cliff.

Cave opening, lover's leap.

1939 photo of the author with a young camper.

Chapter 9
THE LAST RUMRUNNER
1909--2000

As I drove down to Salem for my meeting with "Hubby" Herold, many thoughts played through my mind. Herb had known my mother and dad when we lived up on Prospect Hill in Lawrence in 1929. In our occasional encounters at the pond over the years he had referred to my folks with a familiarity that puzzled me. I guess it was because I wasn't sure whether I should regard him as a contemporary or whether he was a throwback to my parent's generation. But Holy Mackerel...how could this guy still be not only alive, but appear to be as outspoken and aggressive as ever! Could this be the same man who's sister Elsie hung out with my mom in the late 1920s? It didn't seem possible that the guy who raced high-speed hydroplanes on the pond in the late 1930s and early 1940s could still be around. Hell's bells.... He would have to be nearly 90 years old!

I had phoned him to explain that I was writing a story about the pond and that I wanted to talk to him about the old days. During our telephone conversation I brought up the real reason for my interest; I wanted to ask him about his youthful career as a rumrunner during the 1920s. His response was immediate and direct.

"I don't want to talk about that stuff! That was a long time ago and I don't want to talk about it! That's a misdemeanor today, but back then it was a felony and I don't want to talk about it!"

Surprised by his heated response, I backed off and suggested that perhaps we could talk about him racing speedboats in the 1930s. That seemed to pacify him and, after giving me directions to his house, he cautioned me to be on time:

"I keep pretty busy, Spotty; I kind of run things down at the Senior Citizens Center in Salem. I'm going to pick up my girlfriend and go over there now."

On the way to my meeting with Herb I happened to see his daughter Kathy Woods standing out in her yard next to my boat dock. I walked over to ask her advice.

"I don't know what is the matter with him" she commented adding, "Doesn't he realize that part of his life is history? Who wants to read about the speedboats he built? My daughters don't know anything about that history and, if you don't tell the story, it will all be forgotten. Would he rather you write about the rumors or the truth? Just go down there and get him talking and he might surprise you."

Herb saw me coming, and when I reached the top of the steps he opened the door and boomed:

Hey Spotty, how the hell are ya, come on in."

A tube from his nose had a long lead to a large oxygen tank in the corner of the room. We sat down and began talking about the old days on Prospect Hill and I let him lead the conversation. He was born November 9, 1909 and he was a carpenter by trade. He was a union man and I learned that, in November 1999, he will have held a union card for 70 years. He got his drivers license in 1926 and his father bought him a brand new Model T Ford that set him back $400. With an impish grin on his face he added:

"And the first thing I did was make it into a racing car. My father was mad as hell!

Herb is a tall, lanky guy with big, strong hands and sort of a long neck and a genial face that can darken with anger in a heartbeat. His language is colorful. Four letter words flavor his conversation like hot sauce on a taco. Sometimes he comes out with things that are downright outrageous. The acuity of his mind and his total recall of events that are more than 70 years do not match the profile of a man who will be 90 years old before the turn of this century.

He made his first trip to Big Island Pond in 1919. His mother paid Connie Hilse to drive them up to the pond and bring them back. For many years he stayed at his mother's camp in Chase's Grove. In about 1941 his mother let his cousin use the camp for 10 days over Labor Day and Herb had to move out. When his mother had his cousin install a lock on the door to keep him out, he reacted in a predictable way; he immediately went to work and built a camp of his own near the entrance to the dam cove. With a sheepish grin on his face he concluded:

"After I built that camp, my mother wouldn't talk to me for three years."

He had a passion for speed. No matter whether it was an automobile, a boat, or a snowmobile, he wanted to make it go faster. In the late 1930s and early 1940s he used to build a speedboat hull every winter and, after trying it out on the pond, he would sell it to someone. The bellow of the Ford V-8 engines in his custom boats shattered the silence of the pond like the roar of a wounded beast. As a 15-year-old lad camping at Chase's Grove, I was in awe of this bigger than life gladiator of the pond and his flying 3-point speed-boats. He raced boats in Haverhill, Lowell and up in Maine. After the war he developed a passion for snowmobile racing. He showed me a wall full of trophies he won racing with the U.S.S.A. (United States Snowmobile Association). Everyone on the pond knew "Hubby" Herold. He was a great guy, but he had a hair-trigger temper.

There was a lull in our conversation while I made a few notes and then, like a race car driver, he abruptly shifted gears and began to tell his story.

"I got into that other stuff when some of them guys asked me to build some "whiskey hides.""

Unsure whether I had heard him right I asked, "What's a whiskey hide?"

He looked at me as if I were stupid and replied: "That's what they called a place where they hid the whiskey."

"Did you build those whiskey hides out in the woods?"

"Naw, I used to build them under houses and barns and places like that."

Then, as I sat spellbound, he began to tell me about his exciting days working as a rumrunner. Suddenly I was in a time warp, transported back to the Roaring Twenties by one of my boyhood heroes.

In 1920 the U S Congress passed a law that limited the sale of alcoholic beverages to 3.2% beer. At the time people referred to it simply as "Prohibition." The law changed a lot of things, but it didn't stop Americans from drinking. It just made it a lot harder to buy a drink, but where there is a will there is always a way. Prohibition created a nation of scofflaws and produced a new cottage industry of home brewers and wine makers (My father did both). But whiskey making required complicated stills and equipment, and the few entrepreneurs who tried it had to reckon with Federal Agents who made it almost impossible to survive. But there were plenty of offshore sellers eager to satisfy the thirst of American drinkers.

Although they were called rumrunners, their cargo was whisky and high proof alcohol that could be watered down and used in mixed drinks. The suppliers had sales offices at the Mount Royal Hotel in Montreal, Canada. Their warehouse on St. Pierre Island placed them outside the 12-mile limit and outside the reach of U S Law. There were several rum boats that carried the contraband from St. Pierre Island in to remote coves and tiny harbors along the coast of Maine. Lawrence, Massachusetts was a major distribution point for the rumrunners who ran trucks up to Maine to rendezvous with the rum boats. Trucks came to Lawrence from Detroit and New York City to pick up loads of booze. It was a highly organized and dangerous business to be in, but the pay was good.

In 1929 Herb began to build whiskey hides for some of the kingpins of the mob. He was only 20 years old and the pay was good and he was living "la dolce vita". He built a log cabin on Oors Island, Maine for one of the big shots that had a concealed whiskey hide under the floor. The island is near the end of a long peninsula south of Brunswick, Maine. The boss picked the spot because it was ideally situated to off-load rum boats in the isolated, sheltered harbor. Herb had fond memories of this isolated peninsula that was the scene of some of his best stories:

"We used to have a lot of fun up there. Christ, there was some wild women up there. I had a girl friend named Dot Smith. She used to ask me why I hung out with such rough guys, but I told her they were really good guys. She was nice. We used to go dancing at a joint they had up there. The other guys made fun of me because I was the only one going out with a virgin; I was only 20 years old you know. I drove up one day and they put me to work right away unloading whisky from a rum ship in the harbor. It was real cold and, when they finished loading my rowboat, I told them to pile on a few more cases cause I wanted to finish the job. I was rowing the boat wearing a fur coat and spats and the rowboat sank in shallow water and them other guys laughed like hell at me. I had to carry them cases of whiskey to shore in freezing water up to my chest."

One day a driver named Sparky ran a Reo truck loaded with 150 cases of whiskey off a dirt road into a ditch. A local woman named Mrs. Stephens brought over two horses and pulled the truck out of the ditch. Herb said that she was quite proud of the fact that she was a charter member of The Daughters of Pocahontas Association. The men offered her a substantial sum of money for her help, but she wouldn't accept it. Then, with a wry grin, Herb finished the anecdote:

"She wouldn't take the money mind ya, but she told the guys that there was one thing that she would like to have. She said that she would like a bottle of whisky, but she wanted to make sure that they understood it only for medicinal use."

Herb used to store some of his personal belongings down in the whisky hide. The Feds staged a raid and discovered the secret hiding place. They carried off Herb's personal things along with the store of whiskey. Herb was indignant:

"Them damn Feds stole everything I left there. There was a shotgun and six nice sweaters that I bought at McCartney's in Lawrence, and they stole em all. But we had a damn good lawyer, and when he finished with them, the Feds brought my sweaters and gun back the next day."

It was an easy move from building whiskey hides to driving rum trucks and Herb finally arrived in the big time.

"We used to pay $6.00 for a case of whiskey. There was 24 pint bottles in a case and the most popular brand was called Lincoln Inn. We paid $6.25 a case for that stuff. We bought some 3-gallon cans of Blue Belgian Alcohol that had the outline of a black hand printed on the side. Of course, when we got that stuff down to Lawrence we used to get $200 a case at places like the Turn Hall. Them guys would dilute it three or four to one before they sold it."

With total recall and great animation he described an episode that took place in Searsport, Maine.

"I'll never forget it because it was the 13th of the month. We were on shore waiting for the CASSASA to come in with 500 cases (1500 gallons). They named her after the mayor of Revere. Just when she was pulling into port the searchlights came on and all hell broke loose. It was a coast guard cutter and they had her boxed into the harbor. We couldn't do a damned thing. We had to leave the boat and the cargo and we hauled ass out of there. Later we found out that the biggest gun they had on board was a 45 caliber hand gun. "

I was scribbling notes as fast as I could write and I'd interject a question now and then to clarify a point or simply to slow him down:

"Herb, do you mean that the Mayor of Revere was in the business?"

"Naw, they just named the boat after him."

"What about the local authorities?

"Once I was bringing a load down from Maine to Lawrence and I called our headquarters in Lawence like I was supposed to do. They told me that the sheriff was waiting for me at the state line on Route 28. I went to my mother's place at Chase's Grove and dumped the load and then headed for Lawrence like nothing happened. They stopped me and let me go and later I went back and loaded up and came home another way."

I asked him if there was any truth to the story that he once stashed a load of booze out on the ice during the winter that broke through the ice and sank to the bottom. He responded, "I don't know anything about that." He didn't deny it; he didn't seem to want to talk about it. But he went on to describe another occasion when he wheeled into Chases and stashed his load of booze in the main room of his mother's camp. When he came back to pick up the load he discovered that the floor had caved in and all the booze was down in the crawl space under the camp. After he delivered the unbroken bottles to Lawrence, he had to rush back up to the camp and replace the floor joists and the floor before his mother discovered what had happened.

During the rum running days each gang member had an alias.

"I used the name Herb Mason because, being a carpenter, it was easy for me to remember."

By 1932 gang rivalries were increasing the risk factor and disturbing stories were beginning to filter back to Herb. The badly beaten body of a kingpin with the alias of Jack Murphy was found dead in a dory in Nova Scotia. He was known for making passes at the wives of some of the gang members. The brother of one of the Lawrence big shots was killed by the Detroit mob and he retaliated by having someone killed out there.

"I decided that I didn't want to be involved with that kind of stuff and I figured it was time for me to quit the business."

Herb was an outdoor man who enjoyed hunting deer and pheasant with his drinking buddies. Warren Kruschwitz tells the story about a hunting trip to Maine with Herb and some other local men. They were planning to pick up some supplies in Portland, but Herb was dead set against stopping there. When they persisted Herb finally admitted that he was wanted there by the local police. During his bootlegging days he had been picked up and jailed and bail was set pending his appearance in court. Somehow the authorities released him from jail before his compatriots actually posted the bail for his release. When they discovered the screw-up, Herb and his buddies took off for Massachusetts leaving the Portland authorities empty handed; they ended up with neither bail nor Herb.

Herb dominated the local scene with his bigger-than-life-reputation. His flamboyant personality and his reputation for fast cars and boats marked him as someone different. He was only 10 years older than we teenagers were, but his lifestyle seemed a world apart. He was a regular at the Chase's Grove dances on Friday and Saturday night. His tall erect figure and his trademark red plaid shirt seemed to dominate the dance floor. He was an excellent dancer. We watched in awe as he and his dancing partner pivoted, swirled and dipped to 1930s rhythms. His reputation for fast boats, pretty girls, and his chancy lifestyle and devil may care attitude made him a local folk hero.

Roland Korb's father Emil often bemoaned his lost opportunity in the rum business. During that era his bakery trucks ran delivery routes throughout greater Lawrence. Local bootleggers figured that he had the perfect setup to distribute their product but, in the end, he listened to the quiet counsel of his wife Lou and turned them down. Despite his refusal to cooperate with the rumrunners, the Feds stopped and searched his trucks on more than one occasion on trips to the pond. When I stayed with the Korb family in Germantown back in the 1930s I don't recall there ever being a shortage of beer or schnapps (whiskey). These were part of the culture of the period and Prohibition or not, they were not going to be denied.

When developers decided to put in ski trails at Franconia Notch, New Hampshire, Herb was there operating a bulldozer. The mere thought of operating a bulldozer on those slopes would send most men in search of a new occupation. If a machine happened to get sideways to the slope of the hill, there was a real danger of it rolling down the hill. The operator didn't stand much of a chance if he were thrown downhill from the tumbling bulldozer. To solve this problem they anchored winches at the top of the mountain and the dozers did their pushing downhill connected to a safety cable from the winch. The cable slowed things up and limited the maneuverability of the huge machines, but it was much safer for the operators. Everybody thought it was a great idea except Herb.

"I don't want no cable on my machine" he complained. "If it's my time to go damn-it—I'm gonna go!"

And Herb rode those mountains like he did everything else in his life; he was cocky, a little arrogant, and he was very sure he would come out on top.

It is not fair to let 3 years in the life of a 90 year old man mar an otherwise exemplary career. There were no compensating benefits to the problems created by Prohibition and the law turned out to be a disaster for the country. The American public routinely broke the law by patronizing illegal speakeasies. The legendary Robin Hood was also a lawbreaker but, in stealing from the rich to give to the poor, he became a legend. It is 70 years since Herb joined millions of Americans in circumventing a bad law. Yes—he did more than brew beer in his cellar, but then, that was Herb's style.

Herb spent much of his career working as a superintendent for J.F. Fitzgerald Construction Company of Boston. He built several bridges. He spent about three years up at Rumford, Maine building a huge power plant. During the Kennedy administration they asked him to go down to Washington to supervise the refurbishing of the gold dome on The Capitol Building. His wife refused to go and told him that if he decided to go she was going to leave him. People who recall Herb's wife Evelyn describe her as a saint. She is gone, but the husband that she tamed continues to confound those who know him.

As I prepared to leave I asked: "Hey Herb, if you were 20 when you got into that business, and your almost 90 now, do you think you might be the last rumrunner?

He thought for a moment,

"I don't know, Bucky might still be alive down in Lawrence" and then with a serious look, "Most of them other guys got shot off you know."

The look and the remark made it clear why he had been so reluctant to discuss that part of his life.

"Are you still dancing?" I asked.

"Oh yeah, I always loved to dance. We went down to the Lawrence Senior Citizens last week with all those Porto Ricans."

"Geez Herb," I exclaimed, "Did they have you dancing *The Meringue* down there?"

"Naw" he said. "My girl friend likes to line dance. That's what we do most"

A few days later I got a phone call from Herb. He sounded excited.

"Hey Spotty, I got a good story about the rumrunning business that I forgot to tell you the other day."

Laughing silently, I settled into my chair and thought of his daughter's advice:

"Just go down there and get him talking and he might surprise you."

I welcomed the chance to talk to him again because our last session had stirred personal memories. After listening to his story, I explained what was on my mind:

"Herb, when I was 14 I moved up to Milk Street in Methuen and I used to hang around with a kid named Buster. We played hockey together down at Hilsey's Pond and I used to visit him at his big house on Prospect Street. It's all gone now, but it was a big old farmhouse with an attached barn that faced Prospect Street. I knew his mother and brothers, but his father was never around. We had a lot of fun playing in the barn and climbing up to the hayloft and stuff like that. I never asked Buster, but the other kids used to say that his father was a bootlegger. Do you know who I'm talking about?"

"Sure, I used to work for that guy. He was one of the kingpins. He went by the name of Gus Daley."

" I was wondering if there might have been a whiskey hide under that barn?

"Yeah there was, but I never built it."

"Is that where they distributed the booze from?"

"Well yeah, but there was another place down on Park Street in Lawrence, but I ain't gonna tell you the name of that business, and then there was a club over Treat Hardware in Lawrence."

"Geez Herb, you mean you wuz sellin booze right there on the main drag?"

"Naw, it was around the corner on Broadway. That was a big building and there was a staircase on the Broadway side that went up to the Oval Club. It was up there, and oh yeah — we had another place in Haverhill on Water Street — it was 49 Water Street."

"Well I'm gonna use this material in the story Herb, but what about all those names?"

"Hell no, don't use no names, ya wanna get me killed or somethin, and by the way, am I gonna get a book?

"Of course! Maybe we can have an official presentation at the Senior Citizen's Club in Salem when I come up from Florida in May."

"O K Spotty, ya know I just turned 90 last month. There was a newspaper guy at the seniors the other day, and he told me I was the best dancer in the joint. I just hope I'm still here when you come up."

Minzner boys harvesting ice, 1928.

1938 - NOV.

Al Kayworth with 1930 Model A Ford,
at camp with Fred Minzner, November 1938.

1920-s Prohibition Party cartoon.

Chapter 10
AMERICAN STEAM PIONEER
George Eli Whitney
1862--1963

I t has been 51 years since the steamer Ida F last steamed through the tranquil waters of Big Island Pond. For 48 years she cruised the picturesque coves, the channels and the broad reach of the main lake loaded with happy campers and picnickers. She was 31 feet long with an 8-foot beam and she carried 25 passengers under her canopy. The clean lines of her hull and the quiet efficiency of her steam propulsion plant made her queen of the pond and, despite man's talent for innovation, we have not seen her equal on the pond since the summer of 1948. She was the brainchild of George Whitney, an inventor of uncommon talent, who experts of his generation labeled a mechanical genius. Through the research efforts of Captain Richard Jones,[48] of Wellman's Ledge in Hampstead, we can all share the fascinating details of Whitney's long illustrious career as a world authority on steam propulsion systems. After achieving fame as a designer and builder of marine steam engines, his Whitney Steam Carriage was a forerunner of the Automobile Age that began in the late 1800s.

Chief Escumbuit, Benning Wentworth and Alan Shepard rose to great heights on the power of their ambition. Whitney's fame went largely unpublicized, but he was equally driven to excel and his achievements were formidable. Although their talents varied widely, these legends from Big Island Pond's past shared a common

---

[48] *America's Steam-Car Pioneers*, John H. Bacon, Princeton University Press, 1984: All of the details of Whitney's life up until his arrival at Big Island Pond are based on facts presented in this excellent book.

singularity; each of them chose to follow the trail of his dreams with a passion unmatched by others. Chief Escumbuit's quest to drive the English from his ancestral lands carried him from Andover to Newfoundland and then to the Palace of Versailles in France. Benning Wentworth, the first Royal Provincial Governor, established New Hampshire's first summer resort at Big Island Pond in 1741. Alan Shepard followed his boyhood dream into space and then on to the moon itself and George Whitney achieved world fame as a designer and builder of steam powered marine engines and steam carriages before he was 35 years old!

The name Whitney elicits thoughts of inventors, industrialists and entrepreneurs. His father, John Webster Parkins Whitney was a highly skilled engraver who made gold and silver dies for the Philadelphia Mint. Uncle Amos Whitney founded Pratt & Whitney Company, which manufactures over 1/3 of the world's jet engines for the military and the airlines. His Uncle Clarence founded the Whitney Chain Company in Bridgeport and his great grandfather's brother was the famous inventor of the cotton gin. Eli Whitney would have swelled with pride over the mechanical marvels created by his "great nephew" George E. Whitney. Yet, during his years at Big Island Pond he seemed to shun the celebrity his record deserved. He quietly became part of the local scene.

Born in 1862, Whitney was raised in Boston where he displayed his mechanical ability at a very young age. At 12, his favorite playground was the yard of the Boston and Albany Railroad where he spent many hours watching the "iron horses" roll by. Franklin D Child, superintendent of the Hinkley Locomotive Works, took an interest in the young lad with a passion for steam engines and he gave the boy a set of blueprints for a Hinkley locomotive saying, "Here you go lad, take these home and study them." Study them he did and, incredibly, he spent the next 8 years building a small working model from the blueprints. The achievement is tempered only slightly by the fact that he was able to make many of the parts at the Pratt & Whitney plant on weekends and holidays under the critical eye of his uncle Amos Whitney. Of course, without the use of the casting and machining equipment at his uncle's plant, his project would have been impossible, nevertheless, he made every single part himself. This included auxiliary equipment such as safety valve, steam gauge, whistle, cylinder oilers, leaf springs between frame and axles and automatic pumps. These were scale models of the real thing.

Whitney got his early education at the local Boston public schools and he later attended the Massachusetts Institute of Technology where he completed the 2-year course offered by the School of Mechanical Engineering. There were early signs that young George had interests outside the realm of mechanical engineering. He spent a great deal of time building his physique at the Young Men's Christian Union in Boston. Among the many photographs that Dick Jones' research uncovered is a photo of a 22 year old Whitney in a muscle pose revealing a sturdy, handsome young man. Notes on the photo indicate that he was 5' 6" tall and weighed 142 lbs. He had the look of a fit welterweight boxer. After finishing his education at the Massachusetts Institute of Technology he spent a few years working part time for S.H. Roper where he performed various tasks of steam fitting and boiler making. In his spare time he purchased a used boat hull from the athletic director of the W.M.C.U. and fitted it out with a steam engine of his own design. Having come from a close knit, supportive family, it was characteristic of him to name his boat "The Olive" after his mother.

An examination of Whitney's early life reveals a young man whose character seems exemplary in every way. Although an accident in a blacksmith shop had cost him the use of one eye as a boy, he seemed destined to move through life untouched by misfortune, but that was not to be. Ida F. Tufts, the girl he courted and married in 1886, died unexpectedly only two years after they wed. Perhaps it was an early warning that his life would not be without its trials. At the age of 25 Whitney was finally ready to lay down the foundation for his life's work. He formed a partnership with a man named Joseph Crowther and they started a machine shop in Boston near Haymarket Square. Whitney operated the business as a sole proprietorship after his partner left and he was soon building steam launches and yachts. He contracted the hulls to local boat builders, but the overall designs were his own and he equipped them with Whitney designed engines. His reputation grew rapidly and soon he was receiving orders from Maine to Florida. At an age when most men are just settling into their first job Whitney was already famous!

In 1888 He hired an apprentice named Nathanial Coolidge who eventually became his assistant, confidante and lifelong friend. Coolidge later wrote that he met Whitney when he was installing the engine on the steamer Turtle at the Allen Hayes Boatyard in Lynn. He wrote that Whitney was also the captain of a boat in that area. By 1890 Whitney and Coolidge had built or fitted engines to 96 steamboats along the Eastern Seaboard. In 1890 they moved their shop to a permanent location at Mayo's Wharf in East Boston. As non-marine uses for steam power plants grew, Whitney quickly moved to adapt his marine models to serve new markets. A most unusual order came from the Singer Sewing Machine Company. Singer had a ready market for their sewing machines in China, but they found that many of the Chinese women were unable to operate their manual machines. For many centuries the feet of Chinese female infants were bound for cosmetic reasons; Chinese men coveted women with tiny deformed feet. These women lacked the flexibility in their ankles and toes to operate the foot treadle that supplied power to their sewing machines. A Singer agent contracted Whitney to produce 100 small steam engines with integral boilers that were designed to drive standard Singer sewing machines. Before operating these machines the women had to fill the boiler with water and then build a small coal or wood fire in the firebox to generate the steam needed to operate their sewing machine.

The steam carriage bug bit Whitney when Sylvester Roper took him for a ride in an early 1885 model. In the era before the introduction of the gasoline engine, steam seemed to be the power of the future—on land, on the sea and, perhaps, even in the air! Although railway locomotives and boats offered the necessary space to accommodate boilers and fireboxes, designers were under pressure to develop smaller models that could be adapted to a variety of other uses. Whitney became interested when Sylvester Roper asked him to machine two cylinders for an experimental steam bicycle. (Roper later died of a heart attack while road-testing this experimental vehicle.)

In 1885 William Mason of the Mason Regulator Company of Boston came to Whitney and asked him to design a small engine that could be fitted to carriages. Whitney modified a small, high-pressure marine engine and came up with a compact version equipped with a chain drive sprocket. Early steam carriage experimenters quickly adopted this design. Mason was soon producing engines in lots of 100 and shipping them all over the country. Neither Whitney nor Mason had bothered to secure a patent on the engine, and soon other automotive experimenters were copying Whitney's design. Some of the names of companies that used Mason engines still have a familiar ring to old-timers: Stanley Steamer, Clark Steam Car Co, Locomobile Co, Milwaukee Automobile Co, and Overman Carriage Co were well-known companies of the period. And for his design of what has been described as "the first production engine for the American Automotive Industry," William Mason paid George Whitney the princely sum of $200.

Whitney designed several steam carriages before he began construction on a model that he intended for his own use. As he began his construction in 1893, he never could have predicted the problems that lay ahead. As the lioness protects her kill from the hyenas and vultures of the jungle, so does a successful man have to guard against the deceitful and greedy who seek to prey on the hard earned success of others. An 1896 article in The Horseless Carriage describing Whitney's work on a prototype steam carriage appears to have been the catalyst that invited trouble to his shop in East Boston.

The Latest Steam Wagon in Boston

"George E. Whitney, designer and builder of marine engines, East Boston, Mass, is about completing a four-wheeled steam vehicle, the fifth that he has so far designed. The front wheels are 30 inches in diameter and the rear ones 34 inches. All are of wood, and are fitted with 2-inch pneumatic tires. The boiler is 14x20 inches and contains 340 half-inch copper tubes, 13 inches in length. The engine is double, and has 2x4 inch piston valves. It is reversible and is geared to the hind wheels, 2 to 1. The boiler is built for 125 pounds of steam and the engine has cut-off valves at from ¼ to 5/8 stroke. The fuel is kerosene oil. The water consumption on a run of 50 miles, over a road so bad that it requires 125 pounds of steam, half stroke, wide open, is calculated to be about 240 pounds. This, so Mr.

Whitney states, has not been tried, but he believes his wagon would not be run on so bad a road as to require such an expenditure of power for 50 miles in the State of Massachusetts. He estimates the average power required as not more than half this, or two horse power at a speed of 15 miles an hour. He has four horsepower indicated, and can maintain it on a total weight of 600 pounds."

This publicity about a steam carriage that could travel 50 miles in a little more than 3 hours attracted wide attention. Shortly after the article appeared, a man came to Whitney's shop bringing with him a steam engine that he was planning to use in a steam propelled vehicle. Charles D. P. Gibson was a partner in a New York City jewelry business who was obsessed with building a steam automobile. Although he had no engineering experience he had designed his own steam engine. A Providence, Rhode Island machinist had built the engine he brought with him. The engine was worthless and he was hoping that Whitney could salvage his failed venture. Whitney agreed to rent space in his shop where Gibson hoped to salvage his project. Gibson must have been an expert con man to be able to persuade Whitney to go along with his plan. The first thing he did was erect a high partition around his work area so that neither Whitney nor his workers could steal his secret design features. Meanwhile he had the run of Whitney's shop to learn whatever he could about the business. His open access to Whitney's expertise soon made him realize that he would be a fool to spend any more time and money on his own failed design and, after a couple of weeks, he announced that he was abandoning his project. He then focused his attention on buying Whitney's vehicle that was nearing completion. The boiler had not yet been installed, but Whitney managed to give Gibson a demonstration. He connected a flexible steam hose from a separate steam generator to the carriage engine and drove it in forward and reverse around the floor of the shop. Gibson decided he **had** to have that machine! Having spent almost three years building the carriage for his own use, Whitney jacked the price up to $2,500 in order to discourage Gibson. However, Gibson showed up the next day with $2,500 in cash and the machine was his!

Gibson was so taken with his new purchase that he stayed on to watch the completion of his new toy. Two years after the death of his first wife Whitney had remarried a woman named Annie M. Savery. Whitney, always accommodating, invited Gibson to stay at his home during the completion of his vehicle. In a final friendly gesture, Whitney offered to accompany Gibson as far at Wakefield, Rhode Island in his new carriage. Their arrival in Wakefield created quite a stir as it was the first steam carriage that the residents of the town had ever seen. A reporter from a local newspaper interviewed them, and they took some of the prominent citizens of the town out for a trial spin. Gibson, as owner of the vehicle, expounded on the reliability and speed of his new vehicle and Whitney modestly acknowledged being the designer and builder. After spending the night at a local hotel the two men parted company. Whitney boarded a train to Boston and Gibson headed for Stonington where he planned to take a boat to New York City. The closer he got to home the more Gibson's true nature began to reveal itself. The first of the two newspaper articles that follow was written the day the two men arrived in Wakefield. The second article was written after Whitney left for Boston.

The First Horseless Carriage in Town

"The first horseless carriage or motor wagon ever seen in Wakefield wheeled into town Friday night with two occupants who had made the trip from Providence in about six hours. They stayed at the DeLester house over night and Saturday morning one of the gentlemen started off alone bound for New York, while the other returned to Boston by train. This was George E Whitney of Boston, who is the inventor and builder. He has been experimenting for ten years with "automobiles" as these vehicles are called in France. This one was built to order for C.E.P. Gibson of Jersey City, who designed the body and its fittings, and who was taking this trip as an experiment to see how well the machine would run over rough country roads."

The information in the second article was based on an interview with Gibson after he arrived alone in Stoningham Saturday afternoon. With Whitney on a Boston bound train Gibson began to spin a new yarn.

From Boston to Stoningham

"Saturday afternoon a horseless carriage wheeled briskly into Stoningham from the east. The occupant, who said he was the inventor of the vehicle, told a group of interested spectators, which quickly gathered around, that he had come directly from Boston making the trip from the city to Providence in 2 hours and 32 minutes. He said that he had made one mile in 1 minute and 32 seconds and that the carriage had a speed capacity beyond his courage to drive it. The inventor talked freely with the crowd and told them he had just come from East Boston where the machine was built according to his design. He stated further that the cost of the carriage complete was $7,000, but that he could build future vehicles of the same kind for $1,500.

Gibson traveled to New York City by boat from where he drove the carriage to his home in New Jersey. With no one to challenge his claim to be the inventor of his new steam carriage, he proceeded to execute the rest of his plan with incredible chutzpah. He had the vehicle dismantled and had scale drawings made of every single part. He then applied for a patent on his invention and, in 1900 after swearing under oath that he was the true inventor of the vehicle, was awarded U S Patent #622,571--for a vehicle that was 100% designed and built by George Whitney!

When Whitney learned about the fraudulent patent he filed suit. Gibson countered by hiring a New York lawyer named Hotchkiss who did his best to bolster his client's case. During the course of his Boston inquiries he developed an intimate relationship with Whitney's wife Annie. The extent of that friendship became apparent to Whitney after he learned that he was going to receive $40,000 for the patent rights on his prototype vehicle. Having been given the information about this settlement by Hotchkiss, Annie confronted Whitney and demanded half of the money. She threatened to testify at an appeal hearing that Gibson was the true inventor of the steam carriage. Whitney promptly divorced his wife and a short time later she married Hotchkiss.

When one analyzes the twists and turns of this strange chapter in Whitney's life one is led to conclude that he must have been born under a lucky star. After being deceived by Gibson and made cuckold by Hotchkiss, he hadn't fared too badly. In a single stroke of fortune he got $40,000 for his steam buggy design, and he rid himself of an untrustworthy wife without having to pay her alimony.

Throughout this entire fiasco Whitney continued to operate his business successfully and the number of early experimenters in steam car design who visited his shop increased with his fame. Names like J. Frank Duryea, Ransom E. Olds, the Stanley brothers, Albert Pope, Harry K. Knox, J.B. Walker and A. L. Barber were among the visitors to his plant in East Boston. The Stanley Brothers eventually designed and sold the Stanley Steamer, a famous steam car of the day. Their complete lack of formal training, oddly enough, proved an advantage; their farm-bred expertise in solving complicated problems was unencumbered by formal engineering dogma. They were skilled at finding practical solutions to what seemed to be insurmountable engineering problems. Steam pressure and boiler design were two limiting factors in steam engine design. Where conservative engineers like Whitney and Roper believed 150 pounds of steam pressure was excessive, the Stanley Brothers were experimenting with 200 and 300 pounds pressure. Engineers of the period were hung up by the notion that the only way they could achieve higher steam pressures was by designing boilers so heavy that they were impractical. The Stanley brothers discovered that they could achieve the same results by applying a tightly wound layer of piano wire to standard boilers with little increase in the overall weight.

Anyone who has ever been in business knows that success often attracts imitators. There are always envious people who are quick to take advantage of the hard work and sacrifice of successful people. It is not surprising that these are the very same people who, given the opportunity, will attempt to feed off a successful man's achievement without any ethical qualms. Whitney's friendship with the Stanley Brothers began to cool after they began to design their own steam carriage. The brothers had come from a farm in Kingston, Maine and they were frequent visitors to Whitney's East Boston shop. Although they lacked formal engineering credentials, they were good at solving problems using the practical experience they had gained on the farm. They took full advantage of their friendly visits to Whitney's shop. When they set out to build their first Stanley Steamer the gratuitous advice offered by George Whitney was their most valuable asset. They hired two of Whitney's key employees, Frank Killam and George Hatch, to help them build their first model. Frank Killam brought along patterns for Whitney's 14-inch boiler with 298 tubes and this duo proceeded to design a machine for the Stanley brothers using many features already patented by Whitney.

In spite of his generous and open nature Whitney did not hesitate once he learned that his trust had been betrayed. His "friendship" with the Stanley brothers ended when he filed two patent infringements against the brothers. After the Stanley Brothers lost the suit they had to redesign their carriage but that didn't stop them from trying to steal Whitney's ideas. In 1898 Whitney displayed two steam carriages at a giant bicycle exposition held at Mechanics Hall in Boston. In addition to bicycles, there were a number of steam and gasoline vehicles displayed in the main hall. Whitney astutely displayed his vehicle in the basement. Unlike his competitors he had sufficient space to demonstrate his vehicle by driving it in forward and reverse and by demonstrating its braking power. Whitney's live demonstration in the basement delighted the crowds to the huge annoyance of the manufactures on the main floor who had paid premium prices for their space. His vehicle resembled a horse buggy minus the shafts normally used to hitch up the horse. It was equipped with a foot pedal that the operator used to feed kerosene to the firebox. The driver drove the vehicle using a tiller-like device that incorporated all of the necessary controls. A whip mounted within easy reach of the driver was provided to repel attacking dogs and run-a-way horses.

One morning Whitney came into the exposition early and found the Stanley Brothers making a detailed inspection of his vehicle. One was lying under the vehicle taking measurements and the other was taking photos of the vehicle from every conceivable angle. When Whitney complained to the show management, they refused to take action They contended that by signing a contract to display his car he was in fact consenting to having it examined in every detail by any person who bought a ticket to the show.

In connection with this same show there were outdoor events staged at the Charles River Park that were billed as: Motor Carriage Contest, Charles River Park. At the time this park had a 1/3-mile oval track and a 5,000-person grandstand. The list of contestants on the cover of the announcement for the event clearly showed how world competition in automobile design was beginning to heat up. Of the 12 vehicles entered only 2 were steam driven. There were 3 electric contestants and internal combustion gas engines powered the remaining 7 entries. Three of the gasoline-powered models were from France. Another page of the program listed: "Particulars of Competition." Among these particulars were such features as manageability and braking power, but the sponsors only had time to stage a competition for speed and grade climbing ability.

The night before the competition the sports director of the Boston Herald called the show director to make arrangements for the Stanley Brothers to take part in the competition. Their latest model had no reverse gear, but it was very fast due to the high steam pressure they generated in their patented-wire-wound boiler. The show management posted $1,100 in prize money and large crowds turned out to line the parade route of the horseless vehicles from Mechanics Hall to the Charles River Park. The 2-mile pursuit race was the most popular event of the competition. Whitney ran in a heat against 3 gasoline powered vehicles and came in second behind the French Dion gasoline tricycle which made the run in 5m I-2/5 s. They built an 80 foot wooden ramp inclined at 35 degrees to measure the grade climbing ability of the contestants. Each vehicle had to make its run from a stationary start 20 feet in front of the ramp. Both the Whitney and the Stanley steamers did surprisingly well in this competition. In fact they were the only two vehicles to reach the top of the 80-foot ramp. In a final exhibition the Stanley Steamer astonished the spectators by running the one-mile course in 2 minutes and 11 seconds.

The principal message to take from this event was that there was a huge unfulfilled demand in America for an affordable mechanical vehicle. From our modern perspective we know that the handwriting was already on the wall in regards to the future of the steam carriage. At the time, however, the steam carriages more than held their own against the best gasoline vehicles of the day. There was never any indication that Whitney considered going to conventional gasoline engines. He was a steam man.

Throughout this period he continued to design and manufacture boilers and engines for the marine industry, but he continued to experiment with steam carriages and he spent a lot of time touring New England road testing his designs. He was keen on forming a company to build and market steam carriages to the public, but he knew he needed outside capital.

In 1897 he formed a partnership with George P. Upham, a Boston lawyer and former member of the state legislature. The *Whitney Motor Company* was organized with $300,000 capital and Whitney began to tour New England giving demonstrations and distributing printed literature about his car. His uncle Amos Whitney, who was president of Pratt & Whitney in Hartford, followed his progress with great interest. Amos made a proposal to his board of directors that the firm begin producing steam automobiles based on the designs and patents of his nephew, but his board turned him down.

The blossoming automobile industry in the United States was beginning to attract the attention of well-heeled investors who envisioned profits beyond the dreams of avarice. John B. Walker, the owner of the *Cosmopolitan Magazine*, sponsored a road race for steam vehicles in New York City. He approached the Stanley brothers to buy their company. The brothers were reluctant to sell and they tried to discourage Walker by asking $250,000 for their business. Walker responded by saying that $250,000 was exactly the figure he had in mind and the stunned Stanley brothers sold their company. Walker then turned to A. L. Barber, a New York millionaire for the cash he needed to close the deal. For his contribution, Barber got a ½ interest in the company that he and Walker organized in Bridgeport, Connecticut. They named their new venture the Locomobile Company.

At about the same time Whitney and George Upham signed an agreement with the Anderson Manufacturing Company in Boston to manufacture steam cars for them. In 1899 they sailed for France with one of their models hoping to sell the European patent rights for their vehicle. After selling the British rights for $10,000 they ran into A. L. Barber in Paris. He offered Whitney and Upham $250,000 for the Whitney patents with the proviso that they abandon their plans to manufacture cars. His ownership of both the Stanley and Whitney patents gave him a virtual monopoly on American steam carriage production. When Whitney and Upham returned to the United States they paid Anderson $10,000 compensation to cancel their contract and Whitney took a job as chief engineer for the new Locomobile Company in Bridgeport, Connecticut.

Barber wanted to use some of the features from Whitney's latest steam carriage in his new Locomobile, but he wanted to make sure that these engineering changes were sound. He sent Whitney on a 10-day, 1,000 mile trip to road test Whitney's features. Being a canny man, he sent along an observer to insure that he would get an accurate report of the vehicle's performance. The first three days the passenger, who was a high-strung fellow, gave Whitney a hard time with his abusive behavior. The car was performing beautifully, but they had to stop often to repair blowouts in tires that were very fragile in those days. After suffering his passenger's complaints for three days Whitney found a remedy; he discovered that the man was fond of beer. The next time they blew a tire Whitney, who had traveled the route before, limped along on the flat rim to the next tavern where he deposited his passenger. While Whitney struggled to repair and mount a new tire his rider was taking on a load of beer. They continued in that manner until they had completed the 1,000-mile trip. Whitney said later that he suffered no further abuse from the man who spent most of his time between tavern stops dozing in his seat.

In 1901 and 1902 it was becoming obvious that gas was going to replace steam and Barber, seeing the handwriting on the wall, schemed to sell his steam patents to Walker. Walker finally bought the patents, but the Locomobile Company was in financial trouble and Upham and Whitney were having trouble collecting the money owed them for Whitney's patents. They reluctantly took 30 Locombiles worth a total of $15,000 in a last ditch effort to retrieve their money. Whitney sold a few of these carriages for $800 and $900 each, but the cost of storage was high, and he finally ended up storing four of these steam carriages at Big Island Pond. The Locomobile Company changed over to gas in 1902 and continued building quality gas cars until 1928.

A.L. Barber had made his money selling asphalt to New York City and other municipalities. He owned tar pits in Trinidad and his dream of building automobiles to travel on his asphalt pavement looked like a winning parlay. He financed Whitney's development of a massive machine designed to mould asphalt blocks faster and cheaper than had been done previously. These machines became standard for that industry and were sold all over the world. Whitney designed a huge model that was assembled on 8 flatbed railroad cars. It delivered the manufacturing facility right to the job to lower cost and speed up construction. This Barber dream vanished in thin air when the concrete block industry emerged to produce a superior product at a lower cost.

His life long friend and associate Nathanial Coolidge generally oversaw the manufacture of his designs while Whitney was off somewhere turning concepts into inventions. He built a colossal hay press that proved to be a cheap way to bale Texas hay and ship it to France on freighters. He sold his patent rights on a domestic furnace stoker to Link Belt in the 1930s, and in World War 11 he designed a compound steam engine that was used in about 300 submarine chasers that were built to hunt down German U-boats in the Atlantic.

Whitney's work ethic and workmanship were legend in the industry. A man named Ted Middleton of Aberdeen, Washington ordered a compound marine engine from Whitney to be installed in a 35' hull that was being custom-built for him. Whitney's engine arrived before the boat was finished and he had it set up on a cradle in his office where he could admire Whitney's beautiful efficient design and exquisite workmanship. When they finally installed the engine in his new boat the empty spot on his office floor so annoyed him that he had Whitney build him a duplicate engine at a cost of $1,500. This anecdote best illustrates Whitney's credo:

"There is nothing worth doing that is not worth doing well."

George Whitney was an astute businessman and a brilliant engineer, but the horse he entered in the race was not suited to the field; perhaps he felt it was too late to withdraw his entry and begin anew. In fact, steam propulsion is superior to internal combustion, except for the fact that one has to wait for the water or other liquid to heat, and there is the additional problem of maintaining the liquid level in the boiler. If those two problems had been overcome we might all be driving steamers today, and George Whitney may have been remembered as the father of America's automobile industry.

There is a question that hangs unanswered—what motivated George Whitney to come to Big Island Pond? What prompted him to build a camp and a steam launch and sink his roots at this secluded place? The nature of his work brought him into contact with the rich and powerful, and the venue of his activities brought him to resort areas like Bar Harbor, Newport, and Marblehead. I suppose his decision to live at the pond tells us something about the type of person he was. Probably the simple answer is that, after rubbing elbows with the rich and famous, Whitney sought a return to the simple life. The view from his home was the pond and framed in that view was the Ida F. There were no tides to be concerned with nor barnacles to scrape, and his workshop was a few steps away. There he was free to do what he loved best, and there were plenty of things to keep him busy. He could polish his hand-made steam engine and he had his daily routine of lighting a hardwood fire in the firebox for the boiler. He could cast off and head for Howard's Grove to pick up a load of passengers. And, perhaps best of all, it was a place where he could relax and be himself.

The summer of 1900 witnessed a quantum leap in watercraft design on the pond. Local residents watched with interest as George Eli Whitney put the finishing touches to his handsome boat and prepared to launch her. She was 31 feet long with an open cockpit topped by a fringed canopy supported by pipe standards. When Whitney cast off for his maiden voyage from Chase's Grove, folks lined the shore to watch the clean bow of Whitney's new boat cut through the water. And the most spectacular feature of the new boat was that it cruised in almost complete silence because it was powered by a unique steam engine whose firebox was stoked with hard wood.

His large boathouse located on the edge of what is now known as the Whitney Shore had a fully equipped machine shop. Whitney built things to last. He constructed a stone jetty that jutted out into the pond about 100 feet. The jetty acted as a breakwater for waves driven by September winds. A set of rails ran from the front of his boathouse out on to this stone pier. The boat in its wheeled cradle was launched over an inclined set of rails. In the fall, the boat was secured to its cradle and pulled back into the shed for winter storage. Residents still refer to that area as Whitney's Grove.

In a letter to a friend he described the design as a 4x7x6 inch "triangle compound" engine of which only two models were built. The larger 7x14x9 inch engine was fitted to the steamboat Montauk. (Possibly linked to Montauk Point on Long Island) In his letter he drew a simple freehand drawing of his "triangle compound" design. With a few simple strokes of his pen he was able to show the essential components of his design.

Warren Stickney told me that Whitney was interested in a young local boy who became sort of a protégé." Like his famous mentor the boy seemed to have been born with a natural curiosity and urge to tinker with mechanical things. He was an indifferent student in grammar school except for one subject—he got straight A's in math. As his classmates were making plans to go to high school, he was dreaming about going to trade school. As a kid, he spent most of his time down at the pond where he began to hang around Whitney's machine shop on the shoreline. Despite a wide disparity in age and experience, the old engineer and the simple country boy were drawn together by their fascination with mechanical things. The young protégé may have helped fill a void in Whitney's life created by the premature death of his only son. They were an odd pair--an *American Steam Pioneer* and a local *Shade Tree Mechanic*--but their friendship endured.

This protégé is now 72 years old and is the proprietor of Dick's Motor Service on Island Pond Road, which is located just north of Pete's Garage. There, in living quarters connected to the garage where he repairs long haul trucks, lives Russell E Dickey, onetime confidante of George Whitney. Strewn about his large shop are reminders of his former mentor. He has Whitney's drill press and an old metal lathe and large calipers bearing Whitney's stamp. His most spectacular possession is a very large monkey wrench that came from Whitney's old shop. We put a tape to this wrench and it is 48 inches long and weighs 80 pounds. To me that wrench symbolizes the legend of George Whitney; though small in stature he thought big and, like Paul Bunyan, the tools of his trade were big! That prodigious wrench would be a good exhibit in an industrial museum.

Russ says that many years ago someone stole Whitney's steamboat and that it was eventually recovered down by the Merrimac River. They never could figure out how the thieves managed to transport the boat; it would have required a large trailer. Russ says that in 1948 Whitney sold his steamboat to a playboy who owned a nightclub. He came back from a night cruise on the pond at about 2 am and left a coal fire burning in the fire box and forgot to top off the water in the boiler. When the water steamed away, the overheated boiler ignited the hull and burned a hole in the side. They salvaged the steam engine and, according to Russell, it was in service on a steamboat up at Lake Winnipesaukee until about 1990.

Today Mr. & Mrs. Davey own Whitney's old camp. In 1962 their son Joe was swimming and diving off the end of Whitney's stone jetty. One of his flippers uncovered an object on the bottom that he brought to the surface. The old, discolored metal object fascinated him and he began to clean it with some brass polish he got from a neighbor. At first his mother urged him to throw it in the trash, but when his labor produced a shining 8" brass steam gauge from the Ida F, his mother mounted it on the camp wall as an ornament. As I listened to Joe Davey and Russell Dickey reminisce about Whitney, it was clear that *The Steam Pioneer* has become a cult figure to those who remember him well. According to Joe Davey, Whitney was well connected with officials of the Arlington, Pacific and Wood Mills. It was they who persuaded him to build and operate the Ida F to give cruises on the pond during outings for their mill workers.

The most interesting single item in Russell Dickey's collection of Whitney relics is a hot air pump that Whitney used to provide running water to his camp. Russ is presently working on this unique engine and expects to restore it to working order. He has already spent $1400 to have one of the critical parts recast. Henry Wood of England patented the design of the engine in 1759, but it wasn't until 1807 that Sir George Cayley built the first working model. The Caloric Engine Company of England and Roper Caloric Engine Company in the United States later produced improved versions. In 1816 the Rev. Robert Stirling made further improvements for which he is credited to be the inventor of the "Stirling Engine." The Rider Ericsson Hot Air Pumping Engine that Russ is restoring is named after the same Ericksson who built the steel-clad Monitor for the North early in the Civil War. Whitney undoubtedly bought this engine in Boston from his former employer and associate, Sylvester Roper. This unique engine has no carburetor, ignition system, valves or other complicated mechanisms. The source of heat can be wood, kerosene, sunlight or geothermal sources.

Photographs and operating details of this antique engine can be viewed at the web site rustyiron.com. The web site is the brainchild of Robert Skinner of La Habra, California, who owns a rebuilt Ericksson-Rider hot air engine. In the first month of the new millennia Skinner had a surprise visitor. Russ had traveled 3000 miles to see a live demonstration of a smaller version of the engine he is rebuilding in Derry. I asked Russ what motivated him to expend all that money and time to restore an engine that has no practical use in the modern world:

"Well, if you owned it wouldn't you want to see if you could make it work?" he asked.

And, if I read Russell Dickey correctly, he won't rest until that Rube Goldberg contraption from a bygone age is pumping water out in his back yard.

The mechanism consists of a single large cylinder driven by the heat-generated expansion of air. Each stroke pumped approximately 1/3 cup of water to an elevated cistern mounted beside Whitney's camp. The water in the cistern was gravity fed to a faucet in his camp. He started the engine by building a wood fire in the firebox. When the fire got good and hot he gave the heavy flywheel a gentle spin and let the hot air do the rest. When the cistern filled up, George let the fire burn out. Bill Chase says that Whitney also designed a windmill that he used to pump water out of the pond.

Russell Dickey is an engaging guy. One would never guess by glancing at the non-descript collection of buildings and trucks on his property that he once "hung out" with the famous George Whitney and that he is the unofficial curator of Whitney memorabilia. When I asked Russ what kind of a man Whitney was he responded, "Oh, he was a great guy, I never worked for him, we just used to hang out together." To talk to Russell today in his world of trucks and tools and gadgets is to understand what George Whitney saw in him that drew them together so many years ago.[49]

I was in Russ's shop one day with a man named Johnson who is an engineer and a steam engine enthusiast. The rusty parts to Whitney's 100-plus-year-old Rider-Erickson hot air engine were strewn around and we were looking at a heavy cast piece that had a hole in it. It was an inverted bell-shaped part that bolted on top of the firebox. We gazed at it for a moment until Johnson suggested:

"Maybe you can patch it by filling the hole with molten metal."
Russ thought for a few seconds and answered:

"Naw—the whole thing is porous—your ass would be porous too if it hung over a hot fire as long as that thing has."
Russell is not really a profane guy; sometimes he says outrageous things but, like *The Last Rumrunner,* he is always entertaining.

The Ida F was a common sight on the pond for 48 summers and was the highlight of the day for hundreds of people who attended outings at Chase's Grove and Howard's Grove. Bertha MacDougal (now Bertha Smith) of Derry remembers collecting 10-cent fares for rides on Whitney's steamboat. She says that on weekends they headed for Howard's Grove where they knew they could always pick up a boatload of passengers. Whitney developed a regular routine for these cruises. He would stop the boat in a picturesque cove and entertain the youngsters with lurid tales about pirates. Residents could tell the Ida F was out on the pond by listening for the

---

[49] Author's note: My friend Arthur McEvoy triggered the chain of events that led me to Russell Dickey. He told me that he tried unsuccessfully to buy a steam carriage that was stored in Walter Stickney's cellar. When I checked with Warren Stickney, he told me that the steam carriage was already in the cellar when his father bought the house. During the course of my conversation with Warren he mentioned that Whitney had a protégé named Russell Dickey. When I located Russ at his place on Island Pond Road he told me that the steam carriage in Whitney's cellar was a Locomobile that Whitney received as payment on an outstanding debt. It was one of four Locomobiles that Whitney stored at Island Pond. I never found out how the steam carriage got into that cellar, but my friendship with Russell Dickey and the story of his hot air engine began with Arthur McEvoy's lead on Stickney's steam carriage.

distinctive notes of his steam calliope playing "Mary had a little lamb" or "How dry I am." He often prepared a special treat for his personal friends. After a tour of the pond, he entertained them by serving them lobsters cooked in steam he drew from his boiler. In the cleanup that followed, the shells went overboard and today the cove is identified on navigation maps as Lobster Cove. Hundreds of years from now archeologists may scratch their heads as they study the map of a freshwater pond located 30 miles from the ocean and wonder why a certain cove is identified as Lobster Cove, or they might even turn up some of the shells!

Bill Dixon told me that one summer Whitney was appointed the official boat inspector. In stark contrast to high-speed boats manned by uniformed inspectors, Whitney patrolled the pond in his steamboat. Bill Dixon remembers seeing a young lawbreaker, throttle wide open, heading for Hampstead in his small outboard with Whitney's steamer in hot pursuit. He could not say whether Whitney managed to ticket the youngster.

Most men never experience the measure of pride and accomplishment that Whitney must have savored in designing and building his own steam propelled boat. The sheer utility of his craft must have delighted him. 80-year-old resident, Roland Korb tells an interesting tale about a boyhood experience helping Whitney pull stumps out of the channel at the north end of the pond. When the original dam was constructed in the 1878, the raised water level killed many large trees in the swampy passage between the main body of water and the Hampstead shore. In the early 1930s the channel was still littered by submerged rotting stumps. If Whitney deviated from the narrow confines of the channel he could easily run into a submerged stump. By then George Whitney was in his early 70s. He took a liking to the tow-headed youngster, and decided to put him to work. He and Roland steamed down to the channel looking for underwater obstructions. When they located a waterlogged stump, Roland went over the side with a manila line and slipped the loop of a lasso around it. Then, with the free end of the line secured to the stern of the steamer, Whitney opened his throttle wide and when the slack came out of the line, the rotten stump was jerked free of the muddy bottom. The captain then throttled back and cruised up the pond with the waterlogged stump trailing behind until they reached the deepest part. Arriving there, Whitney tied off a smaller line connected to the loop of the lasso. When he released the main manila line the smaller restraining line opened the loop of the towline allowing the stump to sink to the bottom. According to Roland, dozens of stumps were cleared from the channel in this manner.

Jack and Lois Sieg, in their "Researches on Island Pond" quoted a letter in which George Whitney described the design details of the Ida F. Jack, commenting on Whitney's laconic style, suggested that perhaps the efficiency and economy of his words might have been a factor in his longevity. It would be a mistake to judge Whitney by his literary style:

My Dear Frederick:

Mrs. Maxie told me today that on your last visit here you ast me for the enclosed foto of my 31 ft. yot-the Ida F. I named her for my dotter who now lives in Burbank Cal. She was 8½ ft beam (the yot, not the dotter) and was allowed 25 passengers, ran quite regularly summers until 1948--48 summer with no repairs or alterations. Engine was 4x7-1/2x6--Biler was 30" diam. with 428-3/4" tubes 22" long allowed 170 lbs. Pressure.

I got the design of the longitudinal seam from Joseph Ryerson-it was double butt strapped using 8 rows of rivits. She was a success & I never built any one more so. Sold her in 1948 & the guy he got her afire for a finish.

So long for now,
Best wishes, Whit

This short letter tells a great deal about the man. He displays unusual warmth in his salutation: "My Dear Frederick." There is unexpected humor in his remark, "She was 8½ ft. beam (the yot, not the dotter)" and we learn that he probably preferred to be called "Whit" by his friends. His brief letter reveals a warm, engaging, plain talking fellow with a good sense of humor; it is evident that he didn't take himself too seriously.

When Whitney finally sold his beloved steamboat he was 86 years old. His hands had created exquisite machinery for the enjoyment of others during most of those years. He may have felt that it was time to let go of this symbol of his life's work. To own her and not be able to take care of her with his own hands might have destroyed the magic for "Whit." George Eli Whitney died on December I, 1963 having attained his 101st birthday the previous June.[50]

---

[50] Author's note: Several of Whitneys marine steam engines built before 1900 have survived several boat hulls and some are still in use. Models of Whitney engines are on display in the Thomas Newcomen Library and Museum in Steam Technology and Industrial History. It is located in Exton, Pennsylvania and is maintained by the Newcomen Society of the United States. To those who have a particular interest in the history of steam-cars I recommend *American Steam-Car Pioneers, A Scrapbook* by John H. Bacon. It was published by The Newcomen Society of the United States, Exton, Pennsylvania in 1984.

Chapter 11
FIRST AMERICAN IN SPACE
1923--1998

I n the 1930s it was beyond the comprehension of most people to imagine the technological advances that, a mere 30 years later, would make it possible for Alan Shepard to ride a rocket into space and return safely to earth. Actually, there were scientists who were already studying the feasibility of such a feat. Moreover, men were already planning the vehicles that would theoretically enable man to travel beyond the earth's atmosphere and explore space. Alan Shepard's consuming urge to fly became apparent when he crashed a home made glider in Derry in the early 1930s. Later, one of his boyhood rewards from his parents was a flight in a commercial aircraft from Manchester, NH to Boston and return. From this early evidence of his interest in flight to his decision to attend the U S Naval Academy, where he knew he would undergo flight training, the boy seemed to have made up his mind that he was going to be a flyer.

A boy with lofty goals, Alan had the good fortune to be born to a family that was able to encourage his highest ambition having themselves come from a line of illustrious New Hampshire ancestors. His family worked hard to help him avoid the mischief that his precocious personality invited. He got a first rate education in Derry where he attended a private elementary school and later Pinkerton Academy. He learned the value of money by running a paper route, and he learned to work with his hands in his dad's well-equipped shop in the basement of their home. The experience that may have shaped his self-reliance and zest for adventure more than anything else was the 12 summers he spent at the Shepard camp on the north end of Escumbuit Island.

Of those who knew this fun-loving boy in the early 30s, who among them could have predicted that one day Alan Shepard's fame would dwarf that of such legends as Benning Wentworth, Chief

Escumbuit and George Whitney? Who could have imagined that the name Shepard would achieve international recognition?

One evening, seated around a campfire, he pointed up at the full moon that illuminated their campsite on Escumbuit Island and told his companions: "I'm going up there some day."

Like Babe Ruth calling his famous home run in Yankee Stadium, the boy who was destined to become the "First American in Space" had a bold vision and he did not mind sharing it with others. Sixty years later he wrote an endorsement for my novel, *Abenaki Warrior,* that said in part, "Perhaps the thought of flying in space, and then to the moon itself, was being formulated in my mind in those days."[51]

This chapter is a brief account of Alan Shepard's early boyhood in Derry, NH that includes anecdotes from the twelve summers that he spent on Escumbuit Island.

Alan Bartlett Shepard Jr. came from a prominent East Derry family. His mother Renza Emerson came to the town when her father moved his shoe factory to Derry. She married her neighbor "Bart" Shepard and the house they built was flanked on either side by the homes of the two sets of grandparents. Grandfather Shepard had owned a local bank in town and died when Alan was very young. The future astronaut was brought up very much aware of the important role his ancestors played in the history of New Hampshire. The large American flag hanging between two elms in the front yard offered a constant reminder of the family heritage; several early members of the family had been prominent in the history of our country. Alan's father was a direct descendant of General Joseph Cilley who had served under General George Washington in the Revolutionary War. His Grandmother Shepard was a descendant of Josiah Bartlett, whose portrait looked down from the wall of the Council Chamber in the governor's office. He had been one of the signers of the Declaration of Independence. The coat of arms

---

[51] Author's note: Lake resident Dennis O'Riordan got this story first hand from Junior Meir, who was among the group present when Al Shepard made this startling prediction.

displayed in the Shepard house came from the Winslow branch of his mother's family. Only one of seven Winslow brothers who fought in the Holy Land Crusades survived those campaigns.

In her chronicle about camping on the big island between 1878 and 1900, Elizabeth Schneider wrote how, in 1900, "Colonel" Shepard built one of the first permanent camps on the pond. She describes it as a two-story cottage, yellow in color with a bright red roof. It was the first modern structure on Escumbuit Island which legend marked as a stopping place for Hannah Dustin's captors after their raid on Haverhill in 1697. She often saw the Colonel and his three small sons, but noted that many years passed before Mrs. Shepard appeared on the island. She mentioned that her brother belonged to the same fraternity with the older and younger Shepard boys at M.I.T. and that they often visited Black Birch Lodge on the big island while they were in college. She added that the middle boy, Bartlett, went to Dartmouth and later became the father of Alan Shepard Jr., the first American astronaut. In those early days hired help carried baggage and supplies from Derry to the pond in a horse drawn farm cart where it was transferred to the island by rowboat. The Colonel and his three sons drove to the pond in a separate carriage where they rowed a boat to the island. Apparently, like the Sweeney family on the big island, it took some time for the Colonel to accept the fact that females were perfectly capable of adjusting to and enjoying the rustic conditions at the pond.

As a youngster growing up in Derry, Alan Shepard was exposed to all of the ingredients that tend to develop admirable qualities in a young man. His parents and grandparents learned early on that his limitless energy had to be constantly channeled into pursuits that would keep him out of mischief. In spite of the relatively affluent status of his family, he was taught that he must work hard to attain his personal dreams. His youthful experience selling eggs and delivering newspapers came out of efforts by his family to direct his energy in a positive way. He used the proceeds from his egg sales to buy a three-speed bike with lights. He wanted the bicycle to pedal back and forth to Grenier Field (now Manchester Airport) where he had a part time job sweeping out hangers. It gave him an opportunity to be around airplanes, mechanics and pilots. In an early exploit he crashed a home made glider that was built by one of his friends. His parent's choice to reward him for achievement by paying for a round trip flight to Boston in a propeller-driven plane indicates that they understood his passion. By his own account he spent twelve wonderful summers at the family camp that still stands at the north end of Escumbuit Island. There he learned to swim, row and sail a boat and to live out in the open like an Indian. His mother had uncovered some details about the life of Chief Escumbuit and, like many other children on the pond, Alan was fascinated with his legend. He had heard that the chief was buried on the island together with the silver sword and a purse of gold coins presented to him by the King of France at his knighting ceremony. Young Alan developed his interest in wood working through his father who had a good supply of tools in the cellar of their Derry home. He was enrolled at Proctor Academy where he received training in boat building. With the help of the camp instructors he built a kayak and a wooden skiff that he later used at the pond. After Shepard achieved fame for his exploits in space, his boat was given to Proctor Academy in New Hampshire where the boathouse was named the Alan B Shepard Jr. Boathouse. There a plaque bears his name and the date of his boat building achievement.

During the 1938 hurricane that devastated New England, Alan was on the island with his grandmother Nanzie, together with his sister Polly and his cousin Carol. At the height of the storm they decided to head for safety on the mainland in a wooden rowboat. The high waves driven by hurricane winds drew people to the shores who rooted for their safe passage. With his sister Polly in the bow of the rowboat and Grandmother Nanzie in the stern, Alan and his cousin Carol each manned an oar. A man tried to come to their aid with a powerboat, but he couldn't get his motor started. His grandmother didn't have her purse and she was carrying a $5.00 bill that she planned to give to a man for garage rent. She lost her hat and the $5.00 bill to the wind by the time they reached the safety of the shore. This may have been the first of Alan Shepard's many encounters with danger during the course of his action-packed life.

Lorna, an 86-year-old matriarch of Abenaki Indian descendants for whom Drew Road and Drew Brook are named, still recalls the details of her encounter with young Alan when he was a mere boy.[52]

While out in their rowboat on the pond she and her sister went to the aid of a young lad who had turned over in his kayak. When they came alongside he climbed into their rowboat and they tied the kayak to the stern of their boat and towed it to Escumbuit Island. When they reached the island his grandmother, whom Alan called "Nanzie," was waiting on the shore. She scolded the boy for venturing so far from shore in his frail kayak. Although Lorna knew the boy was a Shepard, she thought little more of the episode for many years. Alan died never learning that the two women who "rescued" him that day were descendants of the Abenaki Indians who captured his imagination as a boy on Escumbuit Island. Indeed their descendants had lived at the pond long before his own illustrious ancestors had come to New Hampshire. Ironically, it was Lorna who savored the memory of the encounter and, on May 5, 1961, she sat transfixed in front of her television and watched the lad she had pulled into her rowboat rocket into space and celebrity as the *First American in Space.*

My first contact with Shepard came in about 1935 and again in 1990, but it wasn't until 1997 that these chance meetings over a period of 65 years resulted in more that a casual acquaintance. It is difficult to define the type of person Alan Shepard was by reading newspaper accounts about him. He had achieved international recognition and, by some accounts, was sometimes inaccessible to reporters and autograph seekers. His relatives say, however, that he often autographed photographs and other articles and returned them at his own expense. According to them, he considered autograph signing, and acknowledging the attention of spectators at celebrity golf tournaments a part of his job. Despite coming from vastly different backgrounds, it was interesting to me how our lives touched

---

[52] Author's note: Lorna's maiden name was Drew. The chapter entitled "The Hidden Nation" examines the history of this Abenaki Indian family for whom Drew Brook and Drew Road are named. Lorna is the 85-year-old matriarch of this family whose connection to Big Island Pond goes back to the 1700s.

briefly through 60 years without actually meeting. Yet, after our initial boyhood encounter in 1934 at Big Island Pond, I followed his career with interest. When we finally met on Escumbuit Island in 1990, neither of us could have predicted the unusual nature of our next contact.

When I was about 14 years old I used to hitch hike to Big Island Pond and camp at Hobo Lodge in Chase's Grove up behind the dance hall. I was a real hobo in the sense that I carried little more than my bathing trunks and a toothbrush. Given my lack of money and supplies, my mother was mystified by my ability to stay at the pond up to a week without coming home. I survived through the generosity of the people who camped in the woods up behind Chase's dance hall.

Although they were people with limited resources, they had found an inexpensive way to spend a vacation out of doors where they could enjoy swimming, hiking, boating and even dancing. It was an ideal situation for low income people most of whom worked in the woolen mills in Lawrence. Like many people with modest incomes, they were ready to help those who had even less than they did. Invariably someone gave me a sandwich at noon and a hot meal in the evening, and most of the time I was offered a blanket and space in a tent to bed down for the night.

From this base I was able to take advantage of all the exciting things that Chase's Grove and Big Island Pond offered. People invited me out in their canoes and rowboats and I even scrounged up the fare to go out on Whitney's steamboat. It was an idyllic existence; there is something about having fun without spending money that enhances the pleasure. Perhaps it the delightful feeling of being completely free of worry and responsibility. It is the state of mind that we try to recapture, mostly unsuccessfully, when we become adults.

The Labor Day swimming and boating events at Chase's Beach were the climax of the season for me. I was particularly anxious to compete in the canoe-tilting contest. A pair of canoes face off with two men in each canoe. One man paddles from the rear seat and his partner stands astride the front seat wielding a bamboo pole with a padded tip. The rules of the contest are simple; push your opponent into the water while holding your own balance and you are the winner. After my partner and I won two jousting matches we had a little break before we faced our opponents in the final match of the elimination series. We knew all of the kids we were competing against except the pair we were to meet in the finals. I suddenly identified the boy who was going to joust against me. He was the boy who lived on the north end of Escumbuit Island; he was the boy who I had seen swimming and towing an empty rowboat with a rope harness around his shoulders. At the time I wondered what in the world the kid was training for. Pushing the thought from my mind I prepared to do battle with this kid.

When one considers the situation it would be easy to dramatize the episode of two young boys from very different backgrounds meeting like young gladiators. It's true, I was existing at the pond by mooching on sympathetic people while Alan came from a family of influential Derry people. But it was really nothing like that. We were simply two youngsters in our early teens that were competing in the canoe tilting competition. And since this lad was not very impressive physically, I was feeling pretty confident. Perhaps I was too confident because, after a few feints and jabs, I lost my balance and fell into the water earning the runner-up prize in the competition. Because of that competition, however, the names Shepard, Shepard Island and Escumbuit Island stuck in my mind.

Twenty six years later I lived in Andover, Massachusetts, my lifestyle infinitely more complex. I still spent my summers at the pond, but now I had a family and we had our own camp. I followed the details of the space race to the moon with great interest mainly because Alan Shepard was part of the effort.

It is a little like watching some kid with whom you played high school football play football in the NFL. It's like saying to your friends, "Hey man, I know that guy. I played football with him." Watching Alan Shepard ride a rocket into space had me on the edge of my seat with sweaty palms. For a few moments hope and elation were tempered by anxiety until relief and then celebration prevailed. I watched the national celebration that followed with quiet pride, feeling a special connection with this new American hero. An equilibrium problem threatened to ground Alan for good, but he finally beat that problem and later flew a mission to the moon. He provided an unscheduled highlight to that mission when he hit a golf ball with an improvised golf club from the surface of the moon. He contrived to have the end of his Astronaut's "probing stick" threaded to match the female thread of a metal golf head he took with him on the mission. That stunt, better than anything, was typical of the young Alan Shepard. He was ambitious, he was bright, he was a prankster, he was a dare devil, and he was an American hero.

The summer of 1990 I was still rebuilding the old camp I had purchased on Escumbuit Island. It was next door to the Shepard camp and I learned from them that Shepard lived in Pebble Beach, California and no longer had a financial interest in the camp. Two families related to Shepard shared the cottage. As part of their festivities celebrating the 90th birthday of Renza Shepard, the entire clan including Alan Shepard and his wife were on the island for the day. Island people respect each other's privacy, but when Alan's nephew, David offered to introduce me to the members of the family I accepted.

Alan Shepard was then a retired U S Navy Admiral, and like retired politicians and doctors, it is customary to address Admirals by their formal title. Having been a naval officer in World War II, I fell easily into the courtesy of addressing Shepard as Admiral and, in an effort to make some light conversation, I recalled the circumstances of our previous meeting when he had beaten me in the canoe tilting contest. He laughed and remarked:

Well that's different. Usually, when people tell stories like that, they end up with me getting knocked on my butt.

He was curious to see how I had rebuilt the old Webster cottage and, after we toured my camp, we walked down to the back of the island to inspect the boathouse I built down there. We had a relaxed conversation and, after we finished our tour, I wished him a pleasant day on the island and he rejoined his family.

The following day during a conversation with David he remarked: "The Admiral said he really enjoyed talking to you. He probably appreciated the fact that you didn't ask him for an autograph."

"Well David, I'm really not an autograph hound," I said, " but hell, maybe he should have asked me for my autograph."

We laughed at my quip and left it at that. It had never occurred to me that there might be a downside to fame. Later, in a more serious moment, I pondered the Admiral's position. It occurred to me that it might be difficult for him to judge the motives of people seeking his friendship. I suppose that is part of the price one pays for celebrity.

By the fall of 1997 I had spent two years doing research and writing my story about the life and times of Chief Escumbuit. My goal was to create something unique for my family, in particular my grandchildren. I distributed a few copies to my neighbors on Escumbuit Island and to several other friends around the pond. Maggie Starrett read the manuscript and brought it to the attention of her fiancé, Adolfo Caso, author of 15 books of his own and a publisher. I was swept up in a series of events that left me with a book contract with Branden Publishing Company of Boston. I prepared for my return to Florida with a full plate of things to do in regard to the publishing of *Abenaki Warrior*.

Before heading for Florida I told Adolfo that I had sent a copy of my manuscript to Alan Shepard and that I had asked him for his endorsement. Adolfo said, "That would be a real coup if you could get an endorsement from Shepard" adding, "You realize his name has international recognition?"

Before leaving for Florida I contacted Kerry Johnson at the Derry News in regard to the upcoming publication of my book. She asked me to forward a copy of the finished book and promised to read it. When I casually mentioned that I had written Alan Shepard to ask him for an endorsement, she said: "Good luck," adding with a laugh, "We find him a very difficult man to get in touch with."

My thought as I headed for Florida was that it had only cost me a copy of my manuscript and $3.00 to send it priority mail; there was little else to lose.

There was four-month supply of junk mail waiting when I arrived at my apartment in Boca Raton, Florida. I sat with a wastebasket in front of me and began to pitch anything that looked like junk into the trash. A box number and the Pebble Beach, California address caught my eye so I opened it carefully and read there:

Dear Al:

Delighted to hear from you and enjoyed reading the proof of ABENAKI WARRIOR! Hope it goes well for you. If you would like a quote, you may use the following:

"Having spent twelve summers as a youngster living at the Shepard camp on Escumbuit Island, I was totally fascinated by Kayworth's novel of Big Island Pond. Chief Escumbuit became a real and important figure instead of the legend he was to me as a boy. Perhaps the thought of flying in space and then, to the moon itself was being formulated in the back of my mind in those days!"

Alan Shepard, Rear Admiral, U S Navy (retired)
First American in Space

Suddenly, I appreciated the full measure of the man and the irony of the moment struck me: At that very moment Alan Shepard should have been literally sitting on top of the world, admired by millions for his accomplishments. To the casual observer he appeared to have everything: He had fame and fortune. He had a stable and loving family. He was the co-author of a successful book entitled "Moon Shot." (He gave his share of the profits to Deke Slayton's widow and son.) He was comfortably retired at beautiful Pebble Beach on the Monterey Peninsula in California. And yet, there was something amiss in the life of Alan Shepard--he was fighting for his life.

Sometimes a small gesture can communicate the true measure of a man. David Sherman had confided to me that his uncle's doctor would not allow him to play golf. To an avid golfer the thought of living at Pebble Beach and being denied the pleasure of being on the golf course is unthinkable. Most golfers would be very frustrated. I like to think that when my manuscript arrived it may have provided Alan with a brief respite from his biggest challenge. Perhaps, for a few days, it allowed him to put aside the thoughts that must have consumed him--thoughts of his mortality. It is in this context that I weigh what he did for me; despite his physical problems he reached out to help me. It was the act of a very nice guy!

My mind kept revisiting all those years since Alan Shepard toppled me from my canoe in 1934 at Chase's Grove. His life and career had been that of an All-American boy. After graduation from the United States Naval Academy he served on a destroyer in World War II. He was a test pilot and was one of the first astronauts selected for the space program. After his daring missions in space, his name had become a part of American folklore.

I wanted to phone him to thank him personally, but knowing that he was still undergoing medical treatment, I decided to respect his privacy. I sent him a thank you note together with two copies of *Abenaki Warrior* and a beautiful 11x14 enlargement of Dr. Keith Emery's 1967 photograph of Escumbuit Island. One year later the inevitable last act was reported in a mid morning television news bulletin: "Alan Shepard, America's First Man in Space, died last night at his home in Pebble Beach, California."

There was a flurry of interest in Escumbuit Island by local newspapers and television and the American flag flew at half-mast at the Shepard camp, but the focus of attention was far from Big Island Pond. Yet, even as the nation mourned the passing of one of its heroes, local people knew it had all begun in Derry.

As a boy Shepard lived with the legends of Escumbuit, Wentworth and Whitney. Through more than 70 years he remained fascinated by these ghosts of Big Island and now, as we prepare to enter the 2nd millennia, one of our own bequeaths us the legacy of his daring exploits and we count him among the *Legends of Big Island Pond*.

P O Box 63
Pebble Beach CA 93953
September 25, 1997

Dear Al,

Delighted to hear from you and enjoyed reading the
proof of ABENAKI WARRIOR! Hope it goes well
for you.

If you would like a quote, you may use the following

> "Having spent twelve summers as a youngster
> living at the Shepard camp on Escumbuit
> Island, I was totally fascinated by Kayworth's
> novel of Big Island Pond. Chief Escumbuit
> became a real and important figure instead
> of the legend he was to me as a boy. Perhaps
> the thought of flying in space and then, to the
> moon itself, was being formulated in the back
> of my mind in those days!"

> Alan Shepard
> Rear Admiral, U S Navy(retired)
> First American in Space

Sincerely,

Alan Shepard

Letter to Al Kayworth from Alan Shepard.

Alan Shepard suiting up for Apollo 14 Mission,
courtesy of NASA.

Chapter 12
THE LEGACY
1878--2000

Big Island Pond may be the largest private body of water in the State of New Hampshire. Swimming beaches at Chase's Grove, Collette's Grove and Sanborn Shores are for the use of the residents of those communities. In addition, fishing permit holders are allowed access to the pond at the public launching ramp adjacent to the outlet dam. The history of the modern era of the pond goes back to 1878 when Mathew Taylor built the first dam. Over the years the "water rights" have been transferred to a series of corporations and individuals that have owned the legal right to control the outflow of water from the pond. It is important for local residents and members of BIPC to know this history and to understand how and why the Big Island Pond Corporation was formed.

Clearly, the pond is the most important asset shared by its residents. The right to own property is a fundamental right that is not shared by the citizens of all countries. Individuals tend to protect their property rights like a female tiger protects her cubs. Men have died protecting their property rights, countries have gone to war over property and millions of men have died defending the borders of their country against foreign invaders. And one of the most important property rights is the right to control the flow of water. The unique thing about the Big Island Pond Corporation is that it owns its own water rights.

In 1878 a local entrepreneur named Mathew Taylor put together a clever money making scheme. He planned to dam the outlet of Islandy Pond in Derry to create a reservoir. He proposed to raise the water level 8½ feet above the low water level of his dam spillway. The natural level of the pond outlet was probably somewhat higher than the low water level of his dam. Two brooks that ran down either side of a big island connected Islandy Pond and Perch Pond. By raising the water level 8 ½ feet, he intended to create a single large pond. Five mill owners on the Spickett River downstream from the Islandy Pond outlet had agreed to pay him for a reliable supply of water for their mills. Most mills of the period were built on rivers or streams in order to link the natural flow of water to waterwheels. The seasonal variations in the flow of water from Islandy Pond made it an unpredictable source of power. In the spring the Spickett was flooded, but by late summer, there was not enough water to drive the waterwheels. Mathew Taylor had a water control plan that would keep the mills operating year round.

He made a proposal to the eleven farmers whose property backed up on the shores of Perch Pond and Island Pond that caught their attention. He paid them the sum of $1.00 and other considerations for the right to raise the water level and occupy the land around the two ponds to a height that would be measured by a stone marker at his dam. A vertical split stone that is still in place was erected to mark the 8½ foot level. He built his dam one hundred rods downstream from the original outlet of Islandy Pond. After the dam was built, and after the water level reached the 8½ mark, each farmer drove a series of stakes to show where the high water mark fell on his property. This information enabled them to calculate the amount by which the newly created reservoir reduced their total acreage. Armed with this information they then applied for tax abatements. It was a good deal for the farmers because, in most cases, they received a tax deduction for giving up land that they had not previously cultivated. As an additional bonus they ended up with valuable waterfront property on a beautiful pond that occupied between 500 and 650 acres depending upon the water level. The stored water in the pond enabled Mathew Taylor to control the flow of water to the five mills with which he had made previous agreements. Everyone was a winner in Taylor's plan. The farmers saved tax money and ended up with prime waterfront property on the pond. The mill owners had a dependable flow of water for their mills and Mathew Taylor prospered from the money he received for his water.

By 1900 all of the New Hampshire mills had either burned down or moved and Mathew Taylor decided to sell his water rights to the

Arlington Mills Corporation. The rights allowed them to control the flow of water to their mills in Methuen. They built a new dam just below Taylor's dam and installed a gauge that accurately measured the water level to the maximum 8 ½ foot mark. But, by the early 1920s the stored water at Big Island Pond was insufficient to fully meet the demands of their mills and they decided to create an auxiliary reservoir by building another dam on the Spickett River at the site of the Wheeler Mill in Salem. By this time The Water Resources Board of New Hampshire was getting into the act. They ruled that the maximum allowable draw of water in any 24-hour period from the combined water resources of Big Island Pond and Arlington Mill Pond could not exceed nine million gallons.

During this period, Arlington Mills moved ownership of the rights through several corporations under their control. The transfer sequence included the Whittman Corp, the Charlot Corp and finally the Spicket River Corporation. By the middle 1950s the Lawrence Mills were beginning to move south and their need for water was drastically reduced. In 1958 they sold the water rights to a local farmer named Walter Stickney who had extensive land holdings in the Conley's Grove area. The deed that transferred the water rights from The Spickett River Corporation to Stickney contained covenants that included maintenance of the dam, water quality, and rules for releasing water for mill use.

Warren Stickney was a farmer and a canny dealmaker. He knew that public access to the pond could not be denied forever. He made an agreement with the New Hampshire Fish and Game department that allowed public access to fishermen. This original agreement is still in force. Under its terms fishermen buy permits that gives them the right to fish in the pond. They are given a key that enables them to access a launching ramp located at the dam. They must sign a contract that limits their activities on the pond to fishing only. Today income from fishing permits is used to pay the administration expenses of the Big Island Pond Corporation. Without this income, residents would probably be asked to pay yearly dues.

During the summer of 1958, after buying the water rights from Arlington Mills, Stickney revealed his plans to dredge the swampy area between the natural outlet of the pond and the dam in order to create waterfront house lots. The dramatic draw down of water beginning in October of that year enabled him to bring in equipment to clean out the marsh to a depth of approximately 7 to 8 feet. In the meantime the Island Pond Water Level Control Organization was becoming concerned with water levels in the pond. They concluded an agreement with Walter Stickney that gave them control of the dam without actually buying the water rights. They raised $2,000 through voluntary contributions to help Mr. Stickney pay his water rights and flowage taxes. In return the agreement gave them the right to control the level of the pond in the best interests of all the residents.

During these years numerous meeting were held with the Water Resource Board and hearings were held to hear the views of residents whose personal preferences were often contradictory. Homeowner deeds were researched to provide a validity of the water rights deed and dam operation and public hearings were held to consider input from all interested parties. The decision to hold the water level as close to the 7 ½ foot level during the summer months and to draw down the pond beginning October 1st was determined to be in the best interest of the majority of the residents. These guidelines are in force today.

President Warren Kruschwitz saw the inherent benefits that ownership of the water rights would provide the residents. He came up with the idea of selling shares in a non-profit entity called the Big Island Pond Corporation. Residents of the pond were allowed to buy up to 4 non-redeemable shares in this corporation. The funds raised by the sale of these shares were used to buy the water rights from Walter Stickney. After the formation of the non-profit corporation in 1978, President Warren Kruschwitz and Secretary Evelyn Shore secured an exemption from paying taxes on flowage and water rights. They argued that paying individual taxes for waterfront property while being taxed for raising the level of the water to create waterfront property constituted double taxation. In turn they agreed never to release water for sale and to continue to maintain water levels in the pond that were suitable for the enjoyment of its residents. A 2/3-majority vote of the Big Island Pond Corporation stockholders is required to change these guidelines.

A random search on the internet using the key words lake pollution turns up a myriad of sites that represent all sorts of organizations that are made up of people who are concerned about the quality of water in their particular lake or series of lakes. Several of them describe lakes that have deteriorated to a stage that is known as "advanced eutrophication." One report on Lake Erie described the effect of phosphorous loading from phosphate detergents, human wastes and agricultural fertilizers during the 1950s and 1960s:

"The resulting algae blooms prevented much of the light from penetrating the surface of the water and when it died the bacteria on the bottom that decomposed the algae used most of the available oxygen. This meant that there was less oxygen for fish and other organisms. The loss of the mayfly was traced to the loss of oxygen due to nutrient enrichment. Mayflies are the main source of food for the fish in Lake Erie. Because of the loss of food, oxygen and light, perch, walleye and bass, that were once abundant, began to disappear. Taking their place were such species as carp and suckers."

The report then goes on to describe the steps that have been taken since 1972 to reverse the trend and how the mayfly, the perch, walleye and bass are returning. Stories like this from such diverse places as Minnesota, Florida, Hawaii and Lake Tahoe headlight the pressing need for vigilance at home. The recurring theme that stands out in all of these discussions is that everyone of us has a role in this battle against pollution."

Another study that was conducted by Keith Knudson, a St. Cloud State University biological science professor, demonstrates graphically how man can make a difference. His report highlights the extended length of time needed to reverse the negative effects of poor water management. The quality in nine Minnesota lakes was monitored over a period of 15 years using the Trophic State Index. This is a composite measurement that combines individual measurements of phosphorus and Chlorophyll-a levels, and water clarity. The lower the number the better the quality. Long, Pickerel and Round Lakes had Trophic State Indexes of 45, 47 and 42 respectively. This represented an average improvement of over 6% during that period. As a point of reference, Lake Superior (a very clean lake) has a Trophic State Index of 20 while the Horshoe Chain of Lakes have an index between 70 and 80. He concludes his study by saying that this was great news for the Tri-lakes residents.

"This confirms that by using no-phosphorus fertilizer, upgrading our septic systems, naturalizing our shorelines and educating ourselves on water quality issues--we can make a difference. Each of these has a small impact on water quality when done individually, but when we all do two or three of these water quality-improving techniques together, it makes a BIG difference."

Big Island Pond is part of a huge watershed that is composed of lakes and rivers and streams that discharge their waters into the Merrimac River. A watershed or drainage basin is generally defined as the total area of land that drains into a lake or a pond. This system may in turn be part of a much larger watershed that drains into a major river or the ocean. It is difficult to determine when problems with a lake begin because the histories of most lakes and ponds are not well documented. But it is known that current practices in a given watershed can be modified in order to slow down the advanced aging of a lake or a pond (a process known as advanced eutrophication).

Advanced eutrophication is primarily caused by non-point source pollution. This includes agricultural run-off from farms and from new residential developments, run-off from lawn fertilizer use, run-off from pet waste, leaking septic tanks, water fowl droppings, leaf litter, and grass clippings etc. Humans are the main cause of non-point source pollution. Rainfall can wash in large amounts of non-point source pollution into many lakes and ponds. Current human activities within a watershed can be modified, however, to reduce the impact of human influence. These modifications include the following:

It helps a great deal to leave a buffer zone of uncut vegetation around the shoreline to aid in binding up nutrients that would otherwise run into the water. The size of this buffer zone depends on the slope of the area. Typically buffer zones are ten to fifteen feet in width, but should be wider for steeply sloped area.

Monitor fertilizer use in the watershed. This includes not fertilizing around a body of water where rainfall can carry the nutrients into the water. If fertilizers must be used in run-off areas, low phosphorus or no phosphorus fertilizer should be used. Studies have shown that the biggest contributor to declining water quality in lakes and ponds is irresponsible fertilizer use. The correlation that what makes grass green will make ponds and lakes green is direct and all too accurate.

Monitor lawn care practices. Direct lawnmower cuttings away from the lake and do not deposit clippings near sewers, drains or ditches that drain into the lake. Grass clippings are high in nitrogen that promotes aquatic growth.

Eliminate miscellaneous sources of phosphorus. Many detergents and cleaners are phosphorus based. Select environmentally sound cleaners when washing cars in areas where the run-off may feed into the pond.

Discourage the feeding of ducks and geese. Feeding may change their migratory practices and make them dependent. Their droppings add to the problem.

Improperly maintained septic tanks and drain fields can pose a special danger to the quality of the water in the pond. The tips listed here can help keep your system in good working order and help eliminate expensive repairs:

Pump your septic tank every two years. Insist that the pumper clean your septic tank through the manhole on top of your tank instead of using the 4-inch inspection pipe that sticks up through your lawn.

If you have a garbage disposal, pump your tank every year or better yet compost your kitchen scraps where any run-off from rain will not drain into the pond.

Do not dispose of kitchen grease in your septic tank. It can clog your drain field.

Space out your laundry load through the week and wash only full loads. One wash can use up to 47 gallons of water and a load a day instead of 7 loads on Saturday can make a big difference to your septic system.

Use liquid laundry detergent. Powdered detergents use clay as a "carrier." This clay can plug your drain field. Use of Sudsavers is recommended.

Minimize the amount of household cleaners (bleach, harsh cleaners) in the system.

Do not use automatic toilet bowl cleaners, such as 2,000 flushes. The slow release of these chemicals into the septic system kills the microorganisms that treat your water.

You do not need to put special additives into your septic system.

It is fair game to question my own compliance with the suggestions I have outlined here. I admit that at least half of what I know about pollution comes from the research I have done to write this chapter. Being an island resident, I carefully monitor what goes into my septic system because there is no way I can get it pumped out. Last fall I personally shoveled 10 inches of sludge from the surface of my septic tank into a wheelbarrow and deposited it in a depression in the middle of the island where there will be no run-off into the pond. There are no camps on Escumbuit Island or the Big Island that have lawns. So far as I can determine most island people prefer trees, pine needles and natural vegetation at the shoreline. I must confess that I occasionally go down to the back of the island with my toothbrush and a bar of soap for my morning ablutions. I do it mostly to remind myself that I was once sixteen. I have a great admiration for people who are willing to give of themselves to benefit their community. Warren Kruschwitz, in his time, performed remarkably well, and now we have the good fortune to have a retired Rear Admiral look out for our interests. In his characteristic, direct way BIPC President Herb Lippold wrote the following message for the residents of Big Island Pond.

"The quality of water in our pond is monitored regularly by President, Herb Lippold and other volunteers of the Big Island Pond Corporation. In 1990 BIPC joined the New Hampshire Department of Environmental Services (DES) Volunteer Lake Assessment Program. The Biology Bureau Staff of DES supply equipment, analyses and technical assistance to Lake Volunteers. Water testing had been done previously by Warren Kruschwitz, EDS and UNH intermittently. Big Island Pond waters are sampled June, July and August of each year to determine water quality and for trends that may adversely affect our Pond in the future. Some of the parameters for which samples are taken include chlorophyll, phosphorus, color, conductivity, ph, dissolved oxygen, and transparency. Is the water of our Pond of good quality? YES! But the aging process is taking its toll, and man is a big contributor to accelerating this process.

Algae, the microscopic free-floating plants or green pigment is a part of the Pond's food chain and is increasing. Good for fish, but poor for the Pond as a whole. Only so much can be done to slow the process down, but poor septics, clear cutting shoreline and lawn fertilizers are contributors to greater nutrients, which regulate the growth of algae and aquatic plants. We should do all we can to maintain a healthy shoreline to slow the aging process down."

It is impossible to control the flow of water from the pond in a way that will satisfy everyone. In the era before the October 1st draw down of the water level, the force of expanding ice routinely destroyed poured concrete retaining walls along the shoreline. When the water level was lowered to eliminate this problem, there were new complaints by residents who wanted to use their boats in October and beyond. The precipitous release of water to relieve high water at Island Pond creates flooding problems for residents downstream. Conversely, during dry spells, the same people clamor for more water. But the consequences go beyond the petty concerns of individuals; there is the habitat to consider. A minimum water level in the Spickett River is essential to the survival of the many species of fish and game that make the stream their habitat.

For the past 15 years Ken Heinrich has managed the water flow in a way that is sensitive to all of these concerns. During the past three years he became aware that there were serious structural leaks in the dam. In the summer of 1999 he pinpointed the leaks by diving down to introduce colored dye in suspect areas that were confirmed by watchers on the downstream side of the dam. The response to his call for remedial action illustrates why **every** property owner on the pond should belong to the Big Island Pond Corporation.

To address the problem, The Board of Directors appointed a planning and supervisory committee composed of Herb Lippold, Ken Heinreich, Skip Lanouette, Tom Schwant, Dave Holigan and Bill Banton. Holes beneath the outlet pipe and along the bottom of the inlet and outlet walls were identified as the source of the leaks. Volunteers filled over 350 sandbags with sand that was donated by Ted Wickson and George Merrill. A sandbag cofferdam was constructed and heavy-duty pumps were used to expose the sections that needed repair. Cement grout was pumped into the voids beneath the outlet pipe and a thick overlay of extra strength concrete was poured over the large aprons upstream and downstream of the outlet pipe. A great deal of debris and rotted timber was also removed from the aprons.

The volunteers helped the workers to construct a cofferdam and to pump grout and pour concrete. The supervisory and planning committee obtained the required material and services and coordinated the labor of volunteers Eric Schoneberger, Robert Kinzler, and Dale Anderson. As they labored in boots and rain gear to spread concrete, one of them commented: "Do you realize that it's been 100 years since guys stood and worked where we are right now."

It was hard and dirty work, but everyone felt that they had been part of an important event. There is a deep satisfaction in knowing that you have created something that will likely endure for another century.

The fall issue of the Big Island Ponderables carried encouraging news about pond water quality confirming that conservation efforts by residents are beginning to produce positive results. The newsletter reported the following:

"After our problems with high chlorophyll (green pigment) last year which could have brought about algae blooms, poor clarity and high phosphorus, we are happy to report much better results this year. Chlorophyll was down to normal throughout the summer. It was obvious that the green pigment was much less than last year. "Clarity" was excellent, 4.5 meters plus. Oxygen was much better than normal. Weeds did not grow as much as normal; therefore less to be cut off by boats which depletes the oxygen as they decay. We hope that this year's good results are an indication of people caring for the future of our pond by taking care of their septic systems and not using regular lawn fertilizer adjacent to the pond."

Guardians of the Wilderness

The golden era on Big Island Pond for my generation was the decade of the 1930s. The Great Depression was receding and our summers at the pond were idyllic. Even as we moved into our teenage years there were no drugs and there was very little alcohol in our experience. To us it seemed as though the good times would roll forever. We had no idea that our generation would be swept up in a Great War soon after the decade ended.

I was living the life of a beach bum that found me staying with friends near Howard's Grove or tenting at Hobo Lodge in Chase's

Grove. I had a brief encounter with Alan Shepard and I met Bill Flanders, Charlie Gabler and others from the big island. I often saw a pretty girl boating or swimming near a camp that was located in a cove near Sweeney's Point. One of my more adventuresome friends had gone sailing with her and told me that her name was Mary Lou French and that she lived in Winchester. Apparently her mother kept a tight rein on her, and we never met. Later I heard that she attended Winsor School and then went on to Vassar College. After finishing college, the winds of war carried me to Saipan, Guam and Okinawa where I dreamed that one-day I would return to my special place.

I finally met this extraordinary woman in 1996 in unusual circumstances. I had written a story about Chief Escumbuit that was later published as *Abenaki Warrior*. Having written the story for my grandchildren and friends, I felt that I might have produced something worthwhile, but I wasn't sure. Wally, a Yale graduate and accomplished writer, edited the Island Ponderables newsletter and two of their children are professional writers. One summer afternoon I showed up at their dock unannounced to ask Mrs. Williams if she would read my manuscript and give me an opinion. She was very gracious and quickly put me at ease. As I motored back to Escumbuit Island I congratulated myself on having summoned the courage to ask her to read my story. It gave my confidence a huge lift when Wally and Mary Lou advised me to seek a publisher.

As I wrote stories about the pond, I found the Williams were a good sounding board for my ideas. As they continued to edit my stories I slowly began to learn more about their interests and their personal conservation efforts in the area. Typically, information about their good work came from other sources. There were persistent rumors about them buying up raw acreage to keep it out of the hands of developers. One day I made a blunt proposal.

"The final chapter of my new book will deal with preserving the legacy of the pond and people tell me that you two have done a great deal to preserve the quality of our pond for our grandchildren. Your contributions are an important part of that legacy. I would like to know some of the details."

It was the scope of Mrs. Williams's involvement that astounded me. As I read through the various newspaper clippings, reports and letters of commendation I noted that she had been an activist and spur to the conscience of local bureaucrats and politicians for almost 30 years. It was her interest in horses and riding that got her started. Back in the early 1970s she and her family and friends often took tiail rides north through Hampstead where they followed an abandoned railroad bed that once ran from Windham to Fremont. The 80-foot right of way of the former Worcester, Nasua & Portland Railroad extended for 23 miles. When she learned that a developer was planning to buy a portion of this land from the Department of Transportation, she effectively blocked the transaction. After contacting conservation organizations in the ten towns through which the rail bed passed, she organized a hike to demonstrate the value of the land to various departments of the State of New Hampshire.

"The effect of the hike was that the people from the New Hampshire Department of Parks and Recreation decided that they wanted it," Mrs. Williams said.

At the department's request she came up with a new name for the property--Rockingham Recreational Trail. Subsequently, the state passed a law requiring that any department wishing to divest itself of property must offer it to all other state departments before offering it for sale to the public.

Ever since its incorporation in 1749, Hampstead had a natural network of trails that linked the various farms of the area. By the middle 1970s these traditional trails were being disrupted and obstructed by new development. Concerned that this network of trails might be lost forever to the residents of the town, Mrs. Williams headed a group who formed a Trails Committee to preserve these historic trails. Its purpose was to create new links to traditional trails in order to create a network of multipurpose trails offering recreational, environmental and educational advantages to the townspeople. The Trails Committee persuaded the town to put up $5,000 to study the feasibility of the plan. Through its foresighted action the Town of Hampstead became the first town in New Hampshire to undertake such a project which established a standard for land stewardship that many other towns in the state eventually copied. From 1988 to 1996 eight sections of the trail system were opened that expanded its length to 50 miles. 35 property owners allowed use of portions of their land, and volunteers put in a great deal of hard work clearing brush and building bridges. At the dedication ceremony for the opening of the 10th section in 1998 Mrs. Williams commented: "We have always had plenty of people to clear brush and build bridges and no one has ever refused to let us pass over their land" adding, "The trail system is a great asset to the town. The trails are forever, for the pleasure of generations to come."

There was much more boat traffic and noise on the pond back in the 1950s and 1960s than at the present time. One would think that the tidal wave of new households created in Southern New Hampshire in the past 25 years would have inundated our community by now. Subdivision and condominium developers would love to have access to raw land on our shores with access to the pond. Wally and Mary Lou Williams have been a major force in turning hundreds of acres of wilderness land over to conservation. Between the two of them, they own 15 parcels of land that range in size from 8 to 50 acres. Among their papers is a map of the local area on which conservation and state owned properties are shaded to distinguish them from commercial property. The most striking example of the Williams activism is shown by a wedge of land bounded on the south by Route 111 and on the east by Main Street in Hampstead. The western boundary of this wedge is the Derry/Hampstead town line that runs in a northeasterly direction along the shore of the Big Island and joining Main Street in West Hampstead. When the shaded areas are combined with the portion of the pond that lies within that wedge, it appears as though 70% of that area is beyond the reach of developers. This unprecedented set aside of land for conservation purposes must be credited to the activities of Wally and Mary Lou Williams. In the northwestern portion of this map there is another band of shaded properties that abuts the previously mentioned rail bed. These properties are identified as Hampstead Conservation Land, Derry Conservation Land, Weber Memorial Forest and the Taylor Mill and Ballard Park property on Island Pond Road. Wally and Mary Lou Williams, either by direct ownership or through financial assistance to the towns, have insured that these areas will survive as conservation land for future generations. These areas are all part of the watershed that drains into our pond. Commercial development of these wilderness lands would have inevitably had a negative impact on the quality of water in Big Island Pond.

Wally and Mary Lou were not always praised for their conservation efforts. Their attempt to acquire land that fronted on Boulder Cove in Atkinson failed. The owner of the land opted to sell his property to a developer who planned a condominium development for low-income housing. The original plans proposed that each condominium owner have dockage for his boat and access to the pond in Boulder Cove. There was a potential over time of adding scores of boats to pond traffic. Through the Williams intervention, the developer eventually agreed to abandon his plan to provide dock space to the buyers of his condominiums.

The 1978 Environmental Merit Award for Region One was presented to Mary Lou Williams by the Environmental Protection Agency (EPA). She was chosen out of a field of 100 nominees from a region that included New Hampshire, Maine, Connecticut, Rhode Island, Vermont and upstate New York. Among the recommendations and newspaper articles about the award were letters from the Governor, state representatives and conservation commissions in Southern New Hampshire. That same year Mary Lou and Walworth Williams received the "Land Stewards Of The Year" award at the annual meeting of the Society for the Protection of New Hampshire Forests in recognition of their outstanding dedication to the conservation of New Hampshire's natural resources.

In 1978 Mary Lou Williams proposed that the Town of Hampstead purchase Randall Forest and the Currier property. She proposed a plan that she had effectively used many times for her own purchases. She knew that the Federal Government would provide matching funds if the land were set-aside for conservation. The purchase of the land would have added only eleven cents per $1,000 valuation to tax bills, but the selectmen vetoed the proposal. Most people would have turned their back on the town at that point, but Mrs. Williams decided to provide the $125,000 that the town needed to complete the deal. She also assisted the towns by provided partial payments for some of their other land acquisitions. A comprehensive plan that outlined certain tax advantages and methods of donating property was presented to owners of wilderness land in the area:

> Land gifted to town with the stipulation that it be designated conservation land. The donor would save money on real

estate taxes. They would also be eligible for an income tax deduction. The town could apply for federal matching funds.

The land could be sold to the town for less than market value. Difference between real and discount price provides a tax break to seller. The town would be eligible for matching Federal funds.

The landowner could retain ownership, but surrender right to develop land. Land would be placed under a conservation restriction. Could grant easements for trails, fishing and other recreational use. The reduction in value would provide tax break to donor. Town could apply for matching Federal funds. 35 local landowners granted trail easements in this manner.

The most sincere praise one can receive may be the accolade one receives from a former adversary. There was an editorial in a 1978 issue of the Derry News that perfectly illustrates this perspective. The title was *Hampstead's Opportunity*:

"We've had our differences with Mary Lou Williams, perhaps because over-enthusiastic people sometimes make others a bit nervous, but there's nobody in Hampstead or anywhere else around here that knows more about conservation than she.

Currently Mrs. Williams is fighting a major conservation/growth battle in Derry that may well save this town's economic skin. Her participation and leadership in 14 conservation organizations, coupled with the wetland seminars she conducted in area towns, plus her single handed victory in getting the old railroad bed designated a public recreation trail are only examples of the kind of service she is anxious to perform for her town-if the selectmen will only draw on her talents. Derry is lucky to have a few activists such as she, but we all could use more!"

Having traveled for many years in Latin American and the Caribbean, this semi-wilderness at the margin of a great population center continues to amaze me with its beauty. The haze of polluted air that hangs over exotic places like Mexico City, Caracas, Buenos Aires, Port of Prince, Haiti and Port of Spain, Trinidad made me long to return to the clean air of New Hampshire. And the soil and water pollution that lies under those blankets of smog is even worse to contemplate. Big Island Pond by comparison is heaven on earth.

I confess that, like many local people, I have taken the unchanging nature of our community for granted. I know that, against all logic, the pond is quieter today than it was forty years ago. I never took the time to seriously contemplate my good fortune. I was only vaguely aware that there were others working quietly with great determination to preserve my favorite place.

A great deal of credit must go to President Herb Lippold and the directors of BIPC. Thanks must be given to past President Warren Kruscwitz and former directors of the corporation. The activities of Wally and Mary Lou Williams of Governor's Island have been much less visible to the average resident of the pond. Without their long range program of converting wilderness to conservation land, this body of water would be awash with boats and people by now. The tenacity of this mild-mannered, soft-spoken woman will have a positive impact on our community for generations to come. She, more than anyone, is the architect and builder of our legacy and, apart from his own contributions, Wally has supported Mary Lou at every obstacle in the long trail of their accomplishment.

At the dedication of the new Ordway Park on North Main Street near Hampstead Road a beautiful shade tree was donated by the Hampstead Trails Association to honor Wallace and Mary Lou Williams for their many contributions to the town. The plaque bears their names and the final three lines of this Robert Frost poem:

The Road Not Taken

Two roads diverged in a yellow wood,
And sorry I could not travel both
And be one traveler, long I stood
And looked down one as far as I could
To where it bent in the undergrowth;
Then took the other, as just as fair,
And having perhaps the better claim,
Because it was grassy and wanted wear;
Though as for that, the passing there
Had worn them really about the same,
And both that morning equally lay
In leaves no step had trodden black.

Oh, I kept the first for another day!
Yet knowing how ways lead to way,
I doubted it I should ever come back.
I shall be telling this with a sigh
Somewhere ages and ages hence:
Two roads diverged in a wood and I-
I took the one less traveled by
And that made all the difference.

Newlyweds, Tami Kayworth and Cagney Stevens,
on their victory lap by Escumbuit Island.

Dam repair, cove side.

Dam repair, discharge side.

BIBLIOGRAPHY

1. *225ᵗʰ Anniversary of Hampstead, N. H.*, by the Anniversary Committee

2. *250ᵗʰ Anniversary of Hampstead, N. H.*, Maurice I. Randall

3. *Atkinson Then and Now*, from Louise Noyes Bartnum Collection

4. *From Turnpike to Interstate*, Derry Historic Society Research Committee

5. *America's First Spaceman*, Jewel Spangler Smaus and Charles B. Spangler

6. *History of the Indian Wars*, Samuel Pennhallow Esq. 1726

7. *History and General Description of New France*, Rev. P.F.X. de Charlevoix, S. J.

8. *Journal of Voyage to North America*, Rev. P.F.X. de Charlevoix, S.J.

9. *France and England in North America*, Francis Parkman, 1910

10. *The Border Wars of New England*, Samuel Adams Drake

11. *The Abenaki*, Colin G. Callaway

12. *Pigwacket*, George Hill Evans

13. *Colby's Indian History*, Solon B. Colby

14. *The Abenaki*, Colin G. Callaway, 1953

15. *Histoire du Abenaquis*, N.F. Maurault, S. J.

16. *Historical Sketches of Andover*, Sarah Loring Bailey

17. *Andover, Symbol of New England*, Claude M. Fuess

18. *Handbook of North American Indians*, Vol 15, Smithsonian Institute, W. C. Sturtevant, editor

19. *The Forts of Maine, 1607-1945*, Robert Bradley, Ph. D.

20. *Abenaki*, Gordon Day

21. *The Expeditions of John Lovewell*, Frederick Kidder, 1804--1885

22. *Americas Steam-Car Pioneers*, John H. Bacon, University Press, 1984

23. *Haverhill Gazette*, 1949, Story of Amesbury Lovers Hampstead Tragedy Recalled

24. *The Portsmouth Press*, 1992: Bruce E. Ingmire, articles on Benning Wentworth

25. *The Walking People*, Paula Underwood, Tribe of Two Press

26. *America's Stonehenge-An Interpretive Guide*, Joanne Lambert

27. *The Celts*, Jean Markdale

28. *Manitou*, Mavor and Dix

29. *Puzzles in Stone*, American Stonehenge Video

30. *The Underground Railroad in Massachusetts*, William Siebert

31. *Abenaki Warrior*, Alfred E. Kayworth, Branden Publishing Co, Boston, 1998

32. *The Ruins of Greater Ireland in New England*, William Goodwin

33. *Mystery Hill Research, Theories Concerning Its Origin*, David Williams

34. *The Plymouth Legacy*, Donald F. Kent

35. *Benning Wentworth* Birch Farm on Island Pond, Lillie Cleveland

INDEX

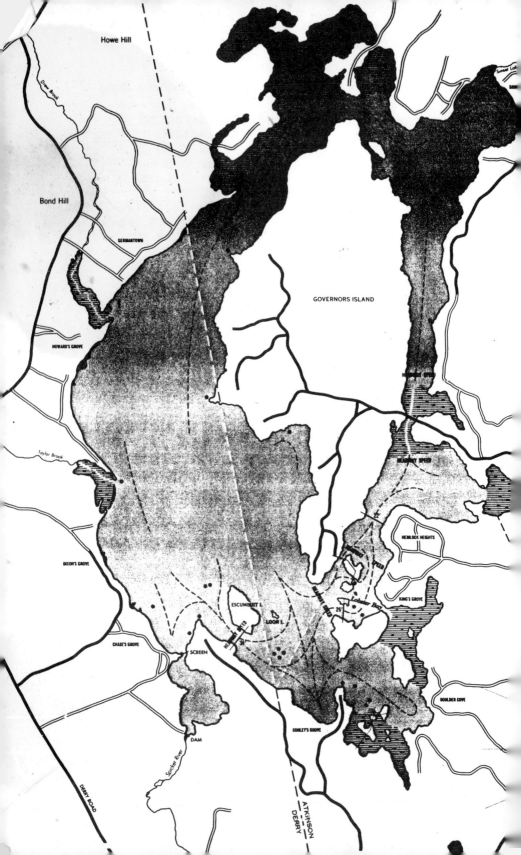